Good evidence-based therapy begins with a coherent and comprehensive theoretical framework for treatment supported by empirical evidence. Smiler provides just that and grounds it in real-world case examples. This is one of the very best books on therapy with men to appear in the past 2 decades and is sure to become a classic.

—**MICHAEL ADDIS, PhD,** PROFESSOR OF PSYCHOLOGY, CLARK UNIVERSITY, WORCESTER, MA

Andrew Smiler has devoted his career to advancing the mental health and well-being of boys and men. From his decades of experience as practitioner and scholar, he provides a highly accessible book that efficiently includes the theory and research needed to better understand this harder-to-engage population. Yet Dr. Smiler's true gift is the rich case studies that clearly identify and illustrate scientifically informed, pragmatic approaches for more effectively helping the diverse men who walk into your office.

—**CHRISTOPHER S. REIGELUTH, PhD,** ASSOCIATE PROFESSOR AT OREGON HEALTH & SCIENCE UNIVERSITY, PORTLAND, AND AUTHOR OF *THE MASCULINITY WORKBOOK FOR TEENS: DISCOVER WHAT BEING A GUY MEANS TO YOU*

Andrew Smiler shows us why it is difficult to engage men in therapy, then demonstrates his expertise about men and masculinity through vivid case examples where he connects to the male experience. Any therapist who works with men should read this book to understand how to make contact with the hurting men who would benefit from treatment and how to help them heal.

—**RICHARD GARTNER, PhD,** TRAINING AND SUPERVISING ANALYST, FACULTY, AND FOUNDING DIRECTOR OF THE SEXUAL ABUSE PROGRAM, WILLIAM ALANSON WHITE INSTITUTE, NEW YORK, NY, AND AUTHOR OF *BETRAYED AS BOYS: PSYCHODYNAMIC TREATMENT OF SEXUALLY ABUSED MEN*

CLINICAL WORK
WITH MEN

CLINICAL WORK WITH MEN

UNDERSTANDING MASCULINITY IN PSYCHOTHERAPY

ANDREW P. SMILER

AMERICAN PSYCHOLOGICAL ASSOCIATION

Published by
American Psychological Association
750 First Street, NE
Washington, DC 20002
https://www.apa.org

Order Department
https://www.apa.org/pubs/books
order@apa.org

Typeset in Charter and Interstate by Circle Graphics, Inc., Reisterstown, MD

Printer: Gasch Printing, Odenton, MD
Cover Designer: Mark Karis

Library of Congress Cataloging-in-Publication Data

CIP data has been applied for.
Library of Congress Control Number: 2025050586

9781433844454 (paperback)
9781433844461 (epub)
9781433850165 (pdf)

https://doi.org/10.1037/0000499-000

Printed in the United States of America

10 9 8 7 6 5 4 3 2 1

To Mike, Richard, and Tony,
who taught me how to be a good therapist.
And to Liz, Carolyn, and Monique,
who taught me how to be a good theorist.

Contents

Acknowledgments

Although my name is on the cover, I didn't get to write this book by working alone. In the 30+ years since I became a therapist, I've learned a lot about how to be a therapist from a great many people. My first mentors were Mike Graziano, Richard Mason, and Tony Goldsmith, all of whom taught me the nuts and bolts of being a good therapist: how to connect with clients, when and how to rely on those connections, and how to pace the therapeutic work. After a few years, I decided I wanted to be an academic. Liz Stine-Morrow, Carolyn Mebert, and L. Monique Ward all taught me what it means to be a good theorist, including the awareness of the assumptions I brought to any piece of work, the depth of thought, and the attention to detail required. I wouldn't be doing this work—and I certainly wouldn't be writing this book—if I hadn't received their guidance.

As I wrote this book, I received feedback from a number of folks, and they deserve thanks. In a first for me, this book generated two different sets of formal reviews. The first was headed by Stephen Wester and three anonymous reviewers on behalf of the academic journal *Psychology of Men & Masculinities*. Those folks helped clarify my thinking and the presentation of the multi-faceted masculinity framework, which forms the spine of my discussion of masculinity throughout the book. The second review started with Chris Kelaher at APA Books, whose feedback on my initial idea, and whose willingness to champion that idea, led to a book contract. Development editor Beth Hatch and copy editor Kathy Savadel left their fingerprints all over the manuscript, which is much clearer and much more readable because of their efforts. I extend my thanks to all of you; this book wouldn't be here without your help.

Closer to home, several friends and colleagues were kind enough to provide feedback on that initial proposal. I thank Laci Green, Doreen Hughes, Travis Jeffords, Bernie Newton, and Amanda Sullivan. There are likely others who were involved in those early conversations and whose names I've forgotten. I'm sometimes bad at keeping records and don't mean any offense. I'd also like to thank Fred Rabinowitz and a handful of anonymous reviewers who provided feedback throughout the formal review processes.

My final thank you goes to all the boys, men, and their family members who have agreed to work with me over the years. Many of you have told me that I helped make your lives better. Knowing you has also helped make my own life better. I've learned a lot from working with all y'all, and I hope that by sharing it here, many more people will be helped.

CLINICAL WORK
WITH MEN

1 HELPING THERAPISTS HELP MEN

Men are struggling. Over the past few years, we have heard about the loneliness epidemic among American men. Richard Reeves (2024) wrote about men's lower levels of academic achievement compared with their female counterparts and the implications this has for employment. And that's just the beginning of men's struggles. Men are also more likely to die by suicide (G. S. Liu et al., 2023), or to overdose (Spencer et al., 2024); these deaths may be understood as the result of difficulty dealing with emotional pain. Our stereotypical image of a young adult who is failing to launch is that of a young man who lives in his parents' basement and spends his time playing video games, and when we think about clients struggling to find employment or strong interpersonal relationships because of attention-deficit/hyperactivity disorder or high-functioning autism we typically think about men.

It would be easy to blame "masculinity" for men's struggles. After all, masculinity directs men to be violent, be independent, ignore their feelings, and seek power without regard to how they get it. Some research offers support for the idea that masculinity contributes to men's struggles, with evidence indicating that men who endorse higher levels of masculinity ideology or who experience more gender role conflict have worse mental health, are

https://doi.org/10.1037/0000499-001
Clinical Work With Men: Understanding Masculinity in Psychotherapy, by A. P. Smiler

more likely to abuse substances, are more depressed, and are less likely to seek therapeutic help (O'Neil, 2015; Wong, Ho, et al., 2017). Online, I have seen people take these results to an extreme and argue that masculinity in any form is toxic and that men can never be healthy unless American culture substantially redefines masculinity or abandons it altogether.

However, masculinity and men's lives are more complicated than that. The reality is that definitions of masculinity in the United States (and other English-speaking countries) have changed over time, and vary across U.S. subcultures, which tells us that men don't all do masculinity the same way (Majors & Billson, 1992; Smiler, 2019; Stearns, 1979). This multiplicity of definitions is also evident in psychological measures of masculinity (Morawski, 1985; Smiler, 2004).

The issue is further complicated by the awareness that any individual man has the ability to choose the degree to which he adheres to our culture's (primary) definition of masculinity, from not at all to completely, with a million points in between. Research-based scales that define masculinity in positive terms, such as Sandra Bem's (1974) Sex Role Inventory and the Personal Attributes Questionnaire, developed by Janet Spence and Robert Helmreich (1978), originally had scores around the scale midpoint, but those averages increased from the 1970s through the early 2010s (Donnelly & Twenge, 2016; Twenge, 1997). In contrast, measures of masculinity ideology, such as the Male Role Norms Inventory—Revised (Levant et al., 2010) and the Conformity to Masculine Norms Inventory (Mahalik et al., 2003), tend to focus on negative elements of masculinity and have relatively low mean scores (Smiler, 2014; Thompson & Bennett, 2015). Clearly, not all men—and not all researchers—are enacting masculinity to the same degree and in the same ways.

The issue becomes even more complicated when we recognize that many of the well-known large-group differences between men and women are driven by relatively small subgroups of men. Although men, when examined at the large-group level, are more violent than women, it is only a relatively small group of men who perpetrate the vast majority of that violence (Cooper & Smith, 2011; Uniform Crime Reporting Program, 2016). Similarly, as mentioned, men are more likely to die by suicide, but deaths by suicide occur among a relatively small group of men (Liu et al., 2023). In addition, although men are more likely to say they want multiple sex partners in the next 30 days (Schmitt & International Sexuality Description Project, 2003), and report more sex partners in the past year (Dariotis et al., 2008; Humblet et al., 2003) than women do, these findings are also driven by relatively small groups (see critiques by Smiler, 2011, 2013). Although these statistics indicate that violence and promiscuity are driven by a minority of men, the ideas that any man could become violent and that most men are interested in sex, but not relationships, are common.

Masculinity's complexities don't stop there. Some scholars have argued that the psychology of men has been dominated by a focus on the negatives and that the field needs to embrace and explore a positive masculinity. Authors such as Mark Kiselica and Matt Englar-Carlson have argued that American definitions of masculinity include a range of positive elements, such as the idea that men demonstrate caring through efforts to protect others; that they demonstrate *action empathy*, by doing things to help others who are struggling; and that they band together for common purposes that promote their communities (Englar-Carlson & Kiselica, 2013; Kiselica, 2010; Kiselica et al., 2016). These scholars believe that most men are fundamentally good, prosocial, and concerned about more than just themselves. Research that has used the positively focused Bem Sex Role Inventory and the Personal Attributes Questionnaire supports this position: Men (and women) with higher masculinity scores report a range of positive outcomes, such as greater self-esteem (Bem, 1993).

When we consider this research collectively, we can see that masculinity is a complicated subject and that men's adherence to masculinity—whatever that might mean to them—is also complicated. In order to work effectively with men in a therapeutic setting, we clinicians need a better understanding of what masculinity is, how men understand themselves, and how to apply this knowledge. That is my goal for this book. I want to expand how you think about men and masculinity and help you move away from cultural stereotypes so you can meet your male clients where they are and recognize the positive and negative components of their masculinity.

CHALLENGES MEN FACE WHEN STARTING THERAPY

Despite the struggles men face, they are less likely than women to attend therapy and less likely to return for a second session even when they do make it to a therapist's office, in the United States and around the world (Addis & Mahalik, 2003; Gough & Novikova, 2020). Recent data from the Substance Abuse and Mental Health Services Administration (SAMHSA; 2021) indicate that less than 10% of adult men report having used any type of mental health service—psychiatric medication, outpatient therapy, or inpatient therapy—in the prior year, a rate that is approximately half of women's use. Usage rates also vary across racial and ethnic lines, poverty status, and insurance coverage (SAMHSA, 2021). Men report that the top three reasons they do not seek mental health services are (a) lack of insurance/cost, (b) structural barriers, and (c) stigma.

Stigma, which we might also think about as shame, may be a particularly strong reason for men to avoid therapy. American expectations of men, and stereotypes about men, position men as being rational, self-sufficient, strong, in control, and able to solve problems—and certainly not controlled by their feelings! In the United States, young men are taught to "take it like a man" and "play through the pain." In order to schedule an appointment with a therapist, and then arrive for that first session, a man needs to acknowledge that he is not meeting expectations in at least one of these areas. In effect, he will need to overcome his own expectations of himself as a man before he can begin to seek support for his mental health needs (Addis & Mahalik, 2003; Real, 1997).

Many people imagine that therapy consists of talking about deep feelings that elicit sadness and tears, or otherwise bearing one's soul. The imaginary interactions probably involve a lot of eye contact while sitting in an intimate setting that has comfortable seating and soft lighting. This exercise in sharing feelings while making eye contact in a comfortable setting fits into masculine conceptions of (heterosexual) romance—it doesn't fit into current-day masculine conceptions of friendship or getting help with a problem. These conflicting images of therapy and expectations of appropriate male behavior create a bad fit between therapy and male socialization (Rochlen & Rabinowitz, 2014).

The SAMHSA (2021) report indicated that structural barriers are the second most common reason men do not seek therapy, after insurance coverage/cost, which is the most common reason. For men who are their family's primary (or only) breadwinner, arranging time off work to meet a therapist may carry a real financial cost. These concerns are magnified for men with relatively low incomes. (This financial dynamic is one of the few ways the gender wage gap adversely affects men.) Asian men may be particularly concerned about lost wages because of the importance they place on supporting their families (Iwamoto & Kaya, 2016).

Among men who do not control their work schedules, who are required to use sick time in half-day increments (instead of hour by hour), or who need to formally ask for time off from a supervisor, leaving work to see a therapist during the work day can be that much more costly and stigmatizing. Travel time to see a therapist, which can be lengthy if one has to use public transportation or resides in a rural area, further compounds the costs and is evident in the racial and ethnic disparities SAMHSA (2021) reported. Those concerns are further exacerbated if he needs to request time off on a regular basis, even if only for a short-term course of therapy that lasts six to 10 sessions. Although virtual (e.g., Zoom) sessions can ameliorate some of these challenges, they are not sufficient to address all of them.

CREATING A GOOD FIRST SESSION

If a man is able to overcome his own shame, the logistical problems, and the financial concerns, he then needs to find a therapist who seems like someone he can work with (and hope that therapist has availability in their schedule). Then he needs to have a good experience during that first session and walk away with the feeling that his therapist can and will understand his concerns. It is important that men not leave a therapist's office believing "You just don't understand," a thought that is consistent with linguist Deborah Tannen's (1990) description of male–female differences in communication patterns.

Creating a good therapeutic relationship—which entails connection, comfort, and confidence between client and therapist—requires *cultural competence*, defined as the development of knowledge, awareness, and skills relevant to a specific cultural group. To be explicit, I am referring to cultural competence in working with men. Psychologist William Liu provided the rationale for doing so in a 2005 article in the *Journal of Clinical Psychology*. He observed that "Men are socialized in a specific culture, with values, norms, customs, and expectations, to which men must adhere" (Liu, 2005, pp. 685–686). The need for cultural competence is exacerbated by the fact that most therapists are female and thus were not raised in masculine cultures. The demographics of the field of clinical and counseling psychology and its student body suggest that the problem will get worse before it gets better. The percentage of male therapists will almost certainly decrease for at least the next 10 years because the majority of students entering the field are female, and the generation currently retiring has a higher percentage of male therapists than the generation replacing them (American Psychological Association [APA], Boys and Men Guidelines Group, 2018; APA Task Force on Race and Ethnicity Guidelines in Psychology, 2019; Salsberg et al., 2017).

APA recognized men's needs when they approved their first set of *Guidelines for Psychological Practice With Boys and Men* in 2018 (APA, Boys and Men Guidelines Group, 2018). In contrast, the first set of guidelines for work with women and girls was published in 2007 (APA, 2007) and updated in 2018 (APA, Girls and Women Guidelines Group, 2018); for lesbian, gay, and bisexual clients the first guidelines were published in 2000 (APA, 2000) and updated in 2021 (APA Task Force on Psychological Practice With Sexual Minority Persons, 2021); and, for transgender and gender nonconforming people, the first guidelines were published in 2015 (APA, 2015).

The 10 guidelines provided in the *Guidelines for Psychological Practice With Boys and Men* (APA, Boys and Men Guidelines Group, 2018) consistently call for the need for psychological services that are sensitive to masculinity (as the male gender role), the unique ways in which boys are raised, and the need to tailor services accordingly. This book specifically fulfills Guideline 9, which states "Psychologists strive to build and promote gender-sensitive psychological services" (APA, Boys and Men Guidelines Group, 2018, p. 17), as well as several other guidelines.

Several authors have recognized and attempted to articulate what male-friendly therapy could look like. Some have written about ways of accepting the client's concerns, awkwardness, and communication difficulties in the clinical setting (Kiselica et al., 2016; Wexler, 2014). Others have argued for using action-oriented language that can help create momentum, build a sense of efficacy, and tap into men's orientation toward problem-solving and task completion (Brooks, 2017; Rochlen & Rabinowitz, 2014). Still others have emphasized the use of colloquial language, humor, and metaphors men are likely to be familiar with (Bhatia, 2014; Kilmartin, 2014). In the seven case studies presented in Chapters 3–9, you will find examples of these strategies.

Zac Seidler et al. (2018) reviewed the literature and identified three common themes across all of the above-mentioned suggestions. One theme was building rapport and a collaborative relationship. Strategies here include adopting a strengths-based approach that includes positive aspects of manhood and masculinity as well as appropriate self-disclosure by the therapist. Each of the case study chapters (i.e., Chapters 3–9) describes the strengths associated with the masculine role highlighted in that chapter.

Another theme Seidler et al. (2018) identified was clarifying the structure or "how" of therapy. This theme includes explanations of how therapy works, including the road map for treatment and specification of short- and long-term goals. Every case study in this book includes a discussion of treatment planning. At a minimum, I ask clients if they want to use therapy time over the next several sessions to address an issue, often with a discussion of the potential benefits and likely challenges of doing so. Some of those discussions are as simple as asking clients if they would prefer to address Issue A or B first.

The final theme Seidler et al. (2018) identified is related to tailoring language to male clients. They observed that many authors emphasize the importance of using language that is action oriented, future focused, and progress driven in order to increase motivation and reduce shame. These strategies often contribute to a problem-solving framework. The sample dialogue in each chapter of this book illustrates this approach, in particular with respect to ways in which the therapeutic conversation is often oriented toward identifying and solving problems, while also providing sample dialogue that does not rely on the explicit discussion of emotions. The linguistic pairing of problem-solving strategies and reducing the focus on emotion is consistent with the idea that many men prefer therapy that is more focused on problem solving to improve a difficult situation instead of learning to cope with that difficult situation.

LAYOUT OF THIS BOOK

My goal for this book is to help you, as a clinician, become more culturally competent in working with men. I do this by explaining and illustrating some elements of masculinity that American culture positions as important elements of how men should be. I focus heavily on ways to conceptualize your work with male clients, given that the authors cited in this chapter have offered a broad range of suggestions for facilitating those interactions.

In the next chapter, I provide a way of understanding and thinking about masculinity: the multi-faceted masculinity framework (MFMF). The MFMF is useful because it taps into a range of psychological and sociological approaches to gender and brings them all together to gain a more thorough understanding of the range of ways that we therapists, and the male clients we serve, might understand masculinity. If Jim thinks his masculine behavior is driven by his beliefs about masculinity, the MFMF explains why. If Neil thinks trying to be what society considers a Real Man is inherently stressful because masculinity has competing directives, the MFMF explains why. And if Ray believes there is a hierarchy of masculinities, and that U.S. culture rewards some versions of masculinity more than others, the MFMF explains why.

The next several chapters, 3–9, contain case studies of seven men. Given my preference for identity work, I titled the chapters using identities, and the identities I have chosen are centered on specific masculine criteria. In Chapter 3, for example, I talk about the breadwinner identity, which emphasizes the masculine criteria of breadwinning and providing financially for one's family. Similarly, the discussion of the player in Chapter 8 is centered on the masculine criterion of promiscuity.

In each chapter's case study, I introduce a client and describe how I conceptualized my work with that client. In doing so, I identify two themes that were the focus of our therapeutic work. For one of these themes, I provide additional detail about what makes this particular issue masculine or particularly important for men. I also provide some cultural context and history, including popular or noteworthy examples from the media.

In each chapter, I address mental health strengths and concerns that are common to the masculine identity being presented. I also discuss ways in which intersectional concerns may appear. I focus on intersectional concerns related to race and ethnicity, social class/socioeconomic status, and ability/disability status.

You, the reader, should also know that each of the case studies I present is an amalgamation of two or three clients who had similar underlying concerns and that I use pseudonyms throughout. If I was actively working with a client while writing this book, I obtained verbal consent to use (part of) their story and offered them the option of providing their own pseudonym. APA's (2017) *Ethical Principles of Psychologists and Code of Conduct* do not require me to obtain consent, written or verbal, when using a brief and anonymized description of a client, so I did not reach out to clients who had completed their work with me to obtain their permission. (And, if any of them are reading this, I hope none of them mind.)

2 THEORETICAL OVERVIEW

"Be a man!"

"Man up!"

These simple sentences are fairly common. A man is a man, so what does it really mean when someone tells him to "be a man?" Do we think he's forgotten that he's a man, that his gender has somehow slipped his mind? And what, exactly, do we want him to do—or to be—while he's manning up? Are we reminding him that he should pee standing up? Would we ever tell a female to "woman up" or "be a woman?" Gender norms, expectations, and stereotypes are things we routinely invoke. They are also a fundamental component of how we see and understand ourselves and other people.

If you are going to work with men in therapeutic settings, this book will help you learn how men understand what masculinity is and some of the ways it shapes their lives. It will also help you identify the mental health benefits and challenges inherent in some ways men choose to demonstrate their masculinity while providing some direction on how to help them.

Before we get started, I'd like you to use stereotypes about men to reply to two prompts. You can do this using the notes app on your mobile device, writing on a piece of paper, or even using Table 2.1—I'm not picky. First,

---

https://doi.org/10.1037/0000499-002
Clinical Work With Men: Understanding Masculinity in Psychotherapy, by A. P. Smiler

TABLE 2.1. Male Stereotypes

Guys should . . .	Guys should not . . .
Be tough	Cry

I'd like you to take a moment or two and list at least five things the stereotype says guys should do, such as "guys should be tough." Then I'd like you to take another moment and list at least five things the stereotype says guys should not do, such as "guys should not cry." If you're with a friend, the two of you can do this together. Go ahead. I'll wait.

Before I ask what you wrote down, I want you to consider how long it took you to make each of those lists. I'll bet it was pretty easy and took you 2 minutes or less for each prompt. I point this out—and I hope I'm right!—to illustrate just how effortless it is to think about masculinity and what it might mean. In just a few minutes, you probably listed 10 attributes, beliefs, or behaviors that set some kind of standard for men's lives. When I have asked these questions in workshops, I have had groups effortlessly develop lists of 30 or 40 items in a span of 10 minutes.

In order to maximize your ability to work with men, you need to understand masculinity. From the outside, masculinity might look like knowing about football and other team sports or being able to fix things. It could also look like doing crazy dumb stuff, like the characters in many movies in which a group of guys make a series of questionable decisions but manage to avoid any serious trouble, often with a lot of laughs—for example, *The Hangover* (Phillips, 2009), *Harold & Kumar Go to White Castle* (Leiner, 2004), and *Bill & Ted's Excellent Adventure* (Herek, 1989).

The reality is that masculinity is much more complicated than that. If you are male, or have ever identified as male, you already knew that. If you are female, and you have always identified as female, then you might be able to get a better understanding of masculinity by considering what it means for women to be pretty. Pretty is complicated, with a million things a woman might choose to do to make herself (more) pretty. Pretty also brings the potential for a woman to be judged on her level of prettiness any time she's doing anything, with those judgments coming from random strangers, coworkers, friends, family, and even herself. The pressure men feel to be masculine is comparable to the pressure women feel to be pretty.

When it comes to being masculine—or manly or demonstrating manhood—I believe most adult men have internalized a version of masculinity that they are trying to enact. I also believe most men are not particularly aware of all the ways in which their behavior and ways of being are shaped by their beliefs about masculinity. Stated differently, I think men's behavior is guided by their beliefs about what it means to be a man, even if they are not always aware of this influence, and I believe part of our job as therapists is to help clients recognize and understand their purposes. From there, we might also help our clients find more effective ways to achieve their purposes or help them develop new purposes.

In 2024, I published a conceptual review of masculinity in the academic journal *Psychology of Men & Masculinities* (Smiler, 2024). In that review, which I summarize in this chapter, I identified four distinct aspects of masculinity that researchers have conceptualized and studied over the years. Taken together, I think these four components describe most of the ways in which masculinity shapes and influences men's lives, and I refer to them during the case studies presented in Chapters 3–9.

THE MULTI-FACETED MASCULINITY FRAMEWORK

As I mentioned, masculinity is a complex construct. In order to better understand it when working with men, you will need a similarly complex framework so you know which elements of masculinity are affecting your client's life, whether for good or for ill. In this section, I present the four components of the multi-faceted masculinity framework (MFMF): (a) masculinity's criteria, (b) masculinity's achievements, (c) masculinity's types, and (d) masculinity's negotiations (Smiler, 2024).

Masculinity's Criteria

Earlier, I asked you to make a list of at least five things a guy should do and five things a guy should not do. We can think of your lists, however short or long they are, as part of *masculinity's criteria*: the expectations about how men will think, feel, and behave. You might also think of these as the rules of masculinity, the boundaries of what is called the "Man Box," or the things a guy needs to do to earn punches on his Man Card.

Psychological theorists and researchers have written about men's independence, endorsement of promiscuity, confidence, violence, emphasis on work, leadership, decisiveness, control of their emotions (or emotional stoicism), and not acting like a girl, among a range of other attributes (David & Brannon, 1976; Pleck, 1981; Stearns, 1979). You might think of these directives as an individual's beliefs (or personal ideology), an individual's traits, or norms to which the individual is conforming. In everyday life, we might also talk about men as doers, their interest in sports, and their ability to fix things. This last item points to a broader interest in technology that ranges from building computers to building cars. By the way, I just listed 11 more things you might add to your lists of things men should and should not do.

Like masculinity for men, women also have a set of criteria to which they are expected to adhere in order to be considered pretty. These criteria tell us what is pretty and what is not, and some of those criteria change from year to year. They also tell us what body parts should be prioritized (e.g., face, breasts) and which ones are less important (e.g., feet, elbows)—at least, that's what it looks like from my perspective as a cisgender male.

Masculinity's Achievements

If masculinity has a set of criteria that direct boys and men to do some things but not others, then we might reasonably ask, what does a guy get for adhering to these directives? Stated differently, what does a guy get for having enough punches on his Man Card? The answer is straightforward: He gets status, primarily (and sometimes exclusively) from other men. Other guys will recognize him as a "Real Man" and, if he is doing a particularly good job of adhering to masculinity's criteria, they might even call him "The Man." The reverse is also true: A guy might be seen as not "Man Enough." In this way, we can talk about *masculinity's achievements*, including the status derived from being judged as having sufficiently adhered to masculinity's criteria.

Social psychologists Joseph Vandello and Jennifer Bosson (2013; see also Vandello et al., 2008) developed the idea of *precarious manhood*. Relying on prior research and commentary, they observed that manhood is a status granted by other men, not the individual himself, and that the criteria and the evaluation process are not always clear to the person being tested. Like others before them, Vandello and Bosson recognized that masculinity's criteria are so broad, and sometimes so contradictory, that no individual can reasonably adhere to all of them. A guy who is good at sports but not the building trades might wonder if he is Man Enough because he doesn't have those skills, or vice versa. He might also question his status if his skill level in one or both of these realms is just OK but not actually good. Therefore, achieving masculine status is an ongoing activity because "manhood is hard won and easily lost" (Vandello & Bosson, 2013, p. 101; see also Gilmore, 1990; Pleck, 1981).

In laboratory research with university undergraduates, Vandello and Bosson (2013) were able to create a sense of anxiety or uncertainty about masculinity achievement using a variety of relatively simple procedures. Some male undergraduates were asked to braid a doll's hair while others braided rope; the young men who had braided the doll's hair demonstrated higher levels of aggression when allowed to play a video game a few minutes later. Similarly, in research that has used the *stereotype threat* paradigm, young men who were told their scores on a gender-related knowledge test were consistent with a feminine gender identity also displayed higher levels of aggression (Vandello et al., 2008; Vandello & Bosson, 2013).

If we take the broad range of masculine criteria and combine them with the tenuous nature of masculine achievement, we can make masculinity itself a competition. This is evident in the form of questions about who is manly and who is not, whereby guys are competing for the title of Man Enough or a Real Man. We can also ask, "Who is more manly?" For example, is singer Harry Styles more manly than actor Vin Diesel? I'm pretty sure the answer for most is "No—Vin Diesel is more manly." If I asked you to compare former President Barack Obama and actor Vin Diesel, you might be less certain about your answer because these two men have different credentials. In both of those comparisons there probably wasn't a moment where you thought the question itself was absurd. But if we try it for women—who is more feminine: Oprah Winfrey or Beyoncé?—the question itself may seem incomprehensible.

We can think about prettiness in the same ways. Women are expected to make an effort to be pretty, and some are beautiful (comparable to being a Real Man and The Man, respectively). Like men, women might know they are pretty, or beautiful, but it is difficult to know exactly what their rank is with respect to other women. And, of course, there's no guarantee a woman will always have that rank or even meet the standard of pretty.

I think it is important that you know the idea of being a Real Man became our standard verbiage around 1980. The term was popularized, and satirized, in Bruce Feirstein's (1982) book *Real Men Don't Eat Quiche*. For Feirstein, real men were characterized by their ambition, focus on individual accomplishments, sexual success with women, and toughness, among other characteristics. Forty years later, these criteria continue to be central to the American definition of manhood.

For boys and men who grew up in the 1940s, 1950s, and 1960s, the goal was to be a Good Guy. Good Guys were self-effacing, expected to be part of their communities by volunteering their time and effort, and worked their way up the corporate and social ladders (Faludi, 1999; Putnam, 2000). They earned the title Good Guy by demonstrating good character. Any man could be a Good Guy, which was part of the reason Bill Lucy and other leaders in the Civil Rights movement adopted the phrase "I Am a Man!" as one of their rallying cries (S. Roberts, 2024).

Masculinity's Types

So far, we have talked about masculinity as a set of criteria that detail what guys should and should not do, as well as the challenges of meeting all these directives. We also have talked about the need to achieve a certain level of masculinity to earn the designation of being a Real Man. Because there are so many criteria that allow a guy to demonstrate masculinity, and because the criteria for proving manhood are somewhat nebulous, our culture provides some prepackaged methods for acting like a typical male. There are different types of masculinity: preexisting images, identities, or stereotypes that are commonly associated with men. Some people call these different types *masculinities,* a term popularized by sociologist Raewyn Connell (1995).

Examples of *masculinity's types* include easily recognizable images such as jock, nerd, player, and rebel, but they also include labels such as "Real Man," "Good Guy," and "Metrosexual." Labels of this sort are easy to generate; when I ask workshop groups to do so, they can easily produce 20 or 30 within 10 minutes. Many labels include specific elements of appearance, the adoption of certain elements of masculinity's criteria, and distinctive patterns of behavior that facilitate masculine achievement (Barber et al., 2001; Green & Ashmore, 1998; Smiler, 2006).

For example, take a moment, close your eyes, and imagine a stereotypical jock. Consider what he looks like, what he does outside of work or school hours, what he chooses to spend money on, and any personality traits that might seem relevant. Go ahead. Imagine. I'll wait.

You have probably imagined a guy who has muscles, from working out or playing sports; tends to wear team jerseys or other athletic gear; has a deep knowledge of the sports he's interested in; and may be very competitive. You might also imagine a preference for partying and objectifying women, although those components are not central to the image; it's possible to be a jock—or, at least, an athlete—without partying or objectifying women. For a teenage boy or an adult man trying to figure out who he is and how to act in the world these kinds of images provide a useful starting point. Because the jock image is widely known and includes external signifiers, such as team jerseys, it provides some guidance with respect to activities a man might choose to engage in (or avoid) and a way to find other people who share his interests. Perhaps this stereotype functions as an identity because a guy sees himself reflected in that image and believes it is a reasonable description of his self. And maybe it functions as a stereotype that is out there but with which he doesn't identify.

You might even think of this stereotype as a template; these templates exist for many masculine types, including rebel, player, and nerd. (Nerds may not have much in the way of masculine achievement, but that's a separate issue; nerd is still a template for how some guys can[not] do masculinity.) Alternatively, you can think of masculine types and their associated stereotypes as roles or identities. There is a lot of flexibility about how one might conceptualize masculine types.

As mentioned, Raewyn Connell (1995; Connell & Messerschmidt, 2005) introduced and popularized the term masculinities, arguing that different types of masculinity have different levels of cultural acceptance. The larger system of patriarchy, which organizes the lives of people of all genders, provides different levels of benefits to different types of masculinity. Hegemonic forms, like jocks and tough guys, show the greatest level of adherence to our culture's stereotype and receive the greatest level of rewards within the patriarchal system. Complicit forms of masculinity, like players, show moderate levels of adherence to the cultural stereotype and receive some benefits. Subordinated forms, like nerds, show low levels of adherence and receive few (or no) benefits. Marginalized forms typically challenge the dominant stereotype and receive no benefits, and they may be persecuted. For most of American history, gay, Black, and Native versions of masculinity have been included in this category (Busette, 2018).

Returning to the parallel with female prettiness, we might talk about different types of pretty. There's cute, and pretty, and beautiful, and sexy, and each has different implications for clothing, makeup, and hair. At the stereotype level, these distinctions also have different implications for flirtatiousness and sexual behavior. We might also think about different types of prettiness, such as classic, stylish, emo, or goth.

Masculinity's Negotiations

If nothing else, I hope you are beginning to appreciate that masculinity is complicated. Navigating the world of masculine criteria, achievement, and types requires a certain amount of effort and decision making, although men may not be consciously aware of all the decisions. In *The Myth of Masculinity*, psychologist Joseph Pleck (1981) argued that the challenges of adhering to stereotypical notions of masculinity are inherently stressful for many reasons, including the expansive and contradictory nature of male role norms, historical changes, social condemnation when one violates norms, and negative psychological evaluations of the self that are due to real or perceived violations of the male role. There are costs and benefits associated with decisions about which criteria to adhere to, the level of masculine achievement desired (Man Enough? The Man?), and which type to enact. I refer to these as *masculinity's negotiations*: the ways in which men make choices about masculinity, as well as the positive and negative consequences of those choices.

In the earlier discussion of masculinity's criteria, I observed that there are a lot of them. These directives cover a broad range of traits, attitudes, and behaviors, and some directives contradict each other. For example, guys are supposed to be good with technology of all sorts, but being too invested in digital technology can lead a guy to be seen as a nerd, which is generally seen as a negative. (Did you ever notice that most of the jokes on *The Big Bang Theory* [Lorre & Prady, 2007–2019] target the nerds the show is about?) Similarly, many men believe heterosexual men should be the primary breadwinner, and we all know that a good education is one key to higher earnings. However, being invested in academics is not a masculine criterion and can be perceived as a loss of masculine achievement. This de-emphasis on academics may explain why girls have had higher grade point averages than boys since mandatory schooling began (Voyer & Voyer, 2014) and why more women now earn college degrees than men (although the number of men receiving degrees has increased year after year; National Center for Education Statistics, 2017; Reeves, 2024). The ambiguity and contradictory nature of masculinity's criteria create stress for men (Pleck, 1981).

Cultural and historical changes can also make it more difficult for men to obtain and maintain masculine achievements (Pleck, 1981). For example, in 1950s and 1960s, American women rarely held managerial roles that included male subordinates. This changed in the 1970s and 1980s because of the efforts of second-wave feminists, and the change was enshrined into law as part of the efforts of the Equal Employment Opportunity Commission, which was created in 1965. The possibility that men would find having a female supervisor inherently stressful has been assessed with a published instrument called the Masculine Gender Role Stress Scale (Eisler & Skidmore, 1987). Research published in the 1990s revealed that men who endorsed the masculine criteria of dominance and antifemininity reacted to a woman being in a "man's job" with some mixture of anger, fear, confusion, and anxiety (Eisler, 1995). Two generations later, public opinion polling by the Pew Research Center revealed that seven in 10 men were comfortable with managers of either gender, and nearly one in 10 preferred a female manger (71% and 7% respectively; Minkin, 2023). That's quite a shift: Men were expected to feel uncomfortable with a female supervisor in the 1970s and 1980s, but 40 years later the majority were quite comfortable with them.

The pressure adolescents place on boys to adhere to masculine stereotypes has been clearly documented in the literature. Researchers have detailed adolescents' efforts to police masculinity through the use of slurs such as "Don't act like a girl" and "That's so gay" (Pascoe, 2007; Reigeluth & Addis, 2016; Rosenberg et al., 2017). The researchers—and the adolescents with whom they spoke—had no difficulty identifying and observing such comments, leading to the conclusion that these efforts to police masculinity and encourage boys to conform to the stereotype were quite common. In my personal and clinical experience, these comments continue into adulthood, where they form internalized beliefs about what is and is not manly.

Viewed comprehensively, teen boys and adult men are expected to find a way to fit into society; efforts to do so are shaped by interests and abilities as well as the opportunities provided by the immediate environment. Larger, national factors (Connell, 1995; Erikson, 1963), such as intersectional influences (e.g., histories of racism and discrimination; Shields, 2008; Wong, Liu, & Klann, 2017) and economic forces, also play a role. A man's negotiation of his masculinity ultimately reflects his own desires as well as his ability to exercise those desires; for example, it's very difficult to be the primary breadwinner when there aren't any good-paying jobs where you live.

Women's choices related to prettiness also require negotiation. At the individual level, these choices include decisions about the amount of time, energy, attention, and money a woman is willing to dedicate to being pretty. The immediate environment provides feedback, in the form of approval or disapproval by others in their reactions to her choices, that may influence subsequent decisions. Cultural notions about prettiness, such as historical efforts to prevent people of color from entering the Miss America competition, can also play a role (Collins, 2020).

Although masculinity has some similarities to prettiness, there is one very important and very substantial difference: Prettiness is about one aspect of women's lives, although that aspect of their lives can be central to who they are, how they see themselves in the world, and how the world sees them. A woman can be pretty as well as smart, accomplished, a doctor, whatever.

When she is home, though, she may have the option to just be her regular self, perhaps not pretty. A man, on the other hand, is expected to be masculine at all times, even when he is alone and unobserved. If you think I'm overstating the alone-and-unobserved part, think of a man in your life who is reasonably masculine, or Man Enough, and definitely not a guy who routinely challenges gender norms. Ask him if he would let you paint his toenails during the winter and keep them painted for a week while he goes through everyday life. This is the kind of thing that no one would know he's doing (although he might not be able to shower at the gym or go swimming), and it isn't inherently sexual, and yet there's a good chance he'll decline because criteria related to masculinity make it uncomfortable for him to have painted toenails.

WHERE DOES MASCULINITY COME FROM?

Feminist theorists and scholars have argued about where masculinity (and femininity) comes from (Butler, 1990; Connell, 1995; Connell & Messerschmidt, 2005; Pleck, 1981, 1995). For researchers and theorists, this question is about the level of analysis. For clinicians, the question highlights the source of the individual's motives or behavior. In the next few paragraphs, I detail three positions related to the source of motivation and behavior as they relate to masculinity: (a) the individual level; (b) the interaction of the individual and their environment; and (c) the broader, cultural level. To continue with the idea that masculinity is complicated, I will tell you right now that my personal answer is "All of these positions are accurate."

The Individual Level

We might think of masculinity as something that exists at the level of the individual. Here, people's beliefs and behaviors are what constitute masculinity; we might also say that masculinity is defined by what (most) men do. For example, sports—team sports and violent sports in particular—are masculine because the majority of athletes and fans are men. Similarly, wearing skirts and trying to look pretty are considered feminine because the majority of people wearing skirts and trying to look pretty are female. This analysis is based on what individuals do. You might think of this type of thinking as bottom-up in nature because it collects information on the basis of the actions of individuals and develops generalizations on the basis of the information collected. When we say a man is trying to be masculine or trying to get punches on his Man Card, we are working at the individual level: He is the (primary) cause of his behavior.

The Interaction of the Individual and Their Environment

We might also think about masculinity as something that exists at the intersection of the individual and their immediate environment. Here, masculinity consists of the things men do primarily because of their immediate environment. Acting in a particular way because he's with the guys, trying to impress his date, or in a sports bar are all examples. This person–environment consideration is a very specific version of trying to fit in or trying to impress other people, which means there's a performance element of masculinity. Similarly, a woman might dress to the correct level (and style) of pretty depending on who she'll be with and where she expects to be. When we say a man is just trying to fit in with the guys, or that he's acting in a particular way in order to impress a potential dating/sex partner, then we are identifying the (primary) cause of his behavior as the interaction between the individual and their immediate environment.

The Broader, Cultural Level

We might also think about masculinity as something our culture expects men to do. In this respect, men follow masculinity's directives because, well, that's what men are supposed to do. From this analytic lens, the culture encourages men to be masculine. That cultural force is typically labeled *patriarchy*. The encouragement here can be mild, such as questioning looks from other people, or it can be direct, like when a guy is told to "man up." And the encouragement to be masculine can be backed up by the force of law. For example, in the mid-20th century a man could be fired from his job and arrested because he engaged in homosexual activity—a clear statement that men should never engage in any same-sex sexual activity or identify as homosexual. Similarly, we might talk about the ways our culture pressures women to be pretty, rewarding those who do it well and penalizing those who do not. When we say a guy's behavior is the result of masculinity, or of the culture in which he is being raised, or when we say his behavior is an example of our culture's definition of masculinity, then we are positioning the culture as the (primary) cause of his behavior.

In this book, I focus primarily on the individual level. I do so because this is a book for clinicians who are working with men individually, in couples, or in therapeutic men's groups. These clinical settings typically emphasize individual behavior. That doesn't mean I won't discuss men and their immediate context or masculinity at the cultural level—I will—but most therapeutic work is about helping individuals cope with their issues by adapting their thoughts, feelings, and behaviors. Sometimes that coping involves changing their immediate environment by changing jobs, terminating a personal relationship, or making some other contextual change.

I also want to be clear that my discussion of masculinity in this book is strictly based on masculinity as cisgender men perceive and experience it. That is where my clinical and academic expertise lies. This book is not designed or intended to guide work with transgender men (Singh & dickey, 2017), or to discuss women's experiences of acting in a masculine way (Halberstam, 1998). Because masculinity has cultural (and historical) bounds, this book focuses on men in the United States, whether they were born here or whether they have been here long enough to have acclimated to and adopted the culture.

THE MULTI-FACETED MASCULINITY FRAMEWORK AND CULTURAL CHANGE

Masculinity's criteria, achievement, types, and negotiations can, and have, changed over time as our culture has changed. I have already mentioned a few of those shifts, such as the change from encouraging men to be Good Guys to encouraging them to be Real Men, the metrosexual type of masculinity, and the expectation that having a female supervisor would be inherently stressful for men. You likely are aware of other shifts, such as the push for fathers to be more involved in the emotional aspects of their children's lives (starting in the 1980s), greater permission for men to acknowledge and verbalize a broader range of feelings (starting in the 2000s), and greater efforts to get men to address their mental health (starting in the 2010s). In later chapters, I briefly address some of the cultural shifts related to specific masculine criteria, such as changes in attitudes toward sex outside marriage (Chapter 8) and changes regarding men's emotional expression (Chapter 9).

We also know that masculinity is defined differently in different cultures. The definition appears in the form of different masculine criteria, requirements for masculine achievement, and masculine types. In each chapter of this book I address, as part of discussions about intersectionality, some of the ways differences might appear. A complete discussion of differences, either within the United States or across the globe, is beyond the scope of this book.

THE MULTI-FACETED MASCULINITY FRAMEWORK IN THE THERAPY ROOM

Now that we have a shared and complex understanding of masculinity, we can discuss how to use the MFMF in therapy. The most direct application is by using your own knowledge and understanding of men's issues. As William Ming Liu argued in 2005, understanding men and masculinity reflects a form of *cultural competence*. The idea behind cultural competence is that good therapy requires the therapist to be knowledgeable about the factors that shape an individual's life and are based on some aspect of their identity (e.g., maleness) and recognize ways in which their clients' experience and ways of being may differ from the therapist's own experiences and ways of being as a result of this influence. This is especially true as I write this in 2025, when the majority of therapy students and therapists identify as female, a trend that has been true for decades in psychology, counseling, and social work.

Thus, using the MFMF can help you better conceptualize your male clients and may provide you with additional (or different) factors to use as the focus of clinical intervention. The MFMF, and the information provided in this book, may also allow you to provide men with some psychoeducation about masculinity, if you choose to discuss and identify the four components of the MFMF with your clients. I often do this with my clients, either in the form of a discussion of masculinity or some version of "That's how our culture expects boys/men to behave." I don't usually direct this into a broader discussion of "What is masculinity?", but some clients take the conversation in that direction.

Some clients have a reasonable level of adherence to some of masculinity's criteria, have achieved Man Enough status, and have a masculine type that describes at least part of their identity. These men typically have self-confidence, self-esteem, and some idea of how and where they fit into the world that is rooted in their masculinity. (They may also have additional sources for these elements of their sense of self.) If they see their lives as going well—and the important people around them agree with that assessment—then therapeutic work may involve small adjustments to their personal construction of masculinity, but it is unlikely to require substantial shifts in their understanding of themselves as men. Chapters 3–6 describe men who fit this description. Other clients have a clear sense of themselves that is based on their masculine criteria, achievement, and type, but it may not be working for them any longer, or it may not work for the important people in their lives. With these men, clinical work is more likely to require them to shift their focal criteria and masculine type, which may also require them to reachieve masculine status. Chapters 7–9 describe such men.

Other clients struggle with masculinity. Most adults have a reasonably clear sense of which criteria are important to them and what their type is, but some struggle to achieve the masculine status they want. If they are struggling to be Man Enough they likely will fit the criteria for anxiety or depression, but they may also struggle with attention-deficit/hyperactivity disorder or be on the autism spectrum and simply be struggling to meet neurotypical expectations. Some guys who struggle to be Man Enough are frustrated and angered by their failure to do so—or by the difficulty maintaining Man Enough status—and direct their frustrations outward. They may present as sexist or racist or homophobic and blame others for their failures, and they may be easily angered. In nonclinical terms, they come across as jerks. With men who are struggling with masculinity, clinical work involves helping them recognize elements of masculinity in which they feel successful (and are potentially Man Enough) and shift their masculine criteria and type accordingly.

The Multi-Faceted Masculinity Framework and Existing Therapeutic Approaches

The MFMF also provides clear points of connection to a range of therapeutic approaches. The goal of this book is to help you, as a clinician, understand your male clients and better conceptualize your work with them. In this section, I describe several points of connection between the MFMF and existing therapeutic approaches. This is not an exhaustive list but rather a way to help you start thinking about how you might incorporate the MFMF into your therapeutic approach.

Masculinity's criteria are directives about what men should (or should not) do. If a man is able to meet these criteria, he likely will gain confidence and self-esteem. There are two common issues here. One occurs when the client's behavior does not match the criteria he has chosen. In this case, clinical work may focus on altering a criterion that is too high so he can attain it; increasing a criterion that is too low, such that he doesn't feel a sense of accomplishment in meeting it; or improving his adherence to that criterion so he can meet his goal. (This may require him to attend a training program of some sort, e.g., a household repair course offered by his local community college, or an assertiveness training program.) The other common issue is when the criteria are inappropriate for the client or inherently problematic (e.g., using violence to solve problems). Inappropriate goals are those for which the client is ill suited, such as an introvert who wants to demonstrate his masculinity by being promiscuous because finding sexual partners requires substantial interaction with strangers.

Conceptually, you might think of masculine criteria as beliefs, values, or norms, or another cognitive structure. As a cognitive structuring technique, you could challenge these norms using principles from cognitive behavior therapy (CBT) or dialectical behavior therapy (DBT) or another approach that helps the client explore and understand their beliefs about appropriate behavior. This approach is especially useful if a particular criterion is too high or too low. For example, if a client believes men should be tough, you might ask—and even have him collect data on—how often he displays toughness during the course of a day, the people toward whom he displays it, the situations that evoke toughness, and the feedback he receives on his demonstrations of toughness. You might also challenge him to intentionally be not-tough in order to determine if the consequences of being not-tough are what he expects.

If you think of masculinity's criteria as core beliefs or personal values, you might ask him a different set of questions that I learned as part of values clarification training back in the 1990s. Here, questions focus on why this is important to the client. You might ask, for example, "Why is it important to be tough?" and prompt the client to distinguish between why this is difficult for guys in general and specifically for him. This approach is useful when his criterion seems like a poor match with his personality or abilities.

Psychodynamic approaches often emphasize early life experiences as shaping subsequent behavior (Blazina & Bartone, 2016), with parental expectations (and punishments) carrying substantial weight in childhood and beyond. Accordingly, you might ask a client about his parents' expectations regarding his behavior, in particular, their standards around male behavior. Did they chide him—or punish him—for "crying like a girl" or "being a sissy"? Tell him to "toughen up" and punish him for not being tough enough? Statements of this sort would contribute to internalized expectations of appropriate (male) behavior.

Masculinity's achievements, the need to demonstrate a moderate or high level of adherence to masculine stereotypes, could also be challenged using CBT or DBT or a similar approach. Achieving masculine status—being a Real Man or even being The Man—is the cumulative result of a variety of efforts over time. Journalistic coverage of and academic research conducted with teenage boys has revealed that they are acutely aware of ways in which their masculinity is being observed and policed by their peers (e.g., Orenstein, 2020; Reigeluth & Addis, 2016; Reiner, 2020; Rosenberg et al., 2017). As one of my clients told me, "It's like having a Greek chorus in your head all the time" that tells you whether or not you are Man Enough. In my work with this client we routinely spoke about the chorus' comments, the volume (or intensity) of those comments, and the frequency with which the chorus was commenting. Over time, he was better able to follow his own perceptions of how to be a man instead of adhering to the standards he had internalized as a child.

Narrative approaches can be useful when addressing masculine achievement because they provide clients with a way to think through some of the what-ifs. With clients who are especially focused on whether or not they are Man Enough, or who seem particularly insecure in their masculinity, I might ask them to tell me the story of their efforts to be seen as manly. Once they have done this, I sometimes ask them to write the next chapter: What comes after they have proved their masculinity? I might also ask for alternative scenarios in which they do not feel as if they have proven their manhood and scenarios in which they are seen as The Man.

As mentioned, the term masculinity's types refers to the different ways to be a man, and they, too, readily lend themselves to therapy. Internal family systems therapy, for example, focuses on an individual's parts and uses labels such as *provider* and *protector*. These two can explicitly been seen as masculine types and thus can facilitate a discussion of how a client's version of masculinity (and his behavior) shift on the basis of which part of himself is present (Schwartz, 2021). I focus on providers/breadwinners in Chapter 3 and protectors in Chapter 6.

The question "What kind of man do you want to be?" is consistent with existential approaches that focus on clients' efforts to make meaning of their lives. Asking this question used to be common, and it still is in communities that emphasize meaning making and living by one's values. In therapy, that question can have a different, subtler power: It can create room for the idea that there are ways to be a man beyond the singular image/stereotype of being a Real Man. I'm fond of using identities and roles as part of therapy, and in the next section of this chapter I describe my approach.

As discussed, masculinity's negotiations encompass the range of ways an individual must negotiate to achieve a balance among his desires, his expectations of what it means to be a man, and the environments in which he finds himself. Stated in this way, it sounds very Freudian; negotiations among the id (desires), the superego (internalized rules), and the ego (mediator) were central to Freud's work. We might also draw from cognitive approaches here, asking what internal and external factors prompted a particular client to emphasize the masculine criteria of toughness instead of breadwinning, for example. Overall, negotiations—helping a client understand what prompts their behavior, especially behaviors with negative outcomes, and how he might change this or cope with it—are the bread and butter of therapy.

When exploring negotiations with a client, I often find myself relying on one of the main tenets of behaviorism: the idea that individual behavior is triggered by a range of environmental cues, such as where the person is (e.g., home, work, exercising) or who they are with (e.g., alone or with friends, coworkers, a romantic partner, family). I then highlight ways these situational differences demonstrate his ability to selectively control his behavior, including the ways in which he meets different masculine criteria or places varying emphases on masculine achievement in diverse settings.

The Multi-Faceted Masculinity Framework in Dr. Smiler's Office

I personally am quite fond of identity-based approaches to therapy. In the 1960s, Erik Erikson (1963) explained that the primary task of adolescence was to develop an identity; he spoke about the *identity crisis* as the process of moving through the adolescent life stage and developing a coherent sense of self. James Marcia (1966) expanded on Erikson's work, emphasizing the importance of exploring different elements of identity before committing to some of those elements.

Our culture changed, and by the late 1990s many youth had not finished this process during their teen years, so Jeffrey Arnett (2000) argued that we should think of identity development as continuing into what he called *emerging adulthood*. Despite the shifts in ages, successful resolution of the identity crisis has not changed. The process is about developing a set of values by which the individual will live and beginning the process of finding their place in the world. For me, the values Erikson (1963) wrote about include acceptance or rejection of each of the many masculine criteria and determining how much masculine achievement a guy wants. These decisions form a masculine type, and he must then negotiate with the self and his environment(s) to enact it; this overlaps with Erikson's ideas about finding one's place in the world.

Within Erikson's (1963) perspective, I often think of a man's capital-I *Identity*—his masculine type—as the central, singular way that shapes how he defines himself and how he interacts with the world. For some guys, a single identity can be so central or strong that it crowds out everything else, and thus their all-caps IDENTITY accounts for 75% or more of who they are. For other guys, it's simply the dominant part of their capital-I Identity—maybe it's 50%–74% of who they are—with the remainder coming from their family, a hobby, an intersectional category, or something else. According to my understanding of Erikson, someone who does not have an identity that is at least 50% of their being has failed to resolve their identity crisis.

I am also influenced by John Turner's (1999) discussion of social identity. Turner worked with his mentor, Henri Tajfel, on foundational research regarding ingroups and outgroups (e.g., Tajfel & Turner, 1979), and his social identity research focused on what it means to be a member of an ingroup and voluntarily take on that identity. Social identity theorists—Turner isn't the only one—emphasize that everyone has multiple social identities. We easily and readily switch between these identities as needed, and each social identity positions us differently by drawing on different elements of our personhood (Thoits & Virshup, 1997). For example, if you asked me for my opinion about the best age to give a child their own smartphone, I would give you a complicated answer that invokes three of my social identities because "As a therapist, I see. . . . But as a researcher, I've learned. . . . And yet as a parent, I've chosen. . . ." Some identities might be transient and be associated with a phase that lasts for a defined period of time, such as being a graduate student, whereas others, such as being a parent, may last much longer.

I like the idea of social identities because they are inherently flexible and changeable. By definition, each person has multiple identities, and we invoke them as needed. This approach allows a man to adopt one—or several!—masculine types as identities (with a small "i"), using the one he needs in that situation. Furthermore, none of these social identities needs to be dominant or the default; he can equally value the different masculine types he uses at work, with his friends, with his partner (and children), and so on. Having multiple social identities that an individual routinely switches between allows that person to be healthy without having an identity that accounts for 50% of their self-definition.

Many of my adult clients who are established in their vocational path Identify themselves through their careers. Their job is often the first part of the answer to "Tell me about yourself," giving me a clue that his work self may represent his Identity or IDENTITY. If he keeps spontaneously returning to his work self to answer questions that don't require it, or if he tells me he doesn't have any hobbies, I'm more likely to see work as his IDENTITY than as an Identity or an identity. Over time, I'll probably want to add more flexibility and talk about other identities he has but doesn't prioritize. (I discuss work and breadwinning in more detail in Chapter 3.)

As I continue getting to know a client, I'll want to know what he likes about his job and more about what he does during his free/discretionary time, including the media he prefers (television programs, movies, musical performers, video games). These things will give me a sense of what is important to him and what he is good at; both of these point to his strengths. A guy who likes mysteries or puzzle-solving video games probably sees himself as smart or clever or a good problem-solver, whereas a guy who works out and plays sports (including sports video games) probably values competition. I might call those "values" or "priorities" in conversation, but in my head I think about them as masculine criteria. I'll also try to assess how much masculine achievement he's seeking: good enough to be seen as a (real) man or striving to be The Man? Or perhaps he really doesn't care about how other people see his masculinity and has opted out. (This is often the case for guys who see themselves as "just a dad.") I'll also want to know about his negotiations—both the successes and the struggles.

During the first session or two, I'll also ask about his sex life. For many men, especially heterosexual men, their sex life serves as a barometer for their primary romantic relationship, their masculinity, or both. It's also one of the few things men typically feel comfortable complaining about. I address men's willingness to complain in Chapter 5 and discuss male sexuality in Chapter 8.

CONCLUSION

Masculinity is complicated. If you remember only one thing from this chapter, I hope that's it. I've tried to delineate some of that complexity by presenting the MFMF, which describes four distinct elements of masculinity, and which I'll return to in each of the case study chapters:

- **masculinity's criteria:** The specific expectations about how men will think, feel, and behave, such as men should be tough, and men don't cry
- **masculinity's achievement:** The status derived from being judged as sufficiently adhering to masculinity's criteria. Men who are sufficiently adherent are Man Enough, and those whose adherence is particularly noteworthy may be described as The Man. Others may "fail" at masculinity.
- **masculinity's types:** Preexisting images, identities, and stereotypes that are commonly associated with men; examples include the Real Man, Good Guy, Jock, Metrosexual, and Rebel
- **masculinity's negotiations:** The ways in which men make choices about masculinity, as well as the positive and negative consequences of those decisions

Masculinity is also complicated by the fact that its criteria can be contradictory, have experienced historical changes, and can vary across cultures and subcultures. Teen boys and adult men feel pressure to adhere to the (dominant) definition of masculinity.

The MFMF can help you, as a therapist, think about men's lives in more detail. Masculine criteria and masculine achievement provide a way to understand the rules and goals a client has internalized that shape his life as a man. These points of shared understanding can then lead to therapeutic discussions and change through the use of techniques from CBT and DBT, existential therapies, narrative therapies, and other approaches.

The MFMF can also help you and your clients adopt a more holistic approach to exploring their masculine type, and it readily lends itself to internal family systems–style part work (Schwartz, 2021), existential therapies, and other approaches. Similarly, discussions of masculine negotiations provides a method to frame struggles of daily life as an inherent part of masculinity.

Regardless of which aspects of the MFMF you find most familiar and useful, I believe that having a complex understanding of masculinity will help you be more culturally competent, and thus more effective, with male clients.

3 THE BREADWINNER

GARY'S CASE

Gary was a 25-year-old, heterosexual, White, college-educated, cisgender male. The only child of divorced parents, he had lived primarily with his mother as a teenager but had regular contact with his father. Gary told me he spent a lot of time and energy worrying about things and always felt as though some aspect of his life was about to go wrong. This had certainly been true in his last romantic relationship: His girlfriend of 3 years cheated on him and then broke up with him.

During our first session, I started by telling Gary I wanted to get to know all of him, not just the problem areas. So I asked, "What do you do for fun? What are the things that make you smile?", and he talked about travel, especially attending music festivals—the 'paloozas and "40 bands in 4 days" kinds of events. We talked about them for several minutes, and I gave him space to talk about some of the bands he had seen and heard over the years.

https://doi.org/10.1037/0000499-003
Clinical Work With Men: Understanding Masculinity in Psychotherapy, by A. P. Smiler

Then I asked about the problems he was having, and the conversation went something like this:

THERAPIST: OK, I feel like I've gotten to know some of the good things in your life. Now it's time to get to the problems. Why are you in a therapist's office today?

CLIENT: I feel like I'm stuck, like my life's not going anywhere.

THERAPIST: What's stuck?

CLIENT: Like, all of it. My job. Especially my job.

THERAPIST: What's wrong with your job?

CLIENT: I'm not getting anywhere, and that's why my girlfriend left me. She basically called me a loser with no future and dumped me. I mean, she said all that after I found out she was cheating on me, but she's right. It's a dumb job, and I'm stuck in it, and that's why I'm never going to find another girlfriend.

THERAPIST: Come back to the job for a second. Tell me what you do for money.

CLIENT: Oh, right. I'm a production supervisor for one of the big food companies. We have a mill here that produces three different cereals. I help oversee the production lines, make sure everything is going smoothly and producing as much cereal as we're supposed to be producing, make our quota. If something goes wrong, it's my responsibility to fix it and get the line going again.

THERAPIST: Like, quality assurance (QA)?

CLIENT: No, there's another person who's responsible for QA, and I coordinate with them. They're responsible for overall quality of the product. The team I'm on is responsible for the production; QA makes sure we're up to standard. I'm one of three managers who make sure the line is operating at all times, 24/7/365. There's only one QA person. That'd be a better job than what I've got now. I might even be able to find a girlfriend again.

THERAPIST: Ah, OK; I get it. I'm curious. You said there were three managers and the line runs 24/7/365. Is there always a manager on duty? Does someone have to work nights?

CLIENT: Sort of. We can run without a manager on site, but then someone has to be on call. Every few weeks, I work nights. Me and the other supervisor. Our boss never works nights.

THERAPIST: So your hours rotate?

CLIENT: Yeah. One week days, one week evenings, one week nights.

THERAPIST: And is that OK with you?

CLIENT: [*Shrugs*] It's OK, I guess. I'm used to it, have been doing it for a couple years now. Actually, I kind of like nights better because my manager isn't there. Neither is the plant director or the QA person.

THERAPIST: Does that mean you're in charge at night?

CLIENT: [*Laughs*] No.

THERAPIST: But it's better when the senior managers aren't around?

CLIENT: I don't feel like I'm going to get in trouble if I can't get the line back up immediately.

THERAPIST: Do you get in trouble often at work?

CLIENT: Not anymore, but the first few weeks were really hard, and I felt like I was always in trouble.

THERAPIST: Was that "new guy" stuff?

CLIENT: I don't know. Maybe.

THERAPIST: Did you used to get in trouble a lot? Was there a time in your life when it felt like you were always in trouble?

CLIENT: My college girlfriend used to yell at me all the time, and we'd fight all the time. But then I'd apologize and we'd make up, and the sex was great. Can I say that? Talk about my sex life?

THERAPIST: Yes. That's an important part of your life, and you can talk about it with me. You can talk about anything here. It's all confidential, unless I think you're going to try to seriously hurt or kill yourself or somebody else.

CLIENT: Cool.

THERAPIST: So, wait. Your college girlfriend would break up with you regularly, you'd apologize, then y'all would have sex?

CLIENT: Yep.

THERAPIST: And that happened a lot?

CLIENT: Yep.

THERAPIST: And how was the sex?

CLIENT: It was awesome! She was probably the best partner I ever had. She would do anything and always had something new she wanted to try.

THERAPIST: Why did the two of you break up so much? Or did you just argue a lot?

CLIENT: Kind of arguing, kind of breaking up. I don't know what all the arguments were about, but a lot of them were about my grades.

THERAPIST: [*Confused*] Your girlfriend got mad at you for your grades?

CLIENT: No. If I did poorly on a test or project or something, I'd get "mopey." That was her word. And she didn't like that, so she'd get mad at me, and we'd argue, and if I didn't stop moping then she'd break up with me. Or threaten to break up with me, anyway.

THERAPIST: And what stopped the arguments?

CLIENT: I'd find a way to stop being upset. Usually by thinking about how awesome the sex was. And once I stopped being sad, I'd apologize and tell her how important she was to me and how much I loved her and wanted to be with her.

THERAPIST: And then y'all would have sex?

CLIENT: Yeah. Sometimes right away, sometimes not for a little while.

THERAPIST: Uh, don't take this the wrong way, but I'm trying to understand and need to ask. Did you ever get mopey so that y'all would argue and then have sex?

CLIENT: Huh? Oh, no. She really liked sex, and I don't think she ever said no. She was a total freak.

THERAPIST: Thanks. I needed to check that out. Sometimes I ask questions that can seem kind of strange.

CLIENT: No problem.

THERAPIST: OK. So, your college girlfriend used to get mad when you'd get upset about your grades, and now you avoid your manager and other managers at work?

CLIENT: Yep.

THERAPIST: And you're worried that if you get fired you won't be able to find a new girlfriend?

CLIENT: Yes. No. Not just that. I'm a production supervisor for a cereal brand, and I'm stuck in my job, and it's kind of a lame job. When I meet a girl, she'll be like "Nice to meet you. What kind of job do you have?" and then I tell her "I run a cereal production line" and it's game over. It's not the kind of job that really attracts women, y'know? It doesn't sound cool. I could bring her samples but "I brought you a box of cereal" isn't romantic. I don't have an office to show off. It's a lame job, and that means I'm lame, and I'm never going to find a girlfriend again because I'm stuck in this job.

I learned several things from this conversation, all of which I would need to explore further. One was that Gary's job had features he liked and features he didn't; his sense of being stuck at work didn't seem to be because his job was awful or he was at some type of dead end. I also learned that Gary was unhappy with his own work performance, and he was very leery of doing anything wrong or being chastised by his superiors, which made me think he was somewhat risk averse. Together, these things suggested that Gary's confidence, and the connection between his confidence and his willingness to take risks, would be important issues in our work. As I got to know Gary over the next few sessions, I also learned that Gary had a hard time setting and maintaining boundaries.

I also learned one other important thing from this conversation: Gary's perception of himself as a productive, effective worker (manager) was clearly and directly tied to his belief that he could find and keep a girlfriend. At the beginning of describing the reasons why he came to therapy, he told me his girlfriend had left him because he was not getting anywhere at work, and he immediately followed that by saying "I'm stuck with this job, and that's why I'm never going to find another girlfriend." Later in the conversation, he told me that when he was disappointed with his academic performance his college girlfriend was unsympathetic: They would argue, and she would (threaten to) break up with him, a pattern that likely strengthened his belief that a good job and a girlfriend were linked. I learned more about the centrality of his work to his self-image and self-confidence as we continued to meet, and this would become a central component of our work together.

Themes in Gary's Therapy

I addressed two main themes in my work with Gary: (a) setting boundaries and (b) taking initiative. We started with boundary work; specifically, our discussions focused on helping Gary become comfortable giving (negative) feedback and directions instead of trying to take care of people's feelings. When someone wasn't doing things properly, he rarely told them so directly; instead, he might work next to them doing the task properly and hope they would notice, or make a suggestion, or encourage them to work faster, but he would go to great lengths to avoid saying "You're doing it wrong." As newly trained therapists in the 1990s, my colleagues and I called this type of work *assertiveness training*. Today, those same principles make up the core of *boundary work*. Whatever you call it, these approaches teach clients to say things like "This is allowed" and "This is not allowed," and that was exactly what Gary needed. Although it was slow and uncomfortable for Gary, he made some progress in directing people's work. Gary's biggest takeaway was that he was not responsible for other people's feelings.

We also identified ways that he could take initiative and thus show leadership, which is not easy in a factory that runs 24/7/365 and has written procedures for everything. Here, we focused primarily on administrative tasks he could create and complete in order to better show his abilities. Gary also struggled here, working slowly at tasks he claimed to feel comfortable with. As we explored his slow speed, Gary acknowledged that the thought of suggesting the company make changes created the same anxiety for him as telling someone they were doing something wrong.

Our discussions of boundary-setting expanded to include his mother after she arrived, unannounced, for a 4-day visit. She lived in a rural area 2 hours away and was coming to town for a weekend-long craft festival where she could buy unique Christmas gifts for the people in her life. Gary's mom expected him to spend all of his nonwork time with her, including attending the festival despite his general lack of interest in buying craft goods. Gary did as expected and didn't complain to her. He told me about it when I saw him the following week.

Discussion of his mother's visit revealed that for most of his adolescence, Gary's role in the family had been to take care of his mother. She didn't date after the divorce, and teenage Gary often served as her companion for events out of the house. Gary's mother also needed a lot of reassurance about day-to-day activities, as well as about the quality of the mother–son relationship, and I suspected that she had an untreated anxiety disorder. Gary's efforts to ensure that other people's emotions stayed level and to reassure them when he was correcting them seemed to have roots in his relationship with his mother.

Approximately 2 months later, something important happened at work. Gary had been a production line manager for 3 years: 1 year at another company and 2 in his current position. He had an assistant manager and manager above him who were responsible for the three lines producing this item. There was also a plant manager (and assistant), as well as a QA manager he had to work with. Gary ultimately imagined himself moving up into one or more of these positions. Within a year of starting to work with me, his assistant manager left for another job. He applied for her position, but it went to a colleague who had slightly less experience.

A year after that, his manager left the company for a similar position with another manufacturer. The assistant manager was promoted, and Gary again applied for the assistant manager position and again was denied. In both cases, his lack of enthusiasm and the inconsistency of his efforts were key reasons why he was not promoted.

Upset, he applied for several comparable positions using one of the big employment websites. To his—and my—surprise, he was offered a position managing a production line for another company, this one a family-owned business based in Europe that had opened a plant in the United States about 2 years earlier. It was time for the family members to head home, and they chose Gary to manage their single production line as part of the transition to a (mostly) American managerial team.

Gary was excited, but things went bad quickly. His difficulty being assertive reemerged. We had worked on the challenges he experienced in telling others to do their jobs more effectively, and Gary had made improvements, but those gains were partly a function of knowing exactly how the production line worked in its entirety. Coming into a new job, where he did not have that knowledge, Gary returned to asking politely or trying to nicely cajole people into doing their jobs properly instead of being more directive and relying on the power and status inherent in his position as a manager (trainee). When he was fired 2 months later, Gary was more relieved than depressed or angry, but he quickly began to worry that his current girlfriend would leave him if he did not immediately find another job.

Being fired was a clinical turning point. With my encouragement, he found and accepted a job doing manual labor: building and installing wooden fences.

He had done work of this sort during high school and didn't mind doing it again, at least for a few months. We positioned this as a temporary gig—and it was, lasting nearly a year—during which time we focused on the practical and symbolic functions of the career path he had been on.

Gary as a Breadwinner

Helping Gary be the breadwinner and financial provider he hoped to be would require us to acknowledge and work with his definition of masculinity. I chose this focus for two reasons. First, Gary had initially talked about not getting anywhere in his professional life and the stress he experienced at work. Second, he would often spontaneously shift from discussing work to the ways in which work would facilitate his romantic life and allow him to get married, which suggested that marriage could not occur without a good job; this connection is exemplified in the conversational segment from our initial interview, which appeared earlier in this chapter. Thus, work was central to Gary's functioning and self-concept. This connection was also evident when he got fired; he quickly shifted from being relieved to no longer have to manage the stress of that workplace to being worried that his girlfriend would break up with him.

The idea that job and career were central to Gary's life and self-confidence made sense to me. Here in the United States, and in many places around the globe, a man's ability to provide for himself and his family are often seen as a central aspect of masculinity (Ng et al., 2008; Sand et al., 2008; Stearns, 1979). In nonindustrial societies, evidence of a boy's ability to provide for kin and clan have often been part of coming-of-age or manhood-focused rites that literally separate boys from men (Gilmore, 1990).

The prioritization of male work is especially important in American culture. As a child of the 1970s and 1980s, I was taught that when I met a man for the first time, I should ask him "What do you do for a living?" He would respond with his job title and maybe hand me his business card. This cultural standard emphasizes men's work in two ways. First, it says that the most important thing I should know about a man is his work and not, for example, whether he has children or what he does for fun. It also positions "his living" with his work; that question literally equates work and life.

Gary was failing in his workplace and thus failing to be a breadwinner or to meet one of masculinity's most prominent criteria—or, more accurately, he wasn't successful at work in the ways American culture pushes men to succeed. He didn't really meet the masculine criterion of being in charge, and he wasn't moving up the corporate ladder. But Gary had absorbed another norm regarding work: It was acceptable, and even expected, that being anxious or unhappy because of work was part of the price of earning a living. He had learned that as a breadwinner, his salary and benefits package were more important than his happiness or mental health.

MASCULINITY AND THE BREADWINNER TYPE

Being a breadwinner is central to current American conceptions of what it means to be a man. For most of the past 100 years, that has typically meant a full-time job with good benefits and good wages, potentially including the ability to move up the company ladder. Over the past 20 years, as we have entered the digital economy, breadwinning increasingly includes options such as having a start-up or a side hustle.

Viewed through the lens of the multi-faceted masculinity framework, which I introduced in Chapter 2, there are several ways to conceptualize and discuss any client's prioritization of breadwinning. If we conceptualize masculinity as a collection of criteria or beliefs, then the primary masculine criterion for breadwinners is their prioritization of work. If we think about masculine achievement and being Man Enough, then we might focus on the size of his paycheck and thus his ability to pay the bills and support his family. He will be labeled a Real Man if he is a high earner, he can support the family at an upper middle–class level (or better) on his salary alone, he is on the path to the C-suite, or he is an owner of a successful business that supports him full time.

If we instead think about masculine types, the most relevant image is the businessman. Analyses of this stereotype indicate that he tends to wear suits and other business attire. The businessman can be differentiated from other masculine types by his emphasis on earnings and work-related prestige. If this is a substantial part of his identity—he's a capital "B" Breadwinner or a BREADWINNER—he will be aware of the earnings of his colleagues, friends, and neighbors, and you likely will notice some competitiveness (and possibly bragging) regarding earnings, vacation, and social status. Even when they are ostensibly cautionary tales, movies like *Wall Street* (Stone, 1987) and *The Wolf of Wall Street* (Scorsese, 2013). illustrate what it means to be a highly successful businessman and breadwinner. The classic romantic comedy *Pretty Woman* (Marshall, 1990) also shows us the benefits of corporate success. We also have stories of disaffected men in the corporate world who see their careers as valueless, such as *Fight Club* (Fincher, 1999). When I first met Gary, he did not see his production supervisor job, or the career that lay ahead, as inherently worthwhile; it was just the way he would earn his paycheck and establish that he was Man Enough.

Benefits of Being a Breadwinner

For men, there are clear benefits to being a breadwinner in the ways that American culture directs them to do. Perhaps the most obvious benefits are the income and status associated with success. Being a breadwinner also fulfills Erikson's (1963) directives to find one's place in the world, especially in an American culture that equates a man's job with his worth. Meaningful employment generates respect, from men and others, that is due to workplace successes and the markers of status that are associated with this type of masculine accomplishment.

The benefits of being a breadwinner go beyond accomplishments and status. Workplace success builds and provides a sense of efficacy—the sense that he is capable of making things happen in the world, even if that occurs through the actions of others he is directing. Confidence is rooted in this sense of efficacy, as is a sense of purpose. Self-esteem also has roots here. Gary's confidence—including confidence in his ability to be a good romantic partner—was clearly tied to his workplace performance.

Among potential dating and sex partners, a breadwinner may be seen as a good catch. He may discover that more attractive partners are more readily available than for a presumably lesser man. If a man has enough money that he can be philanthropic, still other social and cultural rewards become available.

If he works as a manager, there is a good chance he will have good decision-making skills and, depending on exactly what his field and position are, he may have good people skills. Helping him explore life choices using the same diligence and ability to examine pros and cons that he would apply in the workplace can be effective in helping him weigh decisions and new approaches. His ability to manage his staff may mean that he is able to hear their concerns and create effective solutions, possibly including hearing concerns about his own managerial (or interactional) style. These skills can be useful for helping him understand interpersonal relationships, including romantic relationships.

With some clients, in particular those in mid-career or later who are struggling with workplace issues, I sometimes make the distinction between technical experts and administrators. *Technical experts* have extensive field-specific knowledge and are hired for their expertise, and they often lead teams. Their expertise typically generates workplace respect. They differ from *administrators*, whose background is more likely focused on management and who may have less technical expertise. The distinction between technical experts and administrators points to two different career paths and may help clarify future paths and contextualize some workplace conflicts.

Challenges of Being a Breadwinner

Men who are focused on being a provider are at risk for certain mental health issues. Gary's lack of confidence is one such example. This self-doubt can manifest in different ways. As depression, it is characterized by seeing the self as a failure, a lack of initiative and motivation, low energy, feelings of depression, and a reluctance to take risks or put too much effort in because of expectations of poor performance. As anxiety, it appears in the form of self-doubt and insecurity, tentative engagement at their job, and a reluctance to take risks or put too much effort in because of concerns about how he will be judged. Clinical efforts to help clients identify, experience, and accept credit for their workplace successes—small and large—are key to improving confidence and thus diminishing this source of depressive or anxious feelings. Coping skills that help clients get through the daily struggle and continue after failures are also important.

Men who prioritize being a breadwinner, and who also believe men should earn more than their female partner, may also struggle in today's economy. The past few decades have seen women's earnings rise, a continued trend of women earning more college and graduate degrees than men (Reeves, 2024), and an increase in the number of women who earn more than their husbands. These men may report feelings of inadequacy (because one isn't a Real Man if he earns less than she does) and dissatisfaction with their romantic relationship (because of the financial competition). Clinical discussions might help such a client identify other ways in which he is Man Enough/a Real Man, the benefits of finding a partner who helps the marital team do even better financially (and thus shifts the competition from him vs. her to them vs. others), or addressing this element of cultural sexism that he has adopted (although I recommend this approach only if he already views the culture as sexist and thus has a framework from which to work).

Breadwinners are also at risk of neglecting their interpersonal relationships. The obvious version of this is when men don't attend to relationships with their partners or children. Some breadwinners may fill all of their social needs through their workplace relationships. This can be a severe problem when those social needs are filled by people who are colleagues but never become friends, with *friends* defined as people you spend time with in ways that are not connected to work. (I discuss this further in Chapter 4.)

Men who are heavily focused on being a breadwinner and who experience success in their workplace are at risk for overidentification with work, becoming a workaholic, and burnout. Here, work is their capital "I" Identity and possibly their IDENTITY (see Chapter 2). Overidentification is often recognizable in the clinical setting when a client reports that the workplace is the primary or only place where he feels good, when a client lacks hobbies, and when a client lacks social contact outside of his current workplace (and his primary romantic relationship, if he has one). The mental health risk is due to the client's reliance on work as the primary source of positive feelings. There is also a greater likelihood that he is not meaningfully engaging in self-care.

Being a workaholic is characterized by investing more time, energy, and attention to work than is required, with the combination of both extra time and extra energy central to the definition (Andreassen, 2014). Physical symptoms of being a workaholic include signs of stress, such as irritability, high blood pressure, insomnia, and chronic fatigue. Social and emotional signs of being a workaholic include higher levels of work–family conflict and relatively poorer functioning in nonwork settings. Although men and women seem to experience workaholism at similar rates, it is especially common among people with blue collar or manual labor jobs, in particular in the male-dominated construction field (Taris et al., 2012). These fields also have the highest rates of serious workplace injuries and deaths as well as the highest suicide rates (Sussell et al., 2023; U.S. Bureau of Labor Statistics, 2022).

Burnout occurs when the workplace is no longer providing the positive benefits it used to. Although it can occur for any individual, in any context, burnout can be thought of as one possible endpoint of overidentification with a job. The loss of positives may be due to the client's abilities (decreasing abilities, or an inability to meet the expectations of a new role), changes in the workplace (e.g., change in job expectations, change in corporate policies/culture/coworkers), or a combination of the two. A client may feel stuck because of practical and logistical issues (e.g., salary requirements, a field where changing employers is difficult because of noncompete agreements or a lack of options), the extent to which he identifies with that position, or feelings of loyalty (to a company or supervisor). Discussions about other ways to define one's self, generate positive feelings, and maintain status/social standing will be necessary. The idea of a transitional period that will encompass personal changes and job-related changes can be helpful, as exemplified by Gary's new job building fences. When Daniel Levinson et al. wrote *The Seasons of a Man's Life* in 1978 (and when Levinson wrote about it for women in 1996), they wrote about adulthood as alternating between

5- and 7-year periods of stability and 2- to 3-year periods of change. Changing careers can require 2–3 years and could be positioned as one of those periods of change.

Intersectional Issues

In Gary's story, and throughout this chapter, I have focused on breadwinners whose work is sufficient to qualify them as Man Enough and possibly, eventually, qualify as a Real Man. But what of the guys who are struggling to reach that level of achievement, either because of issues of their own (e.g., poor attendance that is due to depression or substance abuse or some other issue) or to contextual factors, such as a lack of decent-paying jobs or discrimination? Men who are failing to achieve breadwinner status, and the masculine status associated with it, may become (more) depressed and see themselves as (more of) a failure, creating a sense of shame. If a man does not have good ways to express and relieve these feelings, he may turn to anger (see Chapter 6). And that anger can come out toward anyone, including his domestic partner, if, for example, they ask a question that triggers his shame.

Not every man can be the primary breadwinner in their family. America's history of racist and discriminatory practices raises distinct barriers for non-White men (APA Task Force on Race and Ethnicity Guidelines in Psychology, 2019; Hannah-Jones et al., 2021). These barriers may be most obvious when considering the school-to-prison pipeline that partly explains why Black men are incarcerated at a rate that is approximately five times than that of White men (McDaniel et al., 2013). The relatively low-quality schools available to poor boys of color also contributes to the challenge of becoming the primary breadwinner in adulthood (Reeves, 2024). Impoverished and lower quality schools are not unique to inner city racial/ethnic minority populations—they also exist in sparsely populated rural areas and tribal lands.

Growing up in a relatively impoverished family, regardless of the geographic locale, can set a boy on the path to lower earnings throughout his life. When boys need to—or choose to—start working full time as teens (and forego college, if that were even an option), that may set them on a path to lower annual and lifetime earnings. This situation is common among boys who become teen fathers (Dariotis et al., 2011), but it also may describe boys who follow their fathers into working on the family farm or another family business that relies on manual labor.

Men who have physical or intellectual disabilities may also struggle to be the primary breadwinner because those limitations may diminish their employment and earning options. Some research has shown that these men are less likely to be promoted than their fully able counterparts (Woodhams et al., 2015).

If a man is the primary breadwinner, which is likely in heterosexual couples because of the gender wage gap, and the family's money is tight or stressed or stretched, financial concerns may substantially influence the day-to-day decisions he makes. This is particularly true for men who do not have professional jobs or are not self-employed because they need to have any requests for time off approved by a supervisor. Furthermore, their employer may require them to use at least 4 hours of vacation or sick time for a single appointment. Job constraints of this sort may make it especially difficult for men to access health care for themselves, or to attend educational or health care appointments for their children when those appointments must occur during the man's work day.

WORKING WITH GARY AND OTHER BREADWINNERS

Gary and I worked together for approximately 4 years. Initially, we met weekly, but after a year or so we switched to biweekly meetings. In the next section, I describe the development of our treatment plan, which includes a brief discussion of three issues that were central to the therapy: (a) vocational issues, (b) Gary's definition of masculinity, and (c) ways to find work–life balance. I also describe some alternate definitions of *provider*—a common synonym for *breadwinner*—and briefly discuss how these alternates may appear in therapy.

Treatment Plan

From my first encounter with Gary, it was clear to me that his symptoms—lack of confidence, low mood most of the time, and difficulty identifying and engaging in pleasurable activities—were coming primarily from his workplace struggles. Those struggles prevented him from developing a sense of himself as competent, and thus he had low self-esteem. This low self-esteem then affected other aspects of his life, making him question his abilities and worth in those realms.

From a treatment perspective, any of these could have been the initial focus. I could have attempted to help Gary develop and bolster his self-esteem and self-confidence through examining and leaning into the things he enjoyed and in which he had found success. We would have done this in the social realm and at work, with the idea that his improved self-esteem would give him the confidence to improve his workplace performance and provide a sense of security in his relationship. This approach would directly address his depressive symptoms, with the goal of helping Gary relieve his symptoms by finding other sources of self-esteem and self-confidence.

Alternatively, I could have helped him cope with a difficult work situation. This approach might have led to the possibility that Gary would need to accept that his work skills were just OK, but not necessarily good, and that a managerial position might not be in his future, or might be available only if he obtained additional training. This approach would lessen Gary's depressive symptoms by improving his ability to cope.

As another option, I could help him improve his workplace functioning by helping him better understand himself and the context in which he made decisions about work, while also addressing the interpersonal skills he would need in the workplace (and in his personal relationships). This approach would help him build the skills that he lacked and thus (ideally) reduce the underlying issues that contributed to his depression.

In consultation with Gary, we prioritized workplace functioning. For Gary, this was a straightforward decision. He knew he was underperforming at work and had entered therapy seeing his poor performance as the primary reason he felt bad. Although I would have been fine with any of the three options I just described, the decision to focus on work meant that I could draw from his existing conception of himself while trying to facilitate some shifts in this conception (but I wouldn't have to try to restructure his personality). I also believe this approach gave Gary the best chance for long-term life satisfaction.

However, adopting a work-centered approach meant I sometimes straddled—and even crossed—the boundary between therapy and vocational counseling. I recognize there is a disciplinary boundary there and that vocational counselors have knowledge, training, and experience that I do not have; I was occasionally aware of my limitations and knew that next steps might require a consultation and possibly a referral. I also believe that therapy is about helping a client gain a better understanding of themselves and develop the personal and interpersonal skills they need and that facilitating these kinds of changes in the workplace is within my abilities.

Over the course of 4 years, Gary and I addressed several issues. First, because it was most readily identifiable, was helping him learn to be assertive and set boundaries. Although our conversations initially focused on his willingness and ability to give (negative) feedback to people he managed, we also identified ways in which he needed to be more direct when speaking to the important people in his life—partners and parents—and how to set boundaries so he wasn't responsible for their feelings.

Another central issue was helping Gary find the right workplace fit. Conceptually, our goal was to help him find a workplace where he could readily show his strengths and hide his weaknesses. For me, this also meant finding a workplace that didn't adversely affect his mental health. It might be someplace that he tolerated, and maybe even a place he liked, but it certainly should not be one he dreaded.

Unmarried and 25 years old, Gary was just starting his career and wasn't really thinking about work–life balance, but I made that part of the therapeutic conversation as well, knowing we were laying the groundwork for the next several years of Gary's life and that those years would likely include marriage and fatherhood. By having discussions about work–life balance now, I hoped Gary would have a straightforward path for making adjustments when those life events occurred. I have also included some parts of our discussion about developing and managing multiple identities. Although this topic wasn't part of my work with Gary, I often address these topics with men in midlife and of retirement age who have prioritized the breadwinner role.

Finding the Right Fit

While Gary was working his temporary gig, we spent time identifying a workplace that would be a good fit instead of talking about careers and job titles. I framed this in terms of a person–environment fit. In doing so, I introduced the idea that Gary might deliberately choose an environment that makes him feel good about work and able to enjoy it instead of choosing an environment that makes him depressed and dreading work. Gary initially struggled with the idea of choosing an environment because of how it would affect his mood; that's not a typical part of men's decision-making process with respect to their jobs. Gary's challenges in conceptualizing his job search based on his comfort weren't unique. Most of the men with whom I have worked expect to make sacrifices for their work, especially regarding their own comfort or convenience. As a result, I often need to repeatedly explain how finding a good fit will enhance their workplace performance. Our conversation went something like this:

THERAPIST: I'd like to help you rethink what you're looking for in your next job.

CLIENT: Uh, OK.

THERAPIST: You sound skeptical.

CLIENT: I'm not sure what you mean. I have a degree in food science. My training and experience are all based in managing corporate production lines, so that's what I'm looking for.

THERAPIST: In the 2 years we've been working together, you've been a production supervisor and a production manager, and you haven't liked either of those jobs. You're taking a break and building fences, and I don't know if you like building fences, but I haven't heard you complain about this job at all.

CLIENT: Huh. You're right. I don't love this job, but I don't really have any complaints about it either. Except the weather.

THERAPIST: [*Laughs*]

CLIENT: So you think I should just keep building fences?

THERAPIST: That's up to you. But I'm wondering if we could figure out a job in food production—or something that uses your degree and experience—that you wouldn't hate.

CLIENT: I guess?

THERAPIST: You sound unconvinced.

CLIENT: It's a job. I mean, I'm looking for a corporate job, and unless I get all the way to the executive suite I'm not going to love it. I just need to make a good salary. That's the most important thing.

THERAPIST: Is the salary the most important thing or the only important thing?

CLIENT: [*Shrugs*] It's probably the only important thing. Anything else is a bonus.

THERAPIST: Do your parents enjoy their jobs? Or did they when you were growing up?

CLIENT: I think my dad does, but I know his job stresses him out. My mom hasn't worked since I was little. And anyway, I'm a man. I'm supposed to earn a big paycheck and that's that. If I don't like my job or it stresses me out, that's just the way it goes. Work isn't supposed to make me feel good.

THERAPIST: What if it doesn't go that way? Or, maybe, what if work didn't suck, even if it didn't make you feel good? Could work be neutral, something that doesn't make you feel bad but doesn't make you feel good either?

CLIENT: That'd be nice, but that's not really a thing, is it?

THERAPIST: What do you mean?

CLIENT: Choosing a job because it makes me feel good. Building fences is fine, and it's been a nice break, but I need to find a real job that's going to give me a good salary and benefits. It doesn't matter if I like it or not. I can't keep going with an hourly job that depends on the weather.

THERAPIST: OK. So what if we helped you identify and find a job that doesn't stress you out any time you think about it or as soon as you show up at work? You don't have to like it, but wouldn't it better to have a job you didn't dread?

CLIENT: Seems weird. Like, I understand the idea. I don't think I can look for a job based on how it's going to make me feel.

THERAPIST: Why not? We talk about how crappy production line work makes you feel. You don't like the hours, you don't like having to manage other people, and the job bores you out of your mind because it is literally doing the same thing over and over and over again.

CLIENT: Yep. That's the way it goes.

THERAPIST: But you don't have any of those complaints about fence building. You don't supervise anyone else, the hours are decent, and every week—sometimes every day—is a different thing.

CLIENT: Yeah, and it pays poorly and I don't have benefits.

THERAPIST: What if we could figure out a job—or really, a job title—that taps into your education and experience but has more of the other stuff you like?

CLIENT: How would we do that?

THERAPIST: Let me ask you a few questions about your ideal workplace . . .

I use some particular questions to help my clients determine not only the field they're interested in but also the workplace environment where they are most likely to feel comfortable and, ideally, their abilities will shine. Once we have identified the environment that seems likely to produce a good fit, we talk about specific types of jobs (and job titles) within the client's field. This is one of the places where the fact that I'm not a vocational counselor is readily apparent: I don't have a good sense of the possible jobs and job titles, but my clients are usually able to fill that gap on their own or with suggestions from the employment websites. The following are some examples of the questions I ask.

- Colleagues: Do you want to work mostly alone, with a small group of colleagues that you'll interact with on a daily basis (perhaps as a member of one to three teams), or work with whoever is on shift that day (e.g., at factory, a big box store)?
- Public: Do you want a job that is mostly external/public facing, mostly internal facing (contact only with coworkers), or a blend of the two?
- Daily routine: Do you want to complete the same task(s) every day, have a routine where the specifics vary day to day (similar to classroom teachers), or have a job where every day can be very different from the day before?
- Work task routine: Do you want a job where you'll work at the same set of tasks pretty much every day, a job where your work tasks vary according to the project(s) you're working on, or a combination of the two?
- Physical activity: Do you want to be in one place/workstation for most of the work day, be moving around from one place to another most of the work day, or a blend of the two?
- Hours/availability: Do you want a job that ends when you leave work each day, a job for which you are occasionally expected to work outside the standard work day, or a job where you can always do work no matter where you are?

As Gary considered each of these questions, we discussed times when he had felt competent and self-assured at various workplaces, as well as academic and other settings that elicited these feelings. We also spoke about other aspects of company culture, such as operating hours (production lines often operate 24/7/365), the potential for (mandatory) overtime, and having multiple managers to whom he was responsible.

Gary's responses pointed to a job that provided a basic structure and routine but also had some variability to help maintain his interest and attention. He wanted to have a small group of colleagues he would work with regularly while also having a task structure such that the details varied day to day or week to week according to the project he was working on. Gary wanted a combination of being on his feet and at his desk, and he wanted to be able to leave work at work, but he was willing to have the occasional overtime or on-call shift. In short, he wanted to be part of a team with a job that had a basic structure as well as some variety.

This pattern of structure combined with variability was also evident in his leisure time activities, which included attending music festivals and traveling. Music festivals have posted lists of performers, but attendees never know what will happen on stage and have the option of arriving and leaving any time within operating hours. Travel worked similarly for Gary. He'd buy tickets in advance for high-priority events or venues that required reservations, but he'd leave the rest of his days available to explore whatever might catch his attention. Music festivals and travel gave him the option of spending all of his time with a group of friends, a subset of the larger group, or going solo for a few hours. These preferences paralleled his desire for regularly occurring sexual activity with lots of variety. (I often find that workplace preferences are similar to other preferences my clients have, which helps build my comfort with these questions.)

Addressing Masculinity

In addition to exploring these questions about his next workplace, Gary and I examined how he had come to see work as the primary element of his adult, masculine self that facilitated and allowed him to have a romantic relationship. His understanding was due in part to the result of our cultural positioning of adult men as breadwinners who provide an income to support their families. Gary's tendency to quickly switch between his job status and the stability of his relationship, as he had done when I first met him, reflected the strength of this cultural dynamic in his life.

Then, one day, Gary told me his father had yelled at him for being a poor manager, getting fired, and taking a break from the managerial track by doing manual labor. As Gary and I processed this conversation, Gary reported that his father was a successful regional manager for a big box store, having risen through the ranks at this chain since starting there at age 18. Gary reported feeling like a failure, not only because he'd been fired but also because he wasn't living up to his father's expectations.

For as long as Gary could remember, his father had always been tethered to his job in some way, including during family vacations. One family vacation was even cut short when his father needed to help manage a store after that store's general manager had been hospitalized. At that point in our conversation Gary realized he didn't want that life. This was the first time he had ever thought and verbalized such a sentiment. He didn't want his work to be the central, defining element of his life the way it had been for his father.

Finding Balance

When I asked about the other men in his life, Gary spoke about his uncle—his father's brother—whom his father was disappointed in (but still loved). With the help of Gary's father, Gary's uncle had become an assistant store manager in the same company. He spent 1 year as a store manager, was very unhappy, and returned to being an assistant manager. Gary saw his uncle as having a good work–life balance, earning a good income and occasionally having mandatory overtime while rarely taking work home with him.

The idea of work–family balance is well known, but from what I have seen most of the research and writing have focused on how women can accomplish this balance; relatively little work has focused specifically on men. In part, this is a historical artifact that results from ways in which American culture has chosen to focus on men as providers who work outside the home but not as caretakers (Smiler, 2019; Stearns, 1979). I believe work–family balance came to the forefront because of feminists' efforts to help women enter the workplace in greater numbers and gain access to a broader range of professions in the 1970s and 1980s, but women subsequently struggled to manage both the 40-hour work week and continue to manage the house and children. The lack of attention to men's struggles to manage career and family, and its implicit positioning as a women's issue, may explain why it often takes effort to convince them they should consider their workplace fit and not just the salary.

Gary spoke to his uncle at length about work–life balance and verified that his perceptions of his uncle's life were accurate. Then he explicitly adopted his uncle's approach and said he would stop seeking his father's professional approval. While Gary built fences, and after we explored the practical and symbolic meanings of being a breadwinner, he rewrote his resumé to match these new goals and emphasize his relevant skills.

Because of Gary's struggles with self-confidence, we allotted part of one session to simulating an interview. I asked some standard questions that tapped into his self-concept and self-confidence, topics that are part of standard therapy: What are your strengths? What are your weaknesses? How do you function in a group setting? Where do you see your career in 5 years? During this conversation Gary mentioned that he found it easy to "speak" and understand government regulations and that he had applied for regulatory positions when he first graduated. He still saw that as a desirable option and altered his job search to include regulatory positions.

Gary was able to interview for two regulatory positions. When he told me about the positions after his interviews, we returned to the questions I had asked earlier about workplaces where he thought he'd fit. He told me that as a food safety inspector (his potential job title), he would be part of a small team of regulators who were responsible for ensuring restaurants met public food safety requirements. Gary also told me the job provided a basic structure—how to complete an inspection—but every day would vary because he would be inspecting different restaurants. He also would split time between the office (to write reports) and the field (to inspect restaurants). Gary was offered one of these jobs, accepted the position and, within a few months, had become a solid and reliable part of the inspection team. Gary now had a job that fit him well and that he (occasionally) enjoyed. More important, he felt confident, his depressive symptoms abated, and he no longer dreaded going to work; after approximately 6 months as a food safety inspector, he told me he liked his job.

During Gary's mandatory training and probation period, we realized he was again having difficulty telling other people they weren't following the regulations properly because it meant telling them they were doing something wrong. We revisited our earlier work on boundary-setting and emphasized that other people's feelings (still) weren't his responsibility. He also paid closer attention to the various ways his trainers would tell people they were making mistakes, with Gary taking notes so he could adopt their verbiage. His ability and comfort telling people they were making mistakes improved, and Gary passed his probationary period. His confidence returned, and he again worried less about his girlfriend leaving him because he wasn't Man Enough. He also told me he felt confident enough to initiate sex more often, and thus the couple were having sex more often, and with more variety, than before. In many ways, Gary's (perception of his) sex life was a barometer for his overall functioning.

Embracing Multiple Identities

Masculinity directs men to strive to be the best, to be strongest or fastest, and, ultimately, to focus on a singular goal and put most or all of their effort into reaching that singular goal. However, balance requires a distribution of effort and making conscious decisions about how to allocate one's time, energy, or attention. Accordingly, men may require a new framework that helps them juggle multiple simultaneous priorities—and multiple identities, as described in social identity theories (e.g., Turner, 1999)—instead of following the cultural standard that encourages men to prioritize work and downplay commitments to their home, their health, or their self. For example, if we shift attention to the nonfinancial aspects of being a provider, as opposed to a breadwinner, then a man might focus on providing the infrastructure necessary to keep the family functioning. This may take the place of household maintenance, maintaining the family's vehicles, managing the family's money, maintaining the family's computers and technology, and other forms of facilitating current-day American life. With respect to child rearing, alternate or expanded definitions of providing might highlight instilling in one's children good morals, a good character, and a sense of right and wrong. These potential redefinitions of what it means to be a provider may be especially important for men who are stay-at-home fathers (Rochlen et al., 2008, 2010). Intersectional factors may be particularly apparent here, especially as they affect a man's ability to complete household repairs, vehicle repairs, and maintain technology.

For my clients who are age 50 or older, I often raise the issue of social preparation for retirement. Men who have primarily defined themselves as a breadwinner can be particularly unprepared for this, and this is reflected in suicide statistics. Among men, suicide occurs in substantial numbers among those age 18–29, and then declines, with a substantial increase again among men in their 50s and 60s. Explanations for the increases in middle age are typically associated with loss of job, income, or job-related prestige. Sylvia Canetto is a leading researcher on gender-related aspects of suicide (Canetto, 2015; Canetto & Lester, 2002). She and her colleagues have demonstrated that men who lack meaningful social involvement with their families are particularly likely to die by suicide (e.g., Chen et al., 2021). Accordingly, I check on clients' roles and identities within their family and elsewhere, with particular attention to whether those connections seem likely to persist once they stop working. A client and I might also speak about building an identity that is based on a range of roles instead of having his identity be primarily defined by his job.

CONCLUSION

In American culture, men are often defined by their jobs. His job is often the first thing he will tell a stranger (after his name), and it's the first thing a stranger is taught to ask a man. Gary had an entry-level job in his desired career, but he was struggling and felt as though he was failing at this central tenet of masculinity. Being a breadwinner was so central to Gary and his conception of masculinity that concerns about losing his job triggered worries about his ability to maintain or start a romantic relationship.

Our work together required an examination of Gary's masculine type of breadwinner role as well as the level of masculine achievement he strove for.

He ultimately decided to aim for being Man Enough but not The Man. Gary came to this decision after we discussed the messages he had received about work, in particular those that told him men might need to suffer through work and (stoically) bear workplace-related stress and that men who didn't do this were somehow lesser. However, Gary's own family provided an example of a man who had made different choices that minimized his stress and prioritized his mental health. We also prioritized Gary's mental health by identifying the characteristics of a workplace that would increase his satisfaction with work and allow him to show off his strengths. After he found a job that fit these criteria, and became comfortable in that position, his confidence increased, his depressive symptoms abated, and he reported greater satisfaction with his life.

Gary's story was also noteworthy for his need to learn how to set boundaries, a problem that plagued him at work and in his personal relationships. Doing so also relieved stress and built his confidence. He seems to have maintained those gains: Gary added me to his Christmas card list after terminating therapy. From those missives, I have learned that he has married the woman he started dated while building fences, they have had a child, and they all seem to be happy.

4 THE SELF-SUFFICIENT MAN

SAM'S CASE

A 50-year-old gay, White, cisgender man, Sam was handsome, stood 6 ft (1.8 m) tall, and was clearly in good shape. He had had two serious romantic relationships, both during the 1980s–1990s, when he was in his 20s. The second occurred at age 27 and had been "the love of his life." Sam had had a few sex partners over the years, some of whom could have been called "friends with benefits" or "hookup partners" depending on the terms of the times (Garcia et al., 2012; Orenstein, 2020). He told me he was not interested in having an ongoing romantic relationship because he didn't have the time, energy, and attention to give to a partner. He was very used to living alone and doing whatever he wanted, and because he made good money Sam could afford to do whatever he wanted, especially if he didn't mind doing it alone.

Six months after I met him, Sam had a stroke. He resumed therapy 6 months afterward, having lost all sense of touch on the right side of his body, all mobility in his right arm, some mobility in his right leg and foot,

https://doi.org/10.1037/0000499-004
Clinical Work With Men: Understanding Masculinity in Psychotherapy, by A. P. Smiler

and some hearing in his left ear. He also had lost some cognitive capacity; his attention span, concentration, and memory were less than they had been before, and his mental stamina was less than it had been. Sam told me he was returning to therapy because he needed to talk about his boyfriend, and our first conversation went something like this:

THERAPIST: It's good to see you again. I'm sorry to hear about your stroke. That sucks.

CLIENT: Thanks. And yes, it does suck.

THERAPIST: What brings you back?

CLIENT: My boyfriend. I need to talk about my boyfriend.

THERAPIST: You weren't dating when we last met, so normally I'd say "Congratulations," but maybe not if the boyfriend is why you're back?

CLIENT: Thanks, but no. His name is Jay. We started dating about a month before I had my stroke. I was in the hospital for about 3 weeks altogether. They were going to send me to a rehab facility, but since Jay could be home with me I was able to skip rehab and head home. Jay being at home made it easier for my family and, quite honestly, I'm glad I went home and not to rehab.

THERAPIST: OK . . .

CLIENT: I've been home for about 7 months now, and Jay is still there.

THERAPIST: And you're not happy about it?

CLIENT: Not really, no. I mean, we'd been together for about a month when I had the stroke. I was trying to decide how much I liked him and if I wanted to keep seeing him, not if I wanted to move in with him. But he was willing to be my caretaker, and I guess my family was OK with him moving in and taking care of me, so that's the decision that was made. I don't remember being part of those conversations. I was so out of it for so long. I might have said yes, but I have no idea. Anyway, Jay moved into my house, and that let me go straight home instead of to rehab. I'm very grateful for that. And for all the help he's provided.

THERAPIST: But?

CLIENT: But I don't think it's working anymore.

THERAPIST: What's the "it" in that sentence? The relationship? Jay as caregiver?

CLIENT: The relationship. I mean, we were still getting to know each other; we'd only been dating for a month. Then all of a sudden we're living together, he's taking care of me because of my . . . limits, and everything is different.

THERAPIST: And if I remember correctly, you haven't had a boyfriend since you were in your 20s? So, not for about 25 years?

CLIENT: Good memory! I went from not having a boyfriend for 20 years to living with a boyfriend I barely know and hadn't even thought about living with.

THERAPIST: Yeah, that's a huge change in your relationship. Two of them, really: living together and Jay as your caretaker. In addition to all the big changes from your stroke. It's a lot to adjust to.

CLIENT: Yeah. And I'm not sure that I'm adjusting well to living with Jay. Or that I want to.

THERAPIST: OK. So what's wrong with living with Jay? The only thing I've got so far is that it happened way too fast.

CLIENT: [*Sighs*] It's . . . there's just . . . I don't know where to start. And I don't want to sound like I'm not grateful. He's been a huge help, and it was so much better being home and with Miles (Sam's dog) than being in a rehab facility for a few months.

THERAPIST: I'll bet. And I hear that you're grateful. But you didn't come talk to me and work your way up my staircase because everything's great, so tell me the bad stuff.

CLIENT: [*Chuckles*] True. OK. I don't think we're a good couple. He's not really my type. I mean, don't get me wrong. He's good-looking, and he's nice, but we don't have all that much in common.

THERAPIST: Such as . . .

CLIENT: [*Pauses*] I don't want you to think I'm petty.

THERAPIST: I won't. I promise. A lot of the guys I work with complain about their partners and sometimes it's [*using air quotes*] "dumb stuff." Relationship problems are one of the most common reasons people see a therapist.

Sam then launched into a litany of complaints and differences between him and Jay. The biggest complaints were their different levels of education (Jay had taken a few college courses, then withdrew; Sam had Master of Arts degree and originally came to therapy because he was struggling to decide if he should return for another advanced degree), their different tastes in food and media, and Jay's high level of physical activity (which suggested hyperactivity) compared with Sam's steady and measured pace. That pacing difference was even more important as Sam learned to cope with the impairments caused by his stroke. Once Sam started talking and realized I wasn't judging him, it was like the floodgates opened, and things he had been holding back had a chance to come out.

There are two other things that are important about this conversation, our first since Sam's stroke. One is that although we referenced Sam's stroke throughout the conversation, we spent less than 5 minutes discussing it directly. When we did, it felt clinical, with Sam reciting the neurology of what had occurred and the physical and mental impact it had on him. There was no real emotion as he spoke about it. The second thing is that Sam's speech was slower than it had been when I first met him; his speech wasn't quite clear, and he sometimes struggled to find a word. I've cleaned that up in the transcript, and by the time another year had passed, Sam's speech had a more typical pace, his diction was clearer, and he rarely struggled to find a word.

Before his stroke, Sam had already spoken about feeling stuck. He had moved up the corporate ladder and was earning an income of more than $100,000/year. But he had become bored with his current consulting-type position and disillusioned with the company he was working for. He had less energy than usual, said nothing really made him feel good or excited anymore, and reported that although he was fine with day-to-day decision making he had long struggled with big decisions. Now, after his stroke, I recognized that ending his relationship with live-in partner Jay fell into the category of big decisions.

Themes in Sam's Therapy

As we continued meeting, I recognized two themes that would dominate our work. One was Sam's avoidant attachment style. *Avoidant attachment* is a form of insecure attachment that is derived from an individual's tendency to avoid becoming attached to other people (Bowlby, 1969). People with an avoidant attachment style are typically described as "distant." They can have good social skills, and even become friends with people, but their relationships tend to be a little more distant or a little shallower than the average relationship.

Like many gay men his age, Sam had grown up in a time (the 1970s and 1980s), place (rural), and with family and community (conservative Christian) that did not approve of homosexuality or homosexuals. Sam wasn't particularly athletic growing up, and he never quite felt comfortable playing with the other boys, which opened him up to some teasing as a child, as it was called then, or *bullying*, as it is called now (Cohen & Brooks, 2014). Born in 1969, Sam turned 18 and graduated high school in 1987, in the midst of the AIDS crisis. Sam said his decision to come out to his parents at age 18 was difficult, but his fears were largely unwarranted. They were initially quiet, then responded with love and acceptance, referencing Jesus's demeanor when faced with people who were "other."

As a gay boy growing up in a rural area where he didn't fit in with the other boys, fearing rejection from his parents, and then experiencing rejection from the country as a whole during the AIDS crisis (described further in the "Intersectional Issues" section), Sam never really opened up to anyone. His avoidant attachment was the result of repeated small-t traumas, not a single capital-T Trauma. This would shape our clinical work while never quite being the subject of our clinical work.

In my experience, avoidant men tend to compartmentalize their lives more than other men with whom I have worked. During his 20s, Sam didn't introduce his boyfriends to his family members. If Jay hadn't shown up at the hospital after Sam's stroke, I don't know that Sam's family would have met Jay. This compartmentalization allows avoidantly attached and self-sufficient men to minimize any emotional spillover from one part of their lives to another.

Clients with avoidant attachment styles can be difficult to work with because they open up slowly and cautiously. Early in our work, I had to remind myself that this was the case and prompt myself to slow down because Sam needed more time than my average client to open up. Doing so helped minimize any frustration I was feeling regarding the pace of our work. The small wins I describe later in this chapter helped me know we were making progress.

The second issue was Sam's intense desire to be self-sufficient, often phrased as "independence." Self-sufficiency is a key element of modern American definitions of masculinity and the presumed answer to questions about why men don't ask for directions. Self-sufficiency is compatible with current American trends to "do it yourself" and take advantage of the gig economy to earn a few extra dollars. When done well, self-sufficiency relies on the ability to manage and plan one's present and future, and it requires both perseverance and fortitude.

I believe the combination of self-sufficiency and his avoidant attachment style both contributed to Sam's difficulty making big decisions and his avoidance of big risks. If he were to make the wrong decision, or the risk went poorly, he would have no one to blame but himself and no one to help him fix whatever had gone wrong.

Sam as a Self-Sufficient Man

Although Sam said addressing losses in physical and mental capacity caused by his stroke would not be a part of our clinical work, he provided updates on his recovery at every session. Sam's desire for self-sufficiency contributed to and facilitated his recovery. At each session, he spoke about the gains he was making physically, including his efforts to walk with only a leg brace instead of needing a cane. And even though my office was on the second floor and the building didn't have an elevator, he insisted on climbing the stairs instead of meeting in a vacant first-floor office my landlord was willing to let me use. Several months after therapy had restarted, about 15 months after the stroke, he was able to walk comfortably without a cane. Sam was good at physical therapy, likely because he had started working out regularly during his 20s.

Sam rarely allowed therapeutic conversations to focus on what he had lost; instead, he consistently focused on his efforts to regain functioning—to return to self-sufficiency. Twenty-four months after his stroke, Sam's legal status changed from temporarily disabled to permanently disabled. Sam did not perceive himself as permanently disabled; he saw himself as having experienced severe loss and recovering more slowly than average. However, he routinely reported having low days, when he lacked energy, didn't want to get out of bed, and accomplished little. In our discussions, he came to recognize these times as depressive episodes that typically lasted 1–3 days, occurred every 2–3 weeks, and were part of his emotional process of recovering from the stroke.

MASCULINITY AND THE SELF-SUFFICIENT MAN TYPE

Drawing from the multi-faceted masculinity framework (MFMF) I described in Chapter 2, the masculine criteria on which Sam centered his construction of masculinity typically comprise what is called *independence*. I've labeled it *self-sufficiency* throughout this chapter because I think that's a narrower and more accurate label. Male independence can take many forms. For Sam, it took the form of being self-sufficient and avoiding any type of ongoing reliance on other people. Other men emphasize being independent decision-makers or leaders (not followers), and yet other men emphasize their independence by assuming a top or dominant role during partnered sex and/or by demonstrating a reluctance to perform oral sex or be anally penetrated.

I have chosen to focus on self-sufficiency because that term narrows the frame to taking care of one's needs without help from others. Self-sufficiency qualifies a man for masculine achievement when he can financially support himself, especially when he chooses to live alone. Sam bought himself a house, took vacations alone, and often did things on his own. He was proud of his independence and his financial accomplishments.

As a method of achieving masculine status within the MFMF, self-sufficiency (and independence more broadly) will help a guy be Man Enough. A guy who isn't independent in some way will certainly face challenges to his masculinity and may not be respected as a man. However, self-sufficiency doesn't really provide a path to being The Man, although it may facilitate other methods of masculine achievement, such as breadwinning (see Chapter 3) and promiscuity (see Chapter 8).

Within the MFMF, the masculine types a guy might adopt or identify with that are based on self-sufficiency could be labeled, for example, "lifelong bachelor" or "loner." "Loner" has some negative connotations. It also has some overlap with "tough guy" and "lone wolf" because of their use in video games and characters from action movies, such as the *X-Men*'s Wolverine (Singer, 2000) and the eponymous *Riddick* (Twohy, 2013). Nonviolent loners do not have well-developed images or stereotypes in American culture. (I discuss anger and violence in Chapter 7.)

Benefits of Being a Self-Sufficient Man

Masculine self-sufficiency has several clear benefits. As I described in Chapter 1, we tend to think of men as doers, and pursuing (and achieving) a sense of self-sufficiency relies heavily on and reinforces the conception of the self as a doer and one who is able. The most obvious benefits, and inherent in Sam's story, is a history of accomplishment, a sense of confidence, and a belief in his ability to do things and get things done.

The successes of self-sufficiency can lead to greater social status. When self-sufficiency is combined with breadwinning and leads to workplace success, rewards include greater income and advancement to positions with greater responsibility and authority, as well as respect from colleagues. It can also generate respect and admiration from friends and family, and he can potentially find masculine achievement as The Man because of his efficacy. Thus, self-sufficiency can provide greater status and self-esteem.

Sam's history of self-sufficiency gave him the motivation and self-efficacy to work toward recovery after his stroke. Relying on a history of being physically and cognitively able, as well as a history of accomplishment, he was able to push himself through various forms of rehabilitation and regain some functioning. Sam isn't unique: Empirical research has revealed that men with a high desire for success and status have better rehabilitation outcomes after a traumatic brain injury or a spinal cord injury (Good et al., 2006).

Self-sufficient Sam had also been able to save a substantial amount of money that helped ensure he could pay for some adaptive services (e.g., automobile modifications) instead of waiting for charitable sources, ask his family for help, or apply for grants. Sam had a professional install grab bars in the bathrooms of his house, which allowed him to do everything he needed to do to live independently, even if those tasks required more time, effort, and attention than he was used to.

As noted previously, self-sufficiency includes independent decision making and is often referred to as "independence." For the self-reliant man, the healthy version of independent decision making involves obtaining the relevant information from reliable sources, obtaining a range of perspectives (for a complex decision), and then making a decision and developing a plan to carry it out. Thus, the decision is uniquely his, and he can lay claim to "being his own man" by making his own decisions. In fact, your self-sufficient clients may describe themselves as "decisive."

The Challenges of Being a Self-Sufficient Man

Although independent decision making can be healthy in many circumstances, too much reliance on one's own judgment without first seeking advice from others can be a problem, and some men choose not to seek input from other people when they need it. They may be seen as overly confident and come across as not open to suggestion.

The pressure to be self-sufficient can be seen in many aspects of U.S. culture. It has roots in the cultural and generational shift away from corporate pensions that were managed by a professional, and medical care that was overseen by your family doctor, to supervising your own retirement portfolio and managing your own health in consultation with your doctors. At the same time, self-sufficiency contributes to today's loneliness crisis because the need for friendship (or *interdependence*) runs contrary to notions of independence.

Researchers have repeatedly examined independence as an element of *masculinity ideology*, which assesses adherence to the (problematic) elements of current American stereotypes about men. One meta-analysis of more than 78 research samples found that greater endorsement of the independence norm was associated with more negative mental health (assessed through depression, general distress, substance abuse, poor body image, and other issues), less positive mental health (as measured via life satisfaction, general self-esteem, and other factors), and lower willingness to seek psychological help (Wong, Ho, et al., 2017). Other authors have addressed the negative impact of masculine independence on men's depression and friendship, among other topics (Addis, 2011; Garfield, 2010).

Intersectional Issues

Intersectional concerns can readily play into a man's desire for self-sufficiency. Sam's story illustrates this in two ways. First, he was a gay man who came of age in a homophobic era: Despite the thousands of deaths, Ronald Reagan's federal government and Ed Koch's New York City administration refused to recognize or meaningfully fund research into and treatment of HIV. Local governments in San Francisco and Los Angeles, as well as the California state government, were much more active in funding treatment and research (Shilts, 1987/2007). The homophobia endemic to American culture shaped Sam's adolescence and young adulthood. These factors likely contributed to his avoidant attachment style and furthered his belief that he could rely only on himself.

A second way intersectionality was evident in Sam's story was through his unwillingness to rely on family members. White conceptions of the nuclear family, which consists of parents and their minor children, provides a basis for this type of self-sufficiency because the children ultimately make their own way and the parents become empty-nesters. But that conception of family and that flavor of independence runs counter to other cultures' beliefs about how families work. The closeness of multigenerational Black families, conceptions of familismo among Latino Americans, familial piety among Asian Americans, and the importance of tribe and family among Native Americans all point to different conceptions of family in which members are more explicitly interdependent. In each of those non-White cultures family members routinely offer and receive help from each other. Help can come from anyone, regardless of generation or degree of connection (e.g., cousins, aunts and uncles, "great"-anythings), unlike White culture's focus on first-degree relatives (parents, siblings, children; Iwamoto & Kaya, 2016; Lee, 2021; Ojeda & Organista, 2016).

Sam was White, male, and highly educated, and he earned a high salary. He had saved quite a bit of money over the years, and these factors gave him the means to be financially self-sufficient and pay for the adaptive supports he needed after his stroke. Clients with more moderate means and those of lower socioeconomic status would have been forced to become less self-sufficient and more reliant on others. This would likely be a substantial challenge to their self-esteem and identity. Given the discrimination in educational and hiring practices (discussed in Chapter 2), such a scenario would be more common among men of color.

WORKING WITH SAM AND OTHER SELF-SUFFICIENT MEN

With the time before and after Sam's stroke combined, as I write this we have worked together for almost 6 years. We have typically met every other week, although the past 2 years have primarily been maintenance therapy, and so we have met every 1 to 2 months. During the initial round of therapy, I made clear efforts to provide Sam with small wins so he would find therapy valuable. After his stroke, our focus shifted to discussions of his romantic relationship, explorations of his other friendships, and some limited work related to his stroke-related losses.

Treatment Plan

When I first met Sam, his treatment and our work seemed fairly straightforward: helping him decide whether or not to return for another advanced degree. I would need to earn some element of his trust in order to learn more about the unstated factors that made it difficult for him to make a decision about pursuing another degree. Within the first two or three sessions, I recognized his avoidant attachment style, and I knew this would make earning his trust more difficult. I also learned he was risk averse, which would affect the decision-making process itself. Sam seemed like someone who I might see fewer than 10 times to address a specific problem.

When Sam returned to therapy after his stroke, he was explicit that our work would focus primarily on helping him determine what he wanted in a romantic relationship and whether Jay fit that description, so that was the treatment plan. Along the way, we would also address his friendships and grieve his stroke-related losses (a little), but those were secondary issues that he agreed to address only "if they came up"—but they weren't an official part of his treatment plan. Because Sam was self-sufficient and had an avoidant attachment style, I knew I needed to build trust by finding some small wins early in therapy. I had done that when he had originally come for treatment, but I provide more detail here. Trust-building is an inherent part of the therapeutic process, but it's not something that typically appears on a treatment plan.

Using the MFMF as a guide, I understood that Sam prioritized the self-sufficiency norm and saw his masculine type as independent/self-sufficient; he described himself as "something of a loner." Sam's descriptions of his behavior indicated that he saw himself and his behaviors as relatively constant and rooted in himself, with minimal changes that varied according to the context he found himself in; he almost never answered a "What would you do in this situation?" question with "It depends." This told me that our work would primarily focus on expanding Sam's self-understanding and his range of potential behaviors with little effort to change the environments he finds himself in (unlike Gary in Chapter 3).

Finding Small Wins to Increase Trust

Men who greatly value their self-sufficiency may do so as an outgrowth of their demonstrated competence but, like Sam, they might also be highly self-sufficient because they have difficulty trusting others and choose to rely exclusively on themselves. Taken together, the desire to be self-sufficient and the reluctance to confide in others can contribute to a strong reluctance to seek therapy. For a man like Sam, what could be more challenging than acknowledging that there's an area in your life where you're not self-sufficient and you need to address that gap by trusting someone else? Results from meta-analyses also have revealed this pattern: Men who score higher on measures of self-reliance report lower willingness to seek help (Wong, Ho, et al., 2017). When I recognize that a man like this has actually arrived in my office and demonstrated a willingness for therapy, I try to quickly recognize his strengths and his accomplishments.

To be effective with Sam and have him value our work, I knew from the beginning that I would need to earn his trust by helping him get things done (because he was a doer). At first, before his stroke, this meant some quick, small wins that he would recognize as progress toward his goal. That win can be something he can see or do outside the office that will provide evidence that talking to a therapist helps his life get better. With Sam, in our first round of therapy (before he had his stroke), this included the process of making a list of the pros and cons of leaving his job and returning to school. Together, we took three sessions to develop this list, and I pushed him to consider factors such as social life, personal values, desire for respect, and other emotional concerns in addition to the professional and logistical factors he could easily generate. Sam was surprised to realize how many of these emotional factors were influencing his decision and the ways they made it more difficult. Once he had completed the list, we looked at the total number of reasons in each column; I sometimes talk about the totals (or the difference between the totals) as *rational feedback*. I also asked Sam to identify the most important pro and most important con in each of his lists; I sometimes talk about these items, which reflect the strongest hope and strongest fear, as *emotional feedback*. Sam found this useful, and it helped him come to a decision. My ability to identify factors he hadn't considered served to demonstrate my competence and the value of seeking therapy and thus contributed to Sam's willingness to continue working with me.

From my perspective, those small wins were the building blocks that would lead to larger and larger changes. They helped Sam identify and adopt new ways of doing things, new ways of understanding things, new skills, and new coping strategies. This approach created a model for our work: Every time he shared a new problem in a new area of his life, I made an effort to make sure he experienced some type of quick, small win that he could see as progress toward resolving that problem, often by identifying emotional factors he hadn't considered. With this therapeutic process in place, Sam could present a new problem and assess both my receptivity and my efficacy helping him address it. I introduced emotional factors in the second session, when I started asking him about differences in emotional openness and trust across different types of relationships.

With other male clients, that quick, small win might be a suggestion that provides stress relief, such as taking 30 minutes for himself each day, or writing out a "punch list" of tasks to be completed instead of keeping them all in his head (which often leads to difficulty falling asleep). Or it might be a way to reduce poor communication with a relational partner by asking some version of "Tell me more" or saying "Let me make sure I understand you . . ." Or it might be some other intervention you think of as a starting point that helps a client address a problem he's asked for your help with. Because he's used to being effective in his life, your helpful suggestion will help him recognize you as effective at helping him improve. Therapy homework can further this element of building a therapeutic relationship.

Addressing Struggles in the Romantic Relationship

Sam hadn't had a serious romantic relationship in more than 20 years and had started dating Jay about a month prior to his stroke. Jay was fairly new to town, having moved here to be geographically close to his sister and her family. He moved out of his apartment and into Sam's house approximately 1 month after Sam's stroke, which allowed Sam to return home quickly instead of spending significant time in a rehabilitation facility. With me, Sam acknowledged that he was not in a good position to make this decision at the time but that it solved a lot of practical problems for him and his family (who would otherwise be providing care).

The majority of our therapeutic time focused on Sam's relationships, in particular his romantic partner, Jay. Over a span of approximately 9 months, starting with Sam's return to therapy, we met every other week and, on occasion, every 4 weeks. Our conversations focused primarily on Sam's relationship with Jay, but because of Sam's high degree of self-sufficiency we also talked regularly about all kinds of intimate relationships more conceptually, addressing friendships and romantic relationships. These conversations helped Sam develop a more detailed conceptualization of the range of possible relationships and the ways in which those relationships differed from each other, and thus they helped him gain some additional perspective on his relationship with Jay. In reality, we'd alternate between discussions about Jay and discussions about friendships. This occurred because of the immediacy of Sam's frustrations with Jay as well as his tendency to start small and build toward the bigger picture while I identified issues he had not previously considered.

In my experience, many men have a broad category called "friends," another called "partner," and very little understanding of the gradations or differences within and between those categories. We had been working on these issues for several months when I began to tie the pieces together. It sounded something like this:

THERAPIST: Before you tell me more about Jay's reselling business, let me ask you a different question. What makes a relationship "good"? Or "great"? Definitely better than "OK."

CLIENT: Hmmm, good question. The couple gets along well and has a lot of things in common, a lot of things they enjoy doing together.

THERAPIST: That's a good start. Keep going.

CLIENT: They approach the world in the same way. Maybe not exactly the same, but their perspectives go together smoothly. [*Slight pause*] They have similar sex drives. [*Slight pause*] They want the same things out of life. Or similar enough things that their goals fit together.

THERAPIST: What about the emotional side? Things like trust, or how they show their feelings and how much they show their feelings, or how they prioritize the relationship?

CLIENT: What do you mean?

THERAPIST: You've talked about the things couples do to fill their time and the values they try to live by. I'm asking about the emotional side—how people show their feelings, how often they do that, how much they prioritize the relationship over the individual, et cetera.

CLIENT: I . . . I really don't know. I don't think about those things. You know I don't really show my feelings, and I guess I want a partner who doesn't show their feelings either. Hmm, maybe. I'm not sure about that. And I'm used to being on my own and not having a partner, so prioritizing the relationship is new for me. I mean, I go out of my way to ask Jay how his day was, how the business is going, and help him when I see he's struggling, so that's prioritizing the relationship, right?

THERAPIST: That certainly sounds like prioritizing the relationship. Or maybe it's really just helping Jay do his thing, because you usually refer to it as his business and not our business.

CLIENT: Hmm, that's a different way to think about relationships.

THERAPIST: Good. Let me try another approach to thinking about relationships. What's the difference between a "best friend" and a "romantic partner"?

CLIENT: Other than sex?

THERAPIST: Yes, in addition to sex.

CLIENT: Oh, uh, uh, I'm not sure. Y'know, I don't know that I've ever had a best friend who wasn't also a romantic partner.

THERAPIST: OK, let me try a different question in the same vein. We might think about your coworkers and the people you consult with as "acquaintances." For me, acquaintances are more than strangers but less than friends. Does that make sense to you?

CLIENT: Yes.

THERAPIST: OK. Then what makes someone an acquaintance instead of a stranger? Or, if it's easier, what makes someone an acquaintance but not a friend?

CLIENT: OK, I think I get it. So, Carol, who was my partner at work, would she be an acquaintance or a friend?

THERAPIST: Did y'all hang out together outside work?

CLIENT: Yes.

THERAPIST: Here in town or only when traveling?

CLIENT: Only when traveling.

THERAPIST: Did y'all talk about personal stuff?

CLIENT: Like family? Yeah. I heard a lot about her husband and their kids.

THERAPIST: For me, Carol might be halfway between acquaintance and friend. She'd be an acquaintance because you only see her at a specific activity—at work—but she might be a friend because y'all talk about some personal stuff.

CLIENT: OK.

THERAPIST: Is there someone else in the office that you don't hang out with at all?

CLIENT: Sure. Christian in accounting.

THERAPIST: OK. Christian is definitely an acquaintance. What are the differences in your relationship with Christian compared to Carol?

CLIENT: Oh, I get it. Christian and I don't text, ever. And we only ever talk about work. I mean, maybe something else, like "Did you see this movie," or "Do you have plans this weekend," if there's small talk before a staff meeting, but that's it. Carol and I talk about pretty much everything. We text some. We have meals together.

THERAPIST: When you and Carol text, is it strictly work related, like logistics or "How's that report coming along?"

CLIENT: [*Thinking*] Pretty much, yeah. Our texting is rarely personal. But in person, we do get more personal.

THERAPIST: And meals together. Do y'all ever get together for a meal that isn't traveling and isn't "Do you want to grab lunch together?" Like, would y'all ever meet for dinner on a Saturday night?

CLIENT: No, it's all work adjacent.

Sam and I continued to identify differences between acquaintances and friends, then shifted to friends versus best friends/romantic partners. With other clients, I would then ask about differences between best friends versus romantic partners, but I didn't ask Sam that question again because he'd already told me he'd never had a best friend who wasn't a romantic partner. Throughout these conversations, I repeatedly asked Sam about his comfort discussing family issues or his love life as a method of introducing the topics of emotional openness and trust.

In the conversation just presented, I was helping Sam develop a more meaningful framework for thinking about the different types of relationships he has (or might have). I structured that by working from least intimate (acquaintances) to most intimate (best friends and romantic partners). This framework helped him clarify what he wanted from his social contacts and more clearly evaluate what he was and was not getting from his social life and his relationship with Jay. I continued with a discussion his relationship with Jay and then addressed Sam's friendships. After we had discussed acquaintances, friends, and best friends/romantic partners at the conceptual level, we shifted to real life. Sam also expressed dislike for some of the "cutesy" things Jay wanted to do when they were in public, like holding hands and other displays of affection. Sam saw these things as performative and felt like Jay was demanding affection. Sam also began to recognize ways in which Jay was more emotionally expressive than he was and eventually realized that he didn't entirely trust that Jay would keep Sam's secrets. Sam never had any reason to believe that Jay did share Sam's secrets, but the combination of his own reluctance to open up and Jay's greater emotional expressiveness made Sam uneasy. Sam ultimately recognized that their approaches toward emotional expression didn't match; neither did Sam trust Jay at the level he thought he should for a romantic partner. Instead, he thought their connection was more friendlike.

As Sam's recovery progressed and he became less dependent on Jay to take care of him and the house, it became increasingly clear to Sam that they had very little in common. After much therapeutic discussion, Sam realized he needed to end the relationship. But because Sam had always struggled with big decisions—part of what brought him into my office to begin with—the decision to break up with Jay required substantial processing time in therapy. Throughout these conversations, Sam repeatedly verbalized feeling very bad because he understood how much effort Jay had invested in Sam's recovery. Sam didn't want to be seen as having taken advantage of Jay. Discussions about repaying what Jay had freely given touched on Sam's self-sufficiency. He was especially concerned about being in Jay's debt, or feeling like he still owed Jay something, in return for Jay's caretaking in those first few months after the stroke.

At a more mundane and more accessible level, Sam struggled with their different tastes and preferences. Sam was more high-brow and intellectual—perhaps not surprising given that he was considering pursuing a second advanced degree—but Jay wasn't. For example, Sam liked intricately plotted television and movies, whereas Jay favored unscripted programs with lots of interpersonal drama. I asked Sam about his preference for both solo time and quiet time, which I expected to be relatively high because he was a self-sufficient man with an avoidant attachment style. Sam told me he wanted much more solo time and more quiet time than Jay.

They also struggled sexually; the sex had been good—fun and fairly easy—when they started dating and before Sam's stroke. But Sam's loss of feeling on his right side extended to the midline of his body, including the right side of his penis, which made for some distracting and odd moments unless Jay was very diligent about where he was touching Sam. Furthermore, Sam had less energy and was more easily tired than Jay, which contributed to very different levels of sexual desire. Even without the stroke, I suspect this would have eventually become an issue, but during that first month of dating, prestroke, when they'd only been together in person five or six times and they were both excited to see each other, they hadn't had any such problems.

Reevaluating Friendships

My discussions with Sam about different types of intimate relationships shed light on the paucity of friendships he had and the limited nature of many of his relationships. This is also reflective of being avoidantly attached; he had only a handful of relationships, and they didn't include much emotional openness and thus weren't particularly intimate even when they were long-standing. Sam's statement that he didn't have a best friend and wasn't sure that he'd ever really had a best friend who wasn't also his romantic partner is common among avoidantly attached men, although I don't think it's unique to this group.

Sam's social life suffered after his stroke. Most of Sam's social contacts were based in his workplace, and these relationships ended within months of his stroke. At work within an organization, or on the road as a consultant, Sam was fairly good at connecting with people. He could always find a colleague to share a meal with, and the conversation would flow. But Sam never got too personal in these conversations, didn't see or text people outside of the workplace, and didn't chat with consulting clients when he wasn't working with them. After Sam's stroke and the end of his work, he stopped talking to those folks. Through the conversation I have excerpted in this chapter, Sam came to recognize these people as acquaintances, not the friends he had originally considered them to be. The tendency to rely heavily on acquaintances with few (or no) friends or best friends is consistent with his self-sufficiency and his avoidant attachment style.

Sam had had two long-time friends, and one of those relationships—based largely on the shared activity of working out—ended because Sam couldn't work out anymore. (Two years after Sam's stroke, he returned to the gym, initially with a physical therapist and then a personal trainer, but his workouts were much more limited than they had been. Sam did not try to reconnect with his lost friend.) Sam spoke about being lonely, but he was also reluctant to reach out to people with whom his friendships had withered. When those people did agree to meet him, Sam often felt as though they had little in common anymore (which is why the friendships had atrophied) or that he were being pitied; his relationship with work friend Carol followed the same pattern.

Grieving Loss

Sam was reluctant to attend a support group for stroke victims, viewing it as a pity party designed to help people get used to being dependent on others. However, he did meet and befriend another stroke survivor around his same age. From a practical perspective, Sam's hearing loss made participation in a support group—or any group—difficult. With only one good ear, he could easily miss some of the conversation and have difficulty identifying who was speaking. Sam also struggled to follow conversations when more than one person spoke at a time, so even dyadic conversations could be challenging when there were other people talking nearby. These were his stated reasons for not wanting to participate in a support group. I suspect he also didn't want to be around other people who spoke about accepting their losses—the "pity party" he was avoiding. Again, I saw this as part of his desire to be self-sufficient.

Throughout our conversations about Jay, I supported Sam while he grieved. He would occasionally acknowledge his losses, but he rarely went into detail and never cried about his losses in my office. Instead, he presented them simply, as facts to be acknowledged and adjustments to be made. For Sam, there was no denial, no anger, no bargaining, and so on, although I would occasionally see some sadness about his losses. His grieving was piecemeal and occurred only occasionally, at least with me. And although I often encouraged him to share more of those loss-related feelings, Sam routinely shied away from his grief and moved the conversation toward other topics. I also believe Sam was unwilling to grieve because it would inevitably raise questions about the self-sufficiency he prized so much.

Sam's unwillingness to grieve in my office was also consistent with his avoidant attachment style. Like many people with avoidant attachments, he was going to open up only so far; he'd gotten this far by not relying on other people and, even though this was therapy, he wasn't going to open up all the way—or, at least, not quickly. As a therapist, I understood Sam's reluctance to open up even though I'm pretty sure that he was more open with me than anyone else in his life. It had just taken longer than usual, from a therapy perspective, and there were times when I believed Sam could be more open but seemed unwilling to do so. I didn't push, but I did make sure he had the therapeutic space to address those emotions.

The concept of *selective optimization with compensation* refers to choices older adults make to reduce their activities in ways that allow them to continue being successful as they age and their abilities diminish (Baltes & Baltes, 1990; Baltes & Freund, 2003). For example, as a man's eyesight changes in ways that make nighttime driving more difficult, he may slowly shift his out-of-the-house activities to daytime hours or choose to carpool with someone who has better eyesight. These seemingly small adjustments allow him to continue engaging in pleasurable activities and fulfilling his responsibilities on his own terms with no (or minimal) reliance on others. After his stroke, Sam demonstrated selective optimization with compensation by relying on a greater number of task lists, which included more details than he had needed before, because of decreases in memory and concentration. When dealing with complex mental tasks, he also took more breaks than he had previously needed. I helped Sam understand these strategies as normal and appropriate and as facilitating his independence.

CONCLUSION

Sam's story illustrates how the masculine criterion of self-sufficiency can shape a man's life. His desire for self-sufficiency led him to seek therapy when he struggled to make some complex decision (return to school, end his romantic relationship); those struggles were partly due to his inattention to emotional factors. Sam's self-sufficiency shaped many parts of his life, including his approach to recovery from his stroke and his ability to connect with others in ways that would facilitate friendships and not just acquaintance-ships.

My recognition of Sam's self-sufficiency pushed me to find small wins that would demonstrate progress, beginning in the first session. Although it is possible that Sam would have returned for a second session anyway, because he felt like I understood him and he recognized the utility of therapy, I believe the need for a quick demonstration of therapeutic efficacy is part of the reason men are less likely to return for a second session than women (Addis & Mahalik, 2003).

I believe that masculine self-sufficiency and the emotionally diminished relationships that are typical of avoidantly attached people can be seen as explanations for the same set of behaviors. For Sam, the lessons of childhood that created his avoidant attachment style were further reinforced by masculinity's directives to be independent. As we explored the challenges he experienced in connecting with others, we routinely addressed both of these sources.

Sam's processing of his grief has been minimal, at least from my perspective, and I suspect this is the result of his desire for self-sufficiency and his relatively low levels of emotional expression. He tends instead to start over. When he returned home from the hospital, he focused on making changes that would allow him to live independently and adapt to—and surpass—his physical limitations, but he rarely discussed his losses. He moved forward. Nearly 5 years after his stroke, and approximately 1 year after he had broken up with Jay, he sold his house and moved into a new place with an existing community. A few months later, he had gotten to know a few people in that community and had been voted onto the board of the homeowners association.

5 THE PROBLEM SOLVER

MURRAY'S CASE

Murray was a 60-year-old, heterosexual, White, cisgender man. He and his wife had been together for nearly 35 years and had three kids, who were all adults and living on their own. Murray and his wife were both medical doctors, and they had moved several times during their adulthood. At one point, they owned a medical practice together in a small town, but as the medical system changed to favor hospital-based networks, and given some of the challenges of running a business with one's spouse, they closed the practice and moved. When I met him, they were both working for large hospitals.

Murray came to therapy because he and his wife, Angela, argued regularly. They were seeing a couples therapist and, at the therapist's suggestion, as well as urging from his wife, he had been strongly encouraged to try individual therapy as well to learn more about his own issues, which were contributing to their arguments. After our first meeting, I asked him to take some notes after he and his wife had their next argument so he and I could

https://doi.org/10.1037/0000499-005
Clinical Work With Men: Understanding Masculinity in Psychotherapy, by A. P. Smiler

better understand what happened when they argued. Murray agreed, and when I saw him 2 weeks later he told me about an argument they had about Angela's painting space. (She had taken a painting class about a year earlier, and it had become a new hobby of hers.)

CLIENT: It was this past Saturday. We had an argument about her painting studio.

THERAPIST: You had an argument about her painting studio?

CLIENT: Yes. I came in to the kitchen after mowing the lawn, and Angela looked frustrated. I asked her what was going on, and she told me the light in her studio wasn't right. So I asked if she needed a different light fixture, or if we needed to buy different lightbulbs—y'know how there are all these different types of lightbulbs now, bright white, and daylight and soft white and whatever else? Probably moonlight; I don't know. Anyway, I'm asking her questions and she keeps saying "No," and "That's not it," and "I don't think so."

THERAPIST: That doesn't sound like an argument?

CLIENT: Then I said I would be happy to go to the hardware store or painting store or lighting store with her and I would install whatever lighting she needed. And she was like "You're not listening to me at all."

THERAPIST: Uh-huh . . .

CLIENT: And then she got really mad, even though I was just trying to help. I could tell because her voice changed. And then she told me I wasn't helping and I said "I'm sorry, but I don't know that much about painting," and she said it was about lighting, and I apologized for saying it was about painting instead of lighting and that I'd been asking about lighting and then she starts to get loud and says I'm "mansplaining" about lighting when I don't know anything about it.

THERAPIST: Whoa. OK. Then what happened?

CLIENT: She was yelling by this point, and so was I. I'm not sure who started yelling first, but I've realized that I simply wasn't patient enough and that's why we started yelling.

THERAPIST: OK . . .

CLIENT: Then she used the code word our couples counselor taught us for when we want to stop an argument instead of getting worse. She looked like she wanted to say something else, but she didn't. I recognized the word and held my tongue—I was still pretty worked up.

THERAPIST: OK, so then what happened the rest of the day Saturday? Or are y'all still mad at each other? (I saw Murray on Tuesdays.)

CLIENT: Oh, no, it blew over after a few hours. I drank some water from the garden hose, did the weed eating, put everything away, did a little cleanup, then went inside the house about an hour later. Angela was in the den, I think. I got a shower, ate lunch, and ran some errands outside the house. At some point, maybe 3:00 or 3:30, I texted her and asked if she needed anything from the grocery store, and she asked me to pick up a few things. I got home around 4:00, and we met friends for dinner at 6:30 and had a good time. I didn't say anything about the argument we'd had earlier and neither has she. I imagine it'll come up tomorrow when we see the couples counselor.

THERAPIST: You sound like you're not sure if you'll tell the couples counselor about this argument.

CLIENT: I'm 95% sure Angela will tell her. I won't have to.

THERAPIST: Do you think it's important for the couples counselor to hear your version?

CLIENT: I'll make sure Angela gets the facts right, but everything else is just her reaction. I think I just wasn't patient enough, and I don't mind saying so.

I didn't think Murray's problem was a lack of patience; I thought it was trying to solve a problem he didn't fully understand. Like many men, Murray was attempting to show his care through doing something helpful, which is called *action empathy*. Broadly speaking, Murray saw himself as a problem solver. He liked fixing things, whether that meant problems Angela or their (adult) children were experiencing, household repairs/maintenance, or his work as a medical doctor.

When presented with an upset person, problem solvers often engage in action empathy by trying to help them solve the problem. They place great emphasis on fixing things; this is demonstrated in Murray's quick suggestion to buy new light fixtures or lightbulbs. Problem solvers are doers, and they want to get things moving and back on track as quickly as possible. Although they may generate viable solutions, they often fail to attend to the emotional side of the problem. This may frustrate the person the problem solver is trying to help because that person doesn't feel heard—their emotions aren't getting through, and thus the suggested solution may continue to cause emotional harm. We see this in Angela's reactions: She doesn't quite finish defining the problem before Murray starts solving it, and her frustrations increase as a result. The problem solver may become annoyed not only by being told he's not understanding but also when none of his solutions are adopted. I often find myself validating my clients' ability to offer practical solutions.

Themes in Murray's Therapy

As Murray detailed their arguments, I noticed two themes that would shape our work. The first theme was that Murray liked to fix things; he was a problem solver. He earned his money fixing people, and he had grown up helping his father fix things around the house. But he wasn't very good at fixing his wife, her problems, or their marriage.

As I got to know Murray better, he told me that he was fundamentally insecure and that he never knew if people liked him. He attributed this to his relationship with his father. Although Murray spent a lot of time playing sports and fixing things with his father, his father rarely showed or verbalized his feelings, which left Murray a little unsure of whether his father truly loved him or if he merely enjoyed Murray's company. I translated Murray's insecurity as anxiety, and his anxiety would be the second theme that shaped our work.

As we explored Murray's motives for helping other people, he spoke about wanting to feel useful—not wanted, but useful. He traced this to his childhood; his father was always working to fix and improve their house. Murray's dad spoke about the ways he and his wife (Murray's mother) divided household tasks to play to their strengths and preferences while covering each other's weaker areas. In this way, the couple improved the two individuals. This conceptualization was common in the 1950s and 1960s, when Murray's parents came of age, and it persisted through Murray's own adolescence in the 1970s.

Murray's dad had coached his Little League baseball team and made the same points to the players. He spoke about the ways individuals came together to form a team that is better than the sum of its parts. When he and Murray watched sports on television, his father was always a little suspicious of players who seemed like they were deliberately attracting too much attention or who otherwise overshadowed the team. Together, these experiences gave Murray a key to being liked and reducing his anxiety: being useful.

As a teenager in the 1970s, Murray realized that if he could make himself useful then other people would seek out his company and his advice. He continued to play baseball; he was good enough to make the high school team, and he could play several positions, but he was never the star. Murray still wasn't sure if the other guys on the team liked him, but he reasoned that because they hung out with him after practice and on weekends they at least enjoyed his company. And if he was invited to get-togethers, and they were enjoying his company, then his anxiety diminished.

Murray as a Problem Solver

Murray's emphasis on being useful continued into adulthood. This is evident in the opening dialogue: As soon as Angela says she's got a lighting issue Murray starts trying to solve the problem. Murray's usefulness took a range of forms, but it mostly came down to listening to people and then trying to help them solve their problems. Because Murray was likable and a good problem solver, everyone came to him to complain: his colleagues, his employees, his friends, and, of course, his patients. And no matter how busy Murray was, he always took a few minutes to listen to their complaints and concerns and offer what help he could. To me, Murray's behavior sounded a lot like action empathy. He showed empathy for people by doing something: solving their problem.

At work, Murray took an open-door approach with his colleagues and subordinates, and many people sought his advice on a broad range of nonmedical issues. This willingness to listen sometimes caused problems with his schedule. He was almost always running behind because he didn't like telling patients to stop talking or inform them that he needed to get to his next appointment. At one clinic early in his career, a nurse was assigned to shadow Murray and keep him on time as best she could.

However, Murray's upbringing did not teach him about handling hurt feelings—or any feelings, really. His parents were attentive, and they told him they loved him, but there was little demonstration of other feelings and no meaningful discussion of feelings. A year or so into our work, Murray and I began to describe the household in which he had grown up as "warm but not demonstrative."

Murray could recall good emotional experiences with only two people. The first was his high school girlfriend; their relationship ended during their first year of college because of minimized contact—this was the landline-only era—and the changes they each experienced. His second girlfriend—Angela—was also open with her feelings, and more than 30 years later they were married and still together.

MASCULINITY AND THE PROBLEM SOLVER TYPE

Within the multi-faceted masculinity framework, the masculine criterion that most accurately describes these men is problem solving. The problem-solving criterion was more central to the Good Guy approach to masculinity and was part of the reason World War II photojournalist Ernie Pyle described that generation of men as being "quietly useful" (Faludi, 1999, p. 17). As a method of masculine achievement, being a reliable and effective problem solver is sufficient to qualify a guy as Man Enough, but it's unlikely to make him The Man. If he is particularly good at fixing things, especially a broad range of things, he might even get called "Mr. Fix It" or "The Fix It Guy," but those descriptors don't really have identities built around them. If his problem-solving skills are mechanical and allow him to fix cars, things around the house, or other tangible products, he may earn his salary through those skills.

Benefits of Being a Problem Solver

It is perhaps not surprising that being able to fix things or get stuff done builds confidence and can be a substantial source of self-esteem and even pride. Depending on exactly what kinds of problems or things a man is able to fix, these skills give him a place in his family, his work, and possibly the world at large. If he is able to save the household money by doing some home or auto repair, his pride may be evident through those stories. Murray's pride was evident in several stories about household repair. And being the problem-solver in a workplace can be particularly important because it provides a man with a way to stand out. Depending on the context, we might label this *practical intelligence*.

Problem solvers also tend to be good at reasoning through a problem and demonstrating logical thought processes. They also have the ability to pay attention to detail, although only in realms where they have sufficient knowledge to do so and when they willingly pay attention. Most of the problem solvers I have met are willing to learn new things (so they can solve more problems). All of these attributes make problem solvers good clients—at least, once they have joined with the therapist and are engaged in the process.

Several of the problem solvers with whom I have worked are good at identifying and naming other people's emotions, but their labels for emotions tend toward the simpler ones, such as *happy*, *sad*, *angry*, *jealous*, *excited*, *surprised*, and *embarrassed*. In my experience, they often struggle with more subtle or complex feelings, such as contentment, shame, or melancholy, and they don't understand that people can feel two different things at the same time. Because they often are judged on a guy standard, they often see themselves as, and receive praise for being, a good listener and especially better than the average guy when it comes to emotional expression. This was certainly true for Murray.

Problem solvers typically demonstrate sympathy for others' concerns; after all, much of their own desire to help other people is driven by a willingness to help someone else in need. These are positives that may need to be highlighted or distinguished as their own unique characteristics, separate from the broader problem solving, especially for problem solvers who see themselves as emotionally incompetent in some way.

Another benefit of being a problem solver is that there is almost always a need for a problem solver—at least, there is always a need if you're an effective problem solver. (Among heterosexuals, this need is partly facilitated by ways in which women are taught to verbalize their complaints and frustrations.) Being needed allows a guy to feel useful and gives him a place in the world. Being needed isn't the same as being wanted, but for Murray, and many men like him, being needed can be an everyday part of life, whereas being wanted is a rare experience.

For me, one of the biggest benefits of working with problem solvers is their ability to use therapy well. Once they have discovered a different way to do something through therapy and have some success with their new strategy, they will look for other situations in which their new strategy might also work. Said differently, problem solvers have the ability to generalize and apply a solution across multiple situations.

Challenges of Being a Problem Solver

Despite their skill at recognizing other people's emotions, problem solvers usually are not good at identifying solutions that address the emotional components of the problem. This is at least partly rooted in their perception that emotions are the evaluation that occurs after an event has happened;

emotions are caused by some action or event and are the effect in some cause–effect sequence. Problem solvers often lack a good understanding of how or why events create Emotional Reaction A instead of Emotional Reaction B. Said more simply, problem solvers often do not have a detailed understanding of why people feel the way they do or what might make someone feel different.

Problem-solving men are often poor at recognizing or expressing their own feelings—at least, the ones I see in my therapy office usually are. They also tend to deprioritize their own emotional needs because they see them as relatively small and unimportant and think of them as a side effect of some particular behavior. Murray routinely described his own feelings as "no big deal" or something he would "get over pretty easily." As a result, these men often try to shift the therapeutic focus away from themselves in ways that may seem like deflecting or being defensive. If you have the sense that a man is hiding something, or that there is an underlying emotion that he's avoiding mentioning, then he might be defensive. On the other hand, if he genuinely seems to be unaware of his own feelings—or, like Murray, simply doesn't value his feelings—then the issue may be a lack of emotional self-awareness (and some strategies from Chapter 9 may be relevant).

Problem solvers may be particularly reluctant to seek individual therapy in the first place, especially when it has been recommended by a couples counselor or their partner. Because they see themselves as problem solvers, they may struggle with the idea that they have problems of their own. This can be a substantial challenge to their capital-I Identity or all-caps IDENTITY, calling into question the masculine criteria that are central to their life and upon which their claims to masculine achievement rest. Similar to self-sufficient men (see Chapter 4), a small win after the first or second session may be especially helpful in building rapport because it demonstrates that you are a problem solver who is capable of helping other problem solvers.

With a romantic partner, a problem solver can generate feelings of safety and security if the partner feels as though he will be able to solve any problem they—or the partner—encounter. However, if this dynamic becomes central to the couple's relationship they may struggle greatly when he is faced with a problem he can't solve. Furthermore, the partner may lose faith in him and question the relationship. And these concerns would occur at the same time he may be having a crisis of confidence in his own abilities.

Problem solvers can create problems for themselves through their efforts to be helpful, especially with their partner. Many of the problem solvers with whom I have worked are good at creating solutions that address the problem at hand. But a problem solver's solutions can create additional problems for him when he repeatedly "solves" problems by taking responsibility for some part of the solution when he wasn't involved in the initial problem at all. For example, one problem solver with whom I worked volunteered to take on responsibility for cleaning their cat's litter box after his wife repeatedly complained about it. She did not volunteer to take on any of his chores in return, and he didn't ask, so his workload increased while hers decreased. This exchange became a pattern, and he eventually ended up with substantially more household chores than she had, and he became resentful. When I hear problem solvers talk about how much they are doing to help their partner and how little their partner does to help them, or complaints that the problem solver is doing (almost) all the household chores and his partner sits around watching TV or playing on their phone, I suspect this dynamic is at play. Here, the problem solver has not only become an active and ongoing part of the solution but he also has done so with little attention paid to the big picture of his daily or weekly activities.

Most of the problem solvers with whom I have worked don't see any point in complaining. One guy told me "You fix it, or you live with it. Complaining doesn't change it." As a day-to-day strategy that might be effective, but from a mental health perspective the lack of complaining means that he's not letting other people know about the stress he's experiencing or the challenges he's encountering.

Many of the problem solvers with whom I have worked view their body as a tool that facilitates their life. As long as they can get stuff done, then any physical or mental health problems are usually labeled "small" and probably ignored. As such, they may engage in maintenance-type behaviors by addressing wounds, taking daily medication, and possibly getting an annual physical. But they don't typically engage in self-care, which entails endeavors such as improving one's physical condition and possibly doing things because they feel good (e.g., getting a massage). This positioning may be an element of masculine selflessness, wherein men don't meaningfully attend to their selves. It also has roots in masculinity's injunctions to avoid anything feminine: Spa days, babying oneself, and the like are marketed to women, but not men. The willingness of gay men and metrosexuals (remember them?) to engage in these stereotypically feminine activities is one of the things that helps define the difference between these masculine types and regular masculinity.

Intersectional Issues

When a man of color is able to solve problems that their White male supervisor cannot, there is a real potential for racial prejudice and discrimination to become a workplace issue. This seems particularly likely to occur if the supervisor is male and insecure about his masculine achievement or his ability to keep his supervisory position and when that insecure male supervisor views the problem-solving colleague as a threat.

Some men who have physical or cognitive disabilities become especially good at solving logistical problems; this is one result of the challenges they face in their daily lives. Unfortunately, other men with disabilities may develop a type of learned helplessness that causes them to give up easily when faced with a new challenge. There is a continuum between these can-do and cannot-do attitudes, and these attitudes may or may not generalize from practical–logistical problems to other types of problem solving.

WORKING WITH MURRAY AND OTHER PROBLEM SOLVERS

I worked with Murray for approximately 4 years. We typically met biweekly, but at times would meet monthly because of scheduling conflicts. In the next two sections, I discuss our work regarding emotion in general, starting with increases in Murray's awareness of his own emotions and the emotions of other people, followed by ways to incorporate this emotional awareness into his problem solving. I then move to our discussions of anxiety, beginning with how we raised Murray's awareness of his own anxiety and then describing the steps he took to address his anxiety. In the final section of the chapter, I review the work we did regarding the source of some of his anxiety: Murray's underlying insecurity.

Treatment Plan

Murray came in with clear goals related to arguing less with his wife, including a desire to better understand what he did to facilitate their arguments. Our efforts to better understand Murray led to his (and my) recognition of his long-standing and persistent anxiety. This became a focal point for our work.

Most of our work directly addressed the couple's arguments, and we would alternate between the two themes of arguing and anxiety. As I listened to Murray's description of their arguments, I recognized that he rarely mentioned any feelings until the point at which anger and frustration changed a conversation into an argument. Over the next few years, and while they continued in couples counseling, we worked on helping Murray increase his awareness of his own feelings, as well as Angela's, and how their feelings contributed to their arguments. Eventually, we used his greater understanding to help him (and the two of them) find better solutions to their arguments. After approximately 6 months of biweekly meetings, we had a conversation that sounded something like this:

CLIENT: Angela and I had another disagreement over the weekend. I heard your voice in my head as we were arguing, and I tried to do the things we talked about.

THERAPIST: How'd it go?

CLIENT: The argument wasn't as bad as usual, so that's an improvement. I still don't understand why we argued though.

THERAPIST: Take me through it.

CLIENT: It was Thursday night, and I'd had a hard day at work. I had clinic in the afternoon and was running late, as usual. My last two clients were both really complicated, one because she hasn't followed her medication regimen, and her condition has gotten worse; she's high risk because she's diabetic and she's not doing good with her diabetes, either. The other didn't say much, and it felt like I had to ask a million questions to figure out what was going on. Those patients always frustrate me.

Anyway, I got home and I'm not 5 feet in the door, and Angela's on me. Our oven seems to be dying, and she started looking at replacements but "Oh my God, they're so expensive" and "There are so many options," and she's just going and going, and I don't even have my coat off yet.

So I asked, "Are you upset?" In retrospect, that probably wasn't the best question, but I wasn't ready. When I'm here, I'm thinking about feelings and our arguments, and you give me time to come up with an answer, but when I was there with Angela I needed something right away, and I was still thinking about those last patients, and that's what I said.

THERAPIST: And how did she respond?

CLIENT: She got mad at me for needing to ask if she was upset. She said it was pretty obvious that she was upset, and she didn't know why I needed her to say she was upset. And then she made some comments about men being emotional idiots.

THERAPIST: OK. I need to go back a minute. How did you feel when you got home and Angela started going on about the oven?

CLIENT: I was surprised. No, that's not right. More like caught off guard. I think about surprise as usually a good thing, like presents at your birthday or Christmas. So, yeah, caught off guard.

THERAPIST: OK, so that's a bad kind of surprised. Anything else?

CLIENT: Looking back on it, I realize that I started to get defensive.

THERAPIST: OK. Did you feel anything else?

CLIENT: I don't think so. I mean, I'd been frustrated when I walked in, but I think that, I don't know, kind of got lost?, when Angela started talking about the oven.

THERAPIST: OK. So you're frustrated when you get out of the car and enter the house. Then surprised in a bad way—"caught off guard"—when you come in and Angela is in your face about the oven, you ask if she's upset and she calls you, and all men, emotional idiots. How do you feel at that point?

CLIENT: I think I might be in a little bit of shock at that point. Like, there's too much going on, and I'm not sure what to do 'cause asking about her feelings didn't work, so I think I didn't say anything for a minute. And that made her more mad. Then I got mad and started yelling back. I think I was defensive? I was definitely trying to clear my name.

THERAPIST: OK. Now we've got the emotional story—your side of the emotional story, anyway. Frustrated to caught off guard, and you try something new but it doesn't work, and then the combination of frustrated about work, trying something new from therapy that doesn't work, and Angela coming at you, gets you defensive and angry. Is that right?

CLIENT: Yeah, that's right.

THERAPIST: Let's see if we can figure out what Angela was feeling.

Increasing Awareness of Emotions: His Own and Others'

As illustrated in this exchange, Murray often struggled to understand why his wife was upset, which prevented him from solving her problems. His stories consistently focused on the external challenge she was facing and never her internal, emotional reaction. The fact that she was upset in some way—hurt, angry, frustrated, disappointed—never entered his story until the point at which their conversation shifted into a fight. His own feelings of hurt, anger, frustration, and disappointment about his advice being ignored were also left out of the tales he would tell me. Emotions simply were not part of his stories until they become the center of the story, especially anger and frustration. So, I would ask for the "emotional story" in a variety of ways. I began by having him retell the story, stopping him at various points and asking if he could name his feelings at that point. I would also ask for his wife's feelings at that point in the argument. At first, Murray struggled with these questions, so I would suggest three or four things they could be feeling when I asked the question (often variations on *hurt*, *angry*, and *disappointed*, as well as something unlikely, e.g., *excited* or "enjoying the argument"). I would then retell the whole emotional story in order to help him focus on the feelings that had caused a simple conversation to become a big argument.

As time went on, and Murray's ability to recognize and name emotions improved, I would stop making suggestions and instead ask for refinements. For example, I would ask him to gauge the extent of the initial feeling as low, medium, or high or, on occasion, to make finer distinctions by introducing a broader range of feeling words. After even more time, I began asking Murray to tell me the emotional story with as little of the rational or logistical content as possible.

Learning to Solve Logistical and Emotional Parts of the Problem

Through our work, Murray learned how to incorporate emotional aspects of the problem into the solutions he generated. At first, he needed his wife's help and would offer tentative suggestions, with "I have an idea for the logistical part of the problem, but I'm not sure if it addresses the emotional piece . . ." As I continued to ask him how his wife would feel and why she would feel that way, Murray began to understand her feelings more. Murray learned from these experiences, as well as from our therapeutic discussions about how emotions worked, and he was able to start generating more complete solutions that addressed both the practical and emotional elements of the situation. This allowed him to produce better solutions and regain his sense of competence at being a problem solver and a good husband. (I discuss teaching men about emotions further in Chapter 9.)

We also discussed the possibility that Murray pause before trying to solve Angela's problems. Our conversations helped Murray understand that his wife sometimes needed to vent, which I defined for him as "releasing emotional energy." In those situations, his job was to listen—patiently. That meant not jumping in or offering solutions. He had had to learn that skill when dealing with hospital administrators, and although he felt sheepish about responding to his wife the way he responded to administrators, he was able to transfer and modify that skill to help at home.

After Murray had learned to avoid immediately solving other people's problems, we discussed the possibility that Angela could solve her own problems. She was a doctor, too, and they had run a business together, so Murray knew she was smart. In conversation, he said she often generated solutions he would never have thought of. He agreed to withhold his ideas unless his wife said she wanted them. When Murray stopped trying to solve her problems and paid more attention to her feelings, their relationship changed. They argued less often, and when they did argue their arguments were usually less vehement. As a result, he was getting greater enjoyment out of the time they spent together, and he was more likely to seek out her company. (He believes she also sought out his company more, but he wasn't entirely sure and decided not to ask.)

At some point, we realized that there were times when Angela became frustrated when Murray sat, listened, and reflected her feelings back without solving a problem. This happened a few times, and when he then offered solutions she became more upset and they reverted to some old patterns of argument. As we explored this dynamic, I asked Murray if his wife ever showed her anger or lost her temper with anyone else. He said that she did not, and we then spoke about ways to release angry energy.

We spoke about ways in which Murray being his wife's only anger outlet created difficulties and was unfair to him. Given that Murray's wife seemed comfortable expressing anger only with him because she trusted him and knew he could handle it, we talked about ways he might serve as her sparring partner to allow her to verbally get her angry energy out without turning the argument into an issue between them. In effect, I taught him how to join with her anger by complaining about "them": bad drivers, hospital executives, insurance companies, and so on. During these conversations, we acknowledged that this dynamic was unfair to Murray by making him responsible for facilitating his wife's processing of her anger. I encouraged him to raise the issue with their couples' counselor.

In his efforts to learn better ways to solve problems, Murray routinely read self-help books. Self-help books (and videos) present new ways to solve people's problems. He routinely reported finding them unhelpful, until he read one of John Gottman's books (e.g., *Why Marriages Succeed or Fail: What You Can Learn From the Breakthrough Research to Make Your Marriage Last*;

Gottman, 1994) and understood the connection between emotional connection and trust in a romantic relationship. This realization furthered his understanding of the benefits of emotions and increased his willingness to engage with his own feelings.

Increasing Awareness of One's Own Stress and Anxiety

As our exploration of the impact of Murray's childhood on his current functioning progressed, he recognized that he wasn't afraid of emotions per se, but he didn't really see the point of feelings in daily life—they just seemed to lead to anxiety or arguments. He strongly preferred peace and quiet, and he typically saw himself as content with life but rarely happy. This led to another realization: Murray had a strong preference for a life with a low level of emotional intensity. If emotions ranged on a scale from –10 to +10, his goal was to keep everything in the –2 to +2 range. He said strong emotions made him "uncomfortable," which I translated as "anxious." Murray could easily identify high-intensity emotional events from his life, ones associated with a score of 7 or more. These were relatively rare and included occasions such as graduation, marriage, closing his and Angela's medical practice, and deaths. But he struggled to identify more moderate events, things that entailed scores from 3 to 6 (positive or negative). We ultimately identified rock concerts and recreational sports leagues (e.g., dodgeball, kickball) as activities where he could let his hair down, so to speak, and show more emotion than usual. I reframed these moderately scored positive experiences as ways to combat stress and thus take care of himself. Murray acknowledged that he had never considered the idea of adding pleasant activities to his own life as a way to counterbalance the negatives or relieve stress.

Murray's low-level anxiety, focus on problem solving, and difficulty with his emotions made him unaware of the extent of stress in his own life. I find this to be common among problem solvers who come for therapy. One day, I was asking Murray about his stress level. He said he was at 4 or 5 on a scale of 1 to 10. I reflected that when he had provided an update on his activities over the past 2 weeks at the beginning of the session, he had spoken about three different challenges at work (reaching his expected number of billable hours, a potential administrative reallocation of his hours across the two venues where he worked, and the departure of the nurse practitioner with whom he worked at one of those venues), two challenges at home (being more emotionally open with his wife, planning their big summer vacation), an ongoing issue with the HVAC system in their house, and the relatively mild pregnancy complications his oldest daughter was experiencing. Murray acknowledged that he hadn't realized he was handling this many things.

Because Murray was a pencil-and-paper kind of guy, I encouraged him to write, over the next 2 weeks, a list of all the things he was stressed about. I suggested that he leave his list on the kitchen table where he and Angela routinely share meals as a method of demonstrating that he was making good use of therapy and of helping her understand the stresses in his life. In addition, although I knew he was reluctant to do so, I encouraged him to discuss his stress with her either at home or in their couples counseling.

When Murray returned 2 weeks later, his list had 15 items on it, almost all of which were ongoing and would take weeks or months to resolve. He was surprised to realize how many things in his life caused him stress, and began to reevaluate how he assessed his general stress level, stating that is was more like a 7 than the 4 or 5 he had originally suggested.

Managing Stress and Setting Boundaries

When Murray realized how high his general stress level was, this opened a pathway for us to start problem solving and fixing his stress level, in part by resetting some of his boundaries. I also suggested he increase the number of pleasurable activities in his weekly schedule as a treatment for his stress.

This strategy was facilitated by teaching Murray to complain. For many men—and, I think, especially problem solvers and other guys who see themselves as doers—there is no clear purpose to or benefit of complaining. They view it as a waste of time and may see it as womanly and pejoratively call it "bitching." With Murray and other men, I reframe this as *venting* and sometimes use examples of mechanical structures that underlie the term; for example, some systems need to physically vent pressure; if that release doesn't occur, they may break down.

To further reduce Murray's stress, we worked on setting boundaries, and we began with his workplace. I gave Murray permission to not help his coworkers and not listen to their problems, and he eventually gave himself permission to do this. We spoke about practical interventions, such as keeping his office door closed when he was writing his clinical notes so that people wouldn't interrupt him. Murray eventually adopted a policy of telling colleagues and coworkers that he had only 5 minutes to talk to them about nonclinical issues, and we discussed how he could enforce this policy. Murray also discovered that he could listen and be sympathetic without solving other people's problems (and do so within 5 minutes). These strategies decreased the number of people who sought Murray's nonmedical advice at work. With each of these strategies, Murray found that he regained control over his time and was less stressed. (Murray adopted some similar strategies at home and found them effective.)

Balancing Being Needed and Being Wanted

Murray had built his identity, and his life, around being a problem solver. As a result, he often felt that he was needed, but it was much less clear that he was wanted. He had had similar experiences during his childhood and adolescence with his father and his baseball team. As we focused on this issue, Murray recognized that this left him perpetually unsure about whether other people liked him and wanted to spend time with him and that this uncertainty was at the core of his perpetual low-level anxiety.

Our discussions here had two focal points. One played off our work regarding understanding other people's emotions, but with a specific focus on signs that people liked Murray; specifically, he began to look for signs that people enjoyed his company, went out of their way to include him in a conversation, or invite him to an event. As he began to differentiate between the people who came to him only to solve problems and those who came to him for other reasons, he became more comfortable with the idea that some people simply enjoyed being with him. Retrospectively, he recognized that his father had genuinely seemed to like him, and so had several members of his high school baseball team.

The second set of discussions were more difficult for Murray. Here, we addressed the extent to which he liked himself. Murray acknowledged that he had never really considered this question, or the related question of why he liked some people but not others. These conversations also revealed that almost all of his ongoing friendships were with people he had met during his education (high school through medical school) and that he hadn't made a new friend in the past 35 years. To the best of his recollection, all the people with whom he had remained friends had initiated the friendship (and Murray was happy to help maintain them). To solve this problem, we discussed ways Murray could initiate activities and reach out to others instead of waiting for others to invite him. (Problem solving is inherently reactive, so acting/initiating was quite atypical for Murray.)

CONCLUSION

Many men see themselves as problem solvers, which fits comfortably within the conception of men as doers. They regularly and routinely help others when those others are stuck, and in doing so are able to achieve status as

Man Enough. This was certainly true for Murray, whose case I used as an example.

Being a problem solver has a range of benefits, most of which are tied to the development of competence and the confidence it generates as well as the creation of a place for oneself in the world. In this way, problem solvers are often needed, although it may be less clear, to them and to you, the therapist, if they are wanted. Murray clearly struggled with this issue.

Among the problem solvers with whom I have worked, the most common focal points of therapy have been their difficulty understanding emotional reactions, solving emotion-related problems, and creating solutions that address emotional needs. Murray also struggled to recognize the extent of his own stressors and the impact they had on him, but once he did so he learned to set effective boundaries.

6 THE PROTECTOR

BENNY'S CASE

Benny was not excited about seeing a therapist. A 30-year-old, heterosexual, White, cisgender man, Benny was plain spoken and direct. He owned a small lawn care business and employed one or two seasonal workers. Physically, he was big; approximately 5 ft, 10 in. (1.8 m) tall, with thick arms and a big belly. I imagined that Benny would come across as physically intimidating to many people.

Benny arrived for the first session accompanied by his wife, Lydia. She had reached out to me about starting therapy, explaining that she was concerned about both his mental health and the quality of their marriage. As Lydia spoke, Benny said little, occasionally expanding on her comments with a few clarifying words. Her primary concern was in the way he responded to their 5-year-old son, Aiden, especially in the evenings after a full day of work; Benny was genuinely distressed about this as well. He acknowledged sometimes losing his temper with Aiden and having slapped the child once or twice. Alone with me during that first session, Benny shared that Lydia

https://doi.org/10.1037/0000499-006
Clinical Work With Men: Understanding Masculinity in Psychotherapy, by A. P. Smiler

had been increasingly upset with him over the past year, since he had disclosed that he had been sexually abused as a young teen. When he told her, she accused him of lying by omission, arguing that she had been open with him about her chronic medical condition, a neurological disorder that periodically kept her in bed for most of a day and prevented her from holding full-time employment.

During our second meeting, which was my first full session with Benny alone, we had a conversation that sounded something like this:

THERAPIST: Last time, you said you were worried about your temper.

CLIENT: That's right.

THERAPIST: Tell me what happens when you lose your temper.

CLIENT: I get mad and start yelling. Sometimes I threaten to hit Aiden.

THERAPIST: And?

CLIENT: [*Shrugs*]

THERAPIST: When you lose your temper, you yell and threaten to hit your son. Lots of guys do that. What's so bad about what you're doing that you're talking to a therapist about it?

CLIENT: I don't want to hit my son. Or yell at him. Or my wife.

THERAPIST: OK. Do you hit your son?

CLIENT: I have.

THERAPIST: How often do you hit him?

CLIENT: Twice.

THERAPIST: Can you be a little more specific? Twice a week? Twice a month?

CLIENT: Twice. In his lifetime.

THERAPIST: And he's 5 years old?

CLIENT: That's right.

THERAPIST: And you don't want to lose your temper and hit him again?

CLIENT: That's right.

THERAPIST: How often do you lose your temper?

CLIENT: Once a week, maybe twice. Lydia would probably say it happens more often than that.

THERAPIST: OK. So, this isn't an everyday thing.

CLIENT: That's right.

THERAPIST: So why do you lose your temper some days but not others?

CLIENT: I think it's because I don't have enough self-control.

THERAPIST: What else is happening on the days when you lose your temper? What kinds of things are going on that threaten your self-control and cause you to yell?

CLIENT: Aiden. Well, sometimes.

THERAPIST: And what does Aiden do those days?

CLIENT: He's just doing kid stuff, really. But for whatever reason, I can't control myself and yell at him.

THERAPIST: Let me try this from a different perspective. When was the last time you yelled at Aiden?

CLIENT: Tuesday. No, Monday. [*Slight pause*] No, Tuesday. I was right the first time.

THERAPIST: Today's Friday. So, 3 days ago Tuesday?

CLIENT: Yes.

THERAPIST: OK. I want you to think about this past Tuesday, 3 days ago.

CLIENT: OK.

THERAPIST: When did you yell at Aiden?

CLIENT: Pretty much when I got home from work.

THERAPIST: Meaning you walked in the door and started yelling at him?

CLIENT: Pretty much. He's got these toy metal trucks, and he likes to bang them together. One of them makes noises on its own, but the metal on metal gets really loud. And he's extra loud when he's playing with them.

THERAPIST: So you walk in, he's crashing the trucks together, and before you've said "Hi," or "Dad's home," or anything like that, and before you've even taken off your shoes, you're yelling at him?

CLIENT: No.

THERAPIST: Can you tell me the story of what happened from the time you walked in until you hit him?

CLIENT: I came in the door, and I was really tired, so I sat down on the bench by the door to take off my work boots. I could hear him from the other room playing with his trucks and yelling and stuff and I'm like "Not tonight. I already have a headache." Then I yelled "Hi" like I always do. Lydia said "Hi" back, and Aiden came running over to me, screaming while he was running, gave me a hug, and ran right back to his trucks, still screaming.

THERAPIST: Doesn't sound like much of a hug.

CLIENT: A fly-by, for certain.

THERAPIST: Then what happened?

CLIENT: I asked him to be quiet. He kept going, and the next thing I know I've got my boots off, and I'm standing in the doorway to the living room where he's playing, and I'm yelling at him. Lydia comes in, stands in front of Aiden—he's crying by this point—and tells me to go shower. So I did.

THERAPIST: Wow. Does that happen a lot?

CLIENT: [*Looking down, the first time he's looked away from me during this conversation*] Yeah. Two or three times a week.

THERAPIST: I'm sorry. And I can definitely help you learn to manage your temper better.

CLIENT: Good. That's what I want. I'm not as bad as my dad was when I was little, but when Aiden is older I don't want his first memories of me to be as an angry man who yelled a lot.

THERAPIST: I can work with that. And just so I know, when you said your dad yelled at you a lot. How much is a lot?

CLIENT: Looking back, it seems like it was every day. As an adult, I know it probably wasn't, but that's what's in my memory.

THERAPIST: Every day meaning 7 days a week, or just the work week?

CLIENT: Uh, I think just the work week. My sense is that he'd yell at me and my brother, and then a short time later we'd be at the dinner table together.

THERAPIST: And did you or your brother get hit a lot?

CLIENT: It was a regular thing, yeah.

THERAPIST: About how often?

CLIENT: I don't know for sure. I'd guess that at least one of us got hit every week. It was never that bad, never left a mark or anything. Just one or two slaps across our bottoms. But hard.

THERAPIST: OK. Thanks for telling me. I want to go back to Tuesday, 3 days ago.

CLIENT: OK.

THERAPIST: You said you had a headache when you got home?

CLIENT: Just starting, but yes.

THERAPIST: Do you often have a headache when you get home?

CLIENT: Maybe once or twice a week. It's a loud job, even with ear protection on most of the time.

THERAPIST: Was there other stuff that made it a bad or difficult day?

CLIENT: Let me think about it for a sec. . . . Uh, yeah, I guess. We have one mower that's got some type of short or something we haven't been able to track down. You'll be going along, mowing just fine, and then all of a sudden, it stops. And you can't restart it right away, you have to wait a couple minutes before it'll restart.

THERAPIST: Sounds frustrating.

CLIENT: It is. You're going along, in your groove, and all of a sudden, *ccccct*. The mower stops and won't restart. And you can't do anything about it except wait.

THERAPIST: Anything else frustrating? Or that made it a bad or difficult day?

CLIENT: We lost a contract.

THERAPIST: You lost a contract?

CLIENT: Yeah, we got to this house. A woman whose lawn we've been cutting for years. We're finishing up, Tim's doing the edging, and she calls me over to tell me thank you for all the help over the years, but they've sold the house and will be moving out in

2 weeks, so they'll need the lawn mowed one more time and then they're out.

THERAPIST: That sucks.

CLIENT: Yeah. She was a nice lady. Big lawn on that house. Said she'd leave our contact info in the house for the new owners.

THERAPIST: That's nice of her.

CLIENT: Yes.

THERAPIST: Anything else frustrating from Tuesday? Or anything that made the day harder than usual?

The conversation continued in this vein, and I learned that Benny works longer hours on Tuesday than any other day of the week; often eats lunch while driving from one lawn to the next (as he had on the day we'd been discussing); doesn't have a break except when he's driving or stops to use a restroom; and gets tired of being with his employee, Tim, because Tim talks nonstop in the car, whereas Benny is on the quiet side. (Tim rides in the truck with Benny instead of following separately in his own car, which would require Benny to pay Tim for his mileage.) I also learned that Benny was worried about their 8-year-old dog because he hadn't been eating as much as usual. Our entire conversation about Benny's stressors took most of that day's session, but it ended with Benny acknowledging that his stress level was higher than usual that day and that his high stress contributed to yelling at his son.

While reading the dialogue, you might perceive me as downplaying Benny's spanking of his child. This was our second meeting, and I was still getting to know him, so I didn't want to come across as being judgmental by immediately saying that spanking is bad or wrong. I did want to get more details about how often Benny hit his son, why exactly it bothered him, and how motivated he was to change. I'm also aware that corporal punishment is legal throughout the United States and, according to one survey, is practiced by approximately one in six parents (Pew Research Center, 2015). I suspect many men see spanking as part of "toughening up" their sons.

Themes in Benny's Therapy

As I got to know Benny, I identified two themes that would dominate our work. The first was Benny's desire to protect his son and his wife from harm as well as from unnecessary stress—and that included any stress he might create. The second was Benny's history of sexual abuse. When we started,

I wasn't sure if Benny would be willing to address that topic with me at all, but he ultimately did.

Benny's job didn't facilitate conversation or personal insight. As the owner of a small lawn care company, his interactions at work were limited to fairly rote conversations with clients and employees about how to best manage a lawn, scheduling, contract negotiations, and the like.

Benny readily answered my questions, on occasion with a story to illustrate his point, but he rarely went off on a tangent, spoke in a stream-of-consciousness manner, or otherwise expanded on any question I would ask. This is evident in the dialogue. If you read closely, you will also notice that Benny rarely uses modifiers of any sort; he doesn't volunteer terms like "a little" or "a lot." Aside from acknowledging his anger, there's no emotional content in his speech. He might feel "good" or be "stressed" or get "mad," but that was about the extent of his emotional vocabulary. In working with Benny, I needed to ask more questions than usual, and I encouraged him to speak more than he otherwise might by asking him to "Tell me about a time in your life when X happened."

Benny had obtained an associate's degree in accounting while also mowing lawns full time. At 21, he was fully self-supporting, and by age 27 he had saved enough money to design and build his own house. Benny's story is one of self-sufficiency (see Chapter 4), and it is also one where he protected himself by learning physical self-defense and avoiding almost any risk. He had always lived with his parents, and thus never had to risk negotiating space and routines with a roommate.

Benny hadn't attended parties in high school and didn't make friends during his associate's program, so he didn't attend parties after high school, either. When I met him, at 27, he had tried a few glasses of alcohol here and there, typically tasting something his father ordered for him. He had never tried marijuana or any other illicit drug. From Benny's perspective, these were all rational choices that were designed to get him on the path to financial independence and secure his future. When I challenged that they were all efforts to create safety so he could never be taken advantage of again—sexually or otherwise—he didn't know how to respond at first. But after some explanation, he was able to understand how I had come to that conclusion.

Benny as a Protector

In addressing his parenting and his marriage, Benny consistently framed issues—and solutions—in terms that indicated he needed to protect Lydia and Aiden from himself. When we talked about ways to de-stress after work and before interacting with his son, he routinely emphasized not yelling at or hitting his son in order to keep his son safe; it would take months of conversation and me directly challenging his wording (and thinking) before Benny started to see being stressed as a problem for Benny himself.

Benny said something similar about having been molested at ages 13–14. The events had been limited to a single perpetrator whom Benny eventually scared off. He didn't believe that being a victim of sexual assault had affected his subsequent life in any meaningful way. Benny had heard about post-traumatic stress disorder, and he was aware of well-known symptoms, such as flashbacks, acting out, and having difficulty fitting in with society, but he didn't have those problems. A small business owner with a good income, he didn't see himself as suffering long-lasting harm and thus didn't think it was important that anyone know about the abuse—not even his wife. In fact, Benny believed telling his wife would have unnecessarily burdened her with a problem he had already resolved. He explained that she had plenty of things to deal with—her medical condition, being the primary parent, managing the household, and so on—so why should she have to deal with something he'd already dealt with? For Benny, not disclosing this part of his past to Lydia was a way to protect her.

Benny saw his role as a man primarily in terms of protecting others he cared for. He needed to protect his 5-year-old son from his temper and, later, would need to teach the boy to protect himself. Benny also believed he needed to protect his wife from unnecessary stress, which could trigger or worsen her neurological disorder; his own past and daily troubles were part of that unnecessary stress. Benny's protection wasn't limited to those issues. He also needed to earn enough and save enough to protect their financial future as well.

I want to be clear that Benny was not paranoid; he did not feel perpetually under threat or that there was anyone out to get him; instead, he believed that life in current-day America was hard and full of challenges and that there were ways to get through these challenges. And he believed that his role was to make sure his wife and son experienced as few challenges as possible and, when they had to face those challenges, had as many resources as possible. Neither was he a bulldozer parent who flattened any challenges his son might run into.

MASCULINITY AND THE PROTECTOR TYPE

According to the multi-faceted masculinity framework (Chapter 2), the masculine criteria around which Benny built his masculinity was protecting others. This is a straightforward and long-standing element of masculinity;

men's roles have always included protecting women, children, property, and livestock. (The adage "Women and children first" is one of the ways American culture communicates our expectations of men as protectors.)

Men, and even teenage boys, are routinely positioned as protectors. Historically, and even today, militaries have been composed primarily, if not exclusively, of men. Demonstrating the ability to protect kin and clan is a common element of coming-of-age or manhood rites around the world (Gilmore, 1990) that help differentiate between juveniles and full-fledged adults.

As a method of demonstrating masculine achievement and acquiring status, being a protector is a well-established path. A man can readily be Man Enough, but it's difficult to become The Man unless he is willing to shift from a defensive mindset to an offensive one. The former relies on preventing others from attacking and having the ability to disrupt any such attacks. Some men with defensive mindsets have the ability to predict or anticipate the bad guys' actions, but protection and defense, by their nature, are based on reacting to others' actions.

However, some protectors believe their efforts to protect others are unrecognized and taken for granted. These men can present as resentful or jerks. With a client like this, I often explicitly give him credit for his efforts in order to help build his self-esteem, sense of confidence, and perception of himself as Man Enough. In my experience, men are unlikely to "get over it" or (easily) abandon their protector identity if they perceive themselves or others perceive them as having failed at protecting others.

We see male protectors regularly on screen. They are the characters in shows like *Criminal Minds*, *Chicago Fire* (and *Chicago P.D.*), *9-1-1*, and other dramas based on first responders. Similar to the characters in those shows, most protectors who come to therapy are not violent. This is a key difference between protectors and the angry men I discuss in Chapter 7.

Protectors position themselves as helping others. Benny was explicit about this, stating that his role was to help his wife and child have the best lives they could. When we discussed this, I pointed out that this positioning made Benny a side character in his own story because the focus was wholly on the people he was protecting. I hear a similar framing from cisgender men who say their primary job in a romantic relationship is to hold frame for women's emotions.

Men who define protection in terms of physical defense are likely to be gun owners. Gun safety—proper training, keeping the gun and ammunition in a gun safe (or separate safes), the use of trigger locks, and so on—can also fit logically within the protection framework because engaging in gun safety is a way to prevent accidental shootings by children. When working with self-identified protectors who have suicidal or homicidal thoughts, I sometimes emphasize that if they are unavailable—because of suicide or incarceration—then they will not be able to protect their family. This provides one reason to avoid suicide or homicide, at least in the short term.

Benefits of Being a Protector

The adoption of a protector identity can lead to careers in law enforcement, the military, or other security-focused careers. Those professions can bring a certain amount of respect, although the pay usually isn't lucrative. They also can facilitate masculine achievement and, if he excels or does something particularly heroic, he'll be The Man.

Protectors are often good at identifying risky elements in their environments because protecting against and eliminating risks is an important aspect of being an effective protector. Doing this requires the ability to analyze different settings and various social situations for risks and potentially includes the assessment of other people's motives. Minimizing and eliminating risks can lead to a sense of accomplishment that helps a man build self-esteem, but it also carries some risks, which I describe later in this chapter.

Protectors' ability to analyze different settings and different social situations, and then identify a solution that would prevent harm, reflects an ability to use reason and logic to solve problems. Protectors' solutions may not be the solutions that we therapists would choose, but that doesn't mean their problem solving doesn't follow some type of logical chain or cause-and-effect system. Like the problem solvers discussed in Chapter 5, protectors may take some pride in their ability to reason things out and see this as one of their strengths. As a therapist who works with these men, I sometimes help them incorporate anger, frustration, and other emotions into their analysis. Benny understood this because anger and frustration caused him to lose his temper. Other protectors with whom I have worked could easily recognize, for example, the ways in which their teenage children would become angry with one or both parents and then violate the safety rules the protectors had created.

For protectors, protecting the family can take many forms and often requires detailed knowledge of that realm. These men may focus on martial arts and other self-defense skills, including, as mentioned, the possession and use of firearms. Alternately, protection could include extensive efforts to ensure digital/online protection and safety, financial safety, and even becoming a (doomsday) prepper. Whatever realms he chooses to protect, doing so requires the ability to gain and apply knowledge and thus demonstrates a willingness to learn and possibly the determination to do learn new things. I sometimes challenge my clients to devote the same willingness to learn to other areas of their lives.

The Challenges of Being a Protector

Protectors can present as always ready to defend and thus be anxious. To be clear, this is a result of looking for external threats to safety. Some protectors with whom I have worked are quite open to feedback on their performance and thus are not defensive. However, always being on guard, or always being prepared for an attack, is a prescription for a relatively high level of anxiety, hypervigilance, and even disturbed sleep. These clients may not be able to accurately assess the risks that occur in a particular setting, or with a particular person; their ability to conduct a threat assessment may be too easily triggered and thus substantially inaccurate. In many cases, as with Benny, it is possible to draw a straight line from an adverse childhood event to becoming a protector.

I find that protectors tend to avoid taking risks and are not eager for change. If you had a plan to protect people and it seemed to be working, you might tweak it via small improvements, but you probably wouldn't make a large-scale change just to try something new. This can be problematic in therapy because much of a therapist's work is about helping clients change their thoughts and actions, often with the goal of generating a different emotional response (e.g., less anxiety and stress). Benny was quite willing to make small changes that helped him handle his stress better, but he was highly ambivalent about making other changes or prioritizing his own emotions. He was reluctant to adopt an additional role, claiming that it might distract him from his efforts to protect his family. (Or himself, I thought.)

When a man's ability to protect others and provide those others with a sense of safety finds a partner who prioritizes those traits in a dating partner, some risks arise. If the partner begins to question the man's ability to provide safety, that can cause substantial relationship problems. I believe that dynamic was central to Benny's eventual divorce. Lydia saw him as having told a lie of omission when she realized he hadn't told her about his childhood abuse, which caused her to no longer feel (emotionally) safe with him. His stress-related outbursts with their child didn't help. Ultimately, I believe she no longer saw him as the protector she originally perceived him to be.

Many protectors are selfless and self-sacrificing. In some ways, this comes with the territory. Being a protector—especially in a law enforcement role or as a member of the military—requires a willingness to put oneself in harm's way in order to protect others. But I find this selflessness often goes farther than that: Many of the protectors with whom I have worked have difficulty asking for or taking their fair share, or even taking anything at all. Some protectors I have had as clients dislike relying on others and tend to be self-sufficient (see Chapter 4). In therapy, they may struggle to see the value of doing something that would improve their daily functioning unless that improvement would enhance their ability to protect others. This was true for Benny, who was never on his own list of people to protect. Like other protectors, positioning selflessness and selfishness as the end points of a continuum helped him recognize that he could do a few things for himself without being labeled selfish.

Intersectional Issues

Most middle-class men, especially White men, rarely need to do more than simply show up to get credit as a protector. Sure, they might need to kill some bugs that have gotten into the house or protect their teenage daughters from boys who may take advantage of them. But for guys whose income doesn't put them into the middle class, and for men whose racial background predisposes them to a certain amount of hostility and prejudice within American culture, serving as a protector might involve some amount of trying to intimidate others as a method of scaring the "bad guys" away in order to keep his family or himself safe.

The highest crime rates and greatest levels of neighborhood violence tend to occur in relatively poor urban areas, and these areas typically have relatively higher numbers of men of color. Guys who grow up in these neighborhoods may be encouraged or required to become protectors from a young age. In this case, becoming a protector may be a rational choice in response to environmental pressures.

The choice to be a protector isn't limited to boys from so-called "bad" neighborhoods. Men who grow up in poor rural areas may also feel a greater need to adopt the protector role because of the lack of access to law enforcement. Rural populations are primarily White and have fewer college graduates than in urban, suburban, and micropolitan areas.

Men from racial/ethnic minority groups—in particular, men of color, can find that enacting the protector role comes with real risks of being misunderstood and labeled as aggressive in White-dominated systems and spaces because of White people's fears of violence by Black men (Alexander & Alexander, 2021). In schools, for example, boys of color are punished more harshly than their White peers and are more likely to be suspended or expelled; equality advocates say these patterns contribute to the school-to-prison pipeline. Similar factors affect the experiences men of color have with law enforcement and the legal system and likely contribute to those groups' overrepresentation in prisons (Nellis, 2021).

Among men who see the protector role as their primary job within the family, midlife can present a challenge. In addition to some age-related decreases in physical ability, what will he do, or what will his role be, once all the kids are out of the house? These concerns can be magnified if he is no longer partnered, or if his partner doesn't feel as though his protection is still necessary.

WORKING WITH BENNY AND OTHER PROTECTORS

I worked with Benny as an individual therapy client for approximately 3 years. During the first 2 years, we met weekly and then shifted to biweekly sessions. During that third year, Benny joined, and continues to attend, a therapeutic men's group I run and eventually stopped individual therapy. Our therapeutic work focused on his approach to protecting others, with particular attention to ways in which his definition of protection caused him stress; I also described strategies for helping clients adjust the criteria they use to evaluate which threats they need to protect people from. I then discuss the sexual victimization of men, exploring how this affected Benny before providing information on some outcomes of victimization that are unique to men and boys.

Treatment Plan

Building a relationship with Benny, as with many protectors, was slower than with other types of men. I had to demonstrate that I wasn't a threat to him so that he wouldn't go into his typical defensive mode, and I had to demonstrate I had something useful to offer him. I suspected that I'd need to have a small win fairly quickly in order to demonstrate that I wasn't wasting his time (see Chapter 4 for more discussion of these small wins). I needed to start by working within Benny's framework, so I adopted his protection framework and began helping him protect his family from himself by reducing his stress and thus reducing the likelihood he would lose control and yell.

We began by addressing protection and safety. Discussion initially focused on how he could better cope with stress in order to protect his son from his temper because that readily fit into his worldview. Our work here included identifying stressful elements of his life, his reactions to increased stress, and ways of coping with stress.

After we had explored the stresses he faced, we made a small shift into discussing his emotions. I had explicitly framed stress as an emotion, and we had a short discussion about ways in which the terms "stress" and "anxiety" were interchangeable so Benny would accept that talking about emotions was a part of our work and could gain some comfort with it. After he had done so, we spoke about the sexual assault he had experienced as a teen.

Protecting People and Reducing Stress

As Benny and I explored things that caused him stress, we were able to start differentiating things that caused stress because they were difficult, such as managing the mowing schedule or equipment that broke down, and things that caused stress because they made him mad, such as employees not showing up for work or his son disobeying him.

We identified a few stress-relieving strategies, including screaming to music on the way home, sometimes taking the long way home because he needed extra time, and taking a long shower that included washing off the physical and mental dirt from the day. (I discuss stress in more detail in Chapter 9.)

THERAPIST: For the past few weeks? Months? We've been talking about things that stress you out during the day and strategies you can use to help you deal with that stress.

CLIENT: That's right.

THERAPIST: Which ones have been most helpful so far?

CLIENT: Showering as soon as I get home and imagining that some of what I'm doing is washing off the stressful things from the day.

THERAPIST: So you [*making air quotes*] "wash off" the daily stresses?

CLIENT: That's right.

THERAPIST: Any other strategies that have been effective that you use regularly?

CLIENT: That's the big one. If we're running early, then I'll take the long way home and scream along to some music.

THERAPIST: Only if you're running early?

CLIENT: Yeah. My wife knows my schedule, and if I'm more than 5 minutes late, she starts texting me.

THERAPIST: And you don't want to be late.

CLIENT: Nope.

THERAPIST: How much extra time would you need if you were screaming along to the music.

CLIENT: About 20 minutes, I think.

THERAPIST: And you'd rather be home and moderately or highly stressed instead of arriving 20 minutes later and having a low level of stress?

CLIENT: It's not that. I don't think it's fair to my wife for me to take an extra 20 minutes to listen to music.

THERAPIST: You're not exactly listening to the music here. You're screaming along to songs that you already know well, and I don't think you're really doing the music-appreciation thing for hard rock songs from the 80s and 90s you've heard a million times.

Benny was very excited by this idea when we first discussed a scream-along playlist and immediately identified several songs from this genre and era.

CLIENT: No, but I am listening to my music instead of being home with Lydia and Aiden, and that seems unfair to Lydia. She doesn't get to spend an extra 20 minutes listening to her music without me and Aiden.

THERAPIST: And I'm guessing you believe it's better to get home as quickly as possible so you can help out around the house, no matter what condition you're in?

CLIENT: That's right.

THERAPIST: When you come home highly stressed and yell at Aiden, or on a night where you're struggling to maintain your self-control, do you think that's easier or harder for Lydia?

CLIENT: It's easier for Lydia because it means she gets a break from Aiden as soon as I get home, and I get home sooner.

THERAPIST: It's easier for her even if she's worried that you might lose control.

CLIENT: Uh, maybe?

THERAPIST: Can Lydia tell when you're highly stressed and you're having a hard time maintaining your self-control?

CLIENT: I'm pretty sure, yes.

THERAPIST: Do you think that stresses her out? That she's not really able to relax and let you watch Aiden on those evenings?

CLIENT: No, probably not. Actually, I'm sure she's not because I know she ends up watching Aiden more on those evenings. Unless she's too wiped out and needs to go lay down. But even then, I think she's trying to stay with us as long as possible so I don't lose control.

THERAPIST: And how long does that last?

CLIENT: What do you mean?

THERAPIST: When Lydia stays with you and Aiden instead of lying down, how long does she stay with you guys?

CLIENT: Until after Aiden has his bath and maybe even until he goes to bed. So, an hour and a half or 2 hours.

THERAPIST: So when you don't take an extra 20 minutes because it wouldn't be fair to Lydia, it costs her an extra hour and a half or 2 hours at the end of the night?

CLIENT: Yeah. I'll need to ask her about taking an extra 20 minutes on my drive home. Maybe I can cut it down to 15. I don't want to burden her. She's already got Aiden all day.

This conversation was the beginning of a revelation for Benny. For the first time, he started to really notice the ways Lydia quietly responded to his mood. It was something he had never considered before, and that realization solidified and expanded our discussion of couple dynamics. That conversation also helped Benny understand that even though his mood wasn't really important to him, it was important to both Lydia and Aiden.

Like many couples, Benny and Lydia texted throughout the day. Benny ultimately came to realize that when his wife complained to him about their son's behavior or another aspect of her day, this increased his stress level because he wasn't there to protect his wife from stress. He was unwilling to ask her to stop sending him texts of this sort, so I met with both of them. Before he was willing to ask her to stop, she had to assure him that she was just venting; she did not specifically need his help with these items, and she had friends she could vent to. She hadn't realized her messages caused him stress and readily agreed to stop texting him about her day-to-day hassles.

I was able to use this focus on stress as a way to demonstrate that therapy could be helpful, that his emotions played an important role in his daily life (by considering stress an emotion), and that change was possible for him and in his relationship. The focus on stress also provided a path to start prioritizing Benny's mood and emotional experiences instead of ignoring them. This was slow work, but Benny was willing to try some new ways to reduce stress and saw the benefits of doing so.

Over the course of 18 months, Benny was able to reduce his stress level and gained ever-better control over his temper, which lessened. He also made gains with respect to his emotional self-awareness and emotional expression, although he was still reticent and slow to initiate a discussion of his feelings. His parenting improved, and so did his relationship with his son, partly because of his ability to feel happy when playing with him.

Addressing Oversensitive Threat Detectors

Examining a protector's *threat detectors* can be a useful element of treatment, especially for men—or their families—who say they're overdoing it. Helping a client examine and adjust his decision-making system can reduce his anxiety and his sense that he always needs to be ready for an attack. Because Benny and his family lived in a neighborhood with a low crime rate, and he didn't voice concerns about being physically attacked, we didn't directly address his beliefs about safety.

One strategy I used with Benny was to make him verbalize his chain of thought/reasoning, as illustrated in our discussion of him getting home from work as quickly as possible. This process helped both of us recognize the assumptions that guided his decision making. His desire to protect Lydia from stress, as well as his difficulty anticipating the ways other people's behavior would change in response to his own behavior, were both issues that we addressed in that moment and would continue to return to. In my experience, protectors often struggle to see the quieter and subtler ways in which other people in the system adjust to the protector's moods, such as Benny's lack of recognition that Lydia would stay with Aiden longer when Benny was in a bad mood.

Another approach I often use is to ask the protectors how their charges will learn to protect themselves for one specific issue at a time, and then I try to expedite the process. Benny and I used this strategy to help him become comfortable leaving 5-year-old Aiden alone in another room or in their fenced-in backyard for more than 2 minutes. Using a technique adapted from systemic desensitization approaches, we talked about the behaviors he needed to see to be comfortable doing so, created a list from least to most anxiety producing, and then worked toward greater time alone for Aiden. As we did so, I spoke about Benny's ability to trust Aiden to protect himself and keep himself safe. We also spoke about times when Benny might be able to skip some steps and jump ahead on the list. Eventually, Benny was able to leave Aiden alone in the yard for as long as 30 minutes and in another room in the house for 60 minutes while periodically checking on him visually (through the window or sticking his head in the room) while not interrupting Aiden. In this way, we reset Benny's threat detector. For subsequent issues, we developed a similar list, and I pushed Benny to start with more freedom and skip more steps (with the goal that his steps would ultimately get bigger).

Many protectors have oversensitive threat detectors because of adverse childhood experiences (ACEs), which are particularly common among men of this type. One recent national study found that approximately 64% of men (and a similar percentage of women) experience one or more ACEs, with approximately 15% of men experiencing four or more (Swedo et al., 2023). Among males, emotional abuse is more common than physical or sexual abuse (34%, 24%, and 7%, respectively), with parental separation or divorce (28%) and household substance use (25%) as the most common categories of adverse events.

Parental separation is the second most common ACE (Swedo et al., 2023). It may lead boys—especially the oldest son—to be told that he is now the man of the house. Although parents typically intend this as a way to encourage the boy to become more responsible, the phrasing invokes manhood and may cause the boy to adopt a broader range of responsibilities than intended, including protection. I typically encourage single parents to talk about "responsibilities" and "maturity" and helping the family "team" instead of promoting the child to the level of the adults. When single mothers have been especially insistent about calling their son the man of the house, I have occasionally asked, will he be sleeping with the woman of the house?

Addressing Sexual Trauma

After Benny's ability to handle his stress and attend to his feelings had improved, we shifted from the process of protecting people to the cause of that desire to protect others. Because I knew from our first meeting that

Benny was a sexual assault survivor, and because he knew that I was on the board of MaleSurvivor (https://www.malesurvivor.org), Benny always expected us to talk about his molestation. He was reluctant to discuss it, but he didn't refuse either.

It took Benny several sessions to tell me the story of his abuse. At age 13, Benny was victimized by another boy who lived in the neighborhood. There were only a few kids who lived in the neighborhood, and this boy, a year older than Benny, was the only boy close to Benny's age, so they played together with some regularity, although Benny said they hadn't spent much time together since the start of middle school 2 years earlier (because the other boy attended a private school). The other boy reached sexual maturity earlier than Benny, and over a span of approximately 9 months convinced Benny to allow some sexual activity, either in the course of imaginary play or, later, as the "price" of allowing Benny to choose how they would spend (the rest of) their time. One time, at the boy's house, he convinced Benny to begin to perform oral sex in order to find out what it was like, promising that he wouldn't orgasm in Benny's mouth and that he'd return the favor, if Benny wanted him to. He climaxed in Benny's mouth and, a moment later, Benny punched him in the testicles, left the house, and never spoke to the boy again.

As experiences of sexual assault go, Benny's was comparatively mild. Benny had not been physically restrained or beaten, hadn't been threatened with violence to himself or his family if he told anyone, had not been anally penetrated, and the duration was "only" a few months. However, between the sexual assault and Benny's history of physical punishment from his parents and the inconsistent emotional safety he experienced from them, the damage was profound. An only child with two working parents, Benny was usually on his own after arriving home from middle school and was used to fending for himself. His parents loved him, but they relied on his self-sufficiency, rarely talked about their feelings, and rarely asked Benny about his own feelings. Benny never told them about being victimized. From Benny's age-13 perspective, he hadn't been physically harmed, and didn't believe he'd need their help to prevent future assaults, so why burden them?

Like many sexual assault victims, Benny blamed himself for what happened by emphasizing the ways he had agreed to sexual activity while ignoring the coercion that created his consent. He responded by closing in on himself, creating boundaries that would be difficult for others to overcome. Benny learned physical protection through Junior Reserve Officers' Training Corps and martial arts. Then he made a series of life choices that allowed him to create a sense of safety and avoid most risks, choosing well-established paths forward.

Benny is one of two male survivors of childhood sexual assault profiled in this book (the other is N'Shawn in Chapter 7). Many therapists learn that one in four girls or young women will be sexually assaulted; according to data from the Centers for Disease Control and Prevention, approximately one in six boys or young men will be sexually assaulted (Basile et al., 2022). The impact for men is similar to that of women: sadness, shame, poor self-esteem, sexual development that can contribute to either abstinence or high levels of sexual risk-taking, greater likelihood of addiction, and so on (Gartner, 1999, 2017a, 2017b; Lew, 2004). Approximately one in seven men will be victimized again (Aosved et al., 2011). Internal research from the organization MaleSurvivor indicates that male victims often wait approximately 20 years before disclosing their assault, and they often do so to only one other person, either a spouse or a therapist, but rarely both.

Three specific elements of masculinity make being a victim of sexual assault very different for boys and men than for girls and women. First, boys and men are expected to be able to defend themselves, and thus the experience of not being able to fight off their attackers adds an extra dose of shame. Second, they are expected to be in control of themselves regardless of the situation, and being victimized clearly indicates they were not in control; this adds an extra dose of shame for male victims. When working with these clients, I help them understand that the fight wasn't fair (especially when an adult man assaults a boy whose body has not yet filled out), that they were given alcohol or drugs that impaired their ability to control the situation, or other factors. I find that I often have to address this topic multiple times over the course of weeks or months before my clients accept that their "failure" may not be shameful. Sometimes, we explicitly shift the shame to the abuser as part of the process of relieving the victim's shame.

Third, boys and men are taught they should want sex, at any time and with anyone, an idea that I dissected in my 2013 book *Challenging Casanova: Beyond the Stereotype of the Promiscuous Young Male*. This framing of male sexuality leaves little cultural space for guys to say they had a sexual experience they didn't want. As a result, sexual assault can be confusing because he's clearly had a sexual experience he didn't want, but he doesn't have a mental framework for explaining that he didn't want sex. This scenario is relatively more common when he's been drugged or when someone (typically an older woman) seduces a teen boy, such as happened with 34-year-old teacher Mary Kay Letourneau and her sixth-grade student ("Mary Kay Letourneau," 2025).

The vast majority of sexual assaults against boys are committed by other males, and anal penetration of the victim is somewhat common (Basile et al.,

2022). Some guys who are exclusively interested in females may be ashamed because they've "had gay sex," especially if they have any type of belief that being gay is wrong. Therapeutically, I emphasize that they didn't "have sex"—they were raped and thus did not have any choice.

For some men—straight, gay, bisexual, pansexual, and so on—having been sexually assaulted as a child may raise questions about their "true" sexual identity, especially if their assailant was male and if they've never thought about the experience as rape. Some men believe they need to have sex with many women to prove they're straight. Other men, some strictly gay and others bisexual or pansexual, have identified their rape as the reason why they like having sex with men. This statement implies they would have been strictly heterosexual and implicitly positions same-sex activity as deviant. In these situations, I provide some psychoeducation about the causes of sexual orientation as primarily biological ("We're born that way") while also exploring homophobic beliefs the client might have in order to determine where any shame related to same-sex activity comes from. I sometimes explicitly state that being penetrated by a penis can't change our sexual preferences; penises aren't that powerful.

American society isn't particularly supportive of male victims of sexual assault, and many agencies struggle to provide adequate support for male victims. However, there are several national organizations in the United States that provide education, support, and some treatment. These include MaleSurvivor; 1 in 6 (https://1in6.org/); the Rape, Abuse & Incest National Network (https://rainn.org/); and MenHealing (https://www.menhealing.org/). As mentioned earlier, I am a former board chair of MaleSurvivor.

I encourage you to review local resources for survivors of sexual abuse to determine if they are willing and able to support male victims. Some venues continue to believe that men cannot be victims and must be perpetrators seeking to regain access to their victims (Machado et al., 2016). Other researchers have begun to document the unique needs of male victims (Cook et al., 2018; Ellis et al., 2020).

Enriching the Inner Life

Approximately 1.5 years into our work together, and 6 months after his wife left him, Benny decided that he wanted to use his carpentry skills to make and sell children's toys online. (He had very good carpentry skills, the result of time spent woodworking with his father and grandfather.) So, he made a few samples, created an Etsy shop, and went into business. A few weeks later, he told me he was frustrated because he had invested time and money into the effort but had made only one sale. This led to a deeper discussion of excitement and disappointment, feelings he rarely shared with anyone.

As we discussed his carpentry business, Benny showed me his online storefront. The first thing I noticed was the protection. On the website, Benny talked about how safe the toys were—rounded edges, finished and sealed in order to prevent splinters—instead of how fun they were. (Benny also struggled with marketing, which involved drawing attention to himself, but that's a different story.)

Benny had once described his (emotional) life as a bunker with concrete walls, a single door, and no windows. He couldn't imagine moving out of the bunker, but he acknowledged that some throw pillows or other decorations, or a window, might make his life in the bunker more enjoyable. Unfortunately, Benny had trouble imagining what those metaphorical decorations might translate to in real life. He had few interests and no one in his personal life to support him while he actively tried new things, or to drag him along to activities he wouldn't have chosen himself.

I mentioned Benny's difficulty moving beyond his bunker. In my experience, this happens for many protectors: Their focus is almost extensively on the well-being of the people they are protecting, rarely themselves, and thus their inner lives are relatively impoverished. They have little sense of what they might want or how they might feel because those concerns don't help them be better protectors. In these situations, I try to highlight to my clients that they deserve the happiness or growth or whatever it is they are trying to create for those they protect, and thus they, too, can enjoy (some) of the fruits of being protected. We also discussed the importance of trying new things, something Benny and Lydia would often express to Aiden, and our talks included the risk that new things might ultimately be evaluated as a waste of time, money, and energy and could leave him feeling disappointed.

CONCLUSION

Benny's story illustrates ways in which men can adopt a protector role toward the important people in their lives. This role is common around the world and readily evident in American history, and thus it offers a masculine type that all people, or at least most of them, are aware of, often from a young age. For those who adopt this role, whether by choice or situational necessity, it offers a place in society, relies on the ability to use reason to solve a specific set of problems, and requires ongoing attention and modification to one's goals (i.e., perseverance). Being a protector also qualifies one as Man Enough.

Benny serves as an example, although he was a bit atypical: He was trying to protect his wife and son from himself. Despite this atypical form of protection, his issues were ones I often see among protectors. Benny struggled to recognize or address his own stress, and thus he inadvertently increased the risk to those he was trying to protect. He also struggled to reduce his sensitivity to threats, which meant the people he was protecting weren't able to develop their own defenses in a way they needed to. Benny, who had been on the receiving end of physical discipline by his parents and was a sexual assault victim, also struggled to experience and enjoy his own inner life as a protector. He was focused almost exclusively on other people: those he was protecting and those who might cause harm.

Unfortunately, Benny's wife opted to end their relationship, and he and I worked through his sadness related to this loss. Two years after he had started treatment, Benny stepped down from weekly to biweekly sessions. He also joined a therapeutic men's group I facilitate and eventually terminated individual therapy while continuing to participate in the group.

7 THE ANGRY MAN

N'SHAWN'S CASE

A 25-year-old gay, Black, cisgender man, N'Shawn had been referred for therapy by his primary care physician (PCP), who was worried he might lose his temper yet again. N'Shawn had a stroke that caused him to become blind and to lose some functioning in his left arm and leg. N'Shawn was living with his mother—herself in poor physical health—and the PCP was worried that N'Shawn's anger might accidentally lead to one or both of their deaths. The PCP had known N'Shawn for several years, and he trusted the doctor's judgment; she was also N'Shawn's mother's PCP. His anger problems were a long-standing issue. They had contributed to two out-of-home placements during his childhood, the second of which, at age 13–14, lasted for approximately 1 year. In the waiting room, I asked N'Shawn how I could best help him walk to the office, and he said he'd like to put his hands on my shoulders and follow me, so that's what we did.

https://doi.org/10.1037/0000499-007
Clinical Work With Men: Understanding Masculinity in Psychotherapy, by A. P. Smiler

N'Shawn was willing to meet with me only because I specialized in working with men. He had had plenty of therapists before and had never liked therapy. He was very personable and chatty and had the social skills to get people to open up. Before his stroke, he had been studying to be a nurse, and he told me he wanted to help other kids like him. N'Shawn was well dressed. He stood 5 ft, 6 in. (1.7 m) and had a slight build. His arms were muscled, but not in a way that made me think he had ever worked out regularly. To me, N'Shawn didn't look like someone who would inspire fear or could be particularly dangerous.

I had been told about N'Shawn's history of violence during the referral process, but I hadn't spoken with him; everything had been arranged through his mother. During that first session, I wanted to assess his desire for therapy. Boys and men with a history of violence are often forced into therapy, and that seemed to be the case here. I knew that people who are forced into therapy are less likely to engage with the therapist and often terminate treatment after a handful of sessions, an outcome I wanted to avoid. Past experience with angry clients told me N'Shawn was likely to test my tolerance for violence and thus my willingness to accept him as he was.

Our conversation during that first session went something like this:

THERAPIST: OK. We've talked about things that make you happy. Can I change the focus?

CLIENT: Sure.

THERAPIST: Why are you in a therapist's office today?

CLIENT: Because I have anger problems.

THERAPIST: Do you think you have anger problems, or is that what other people tell you?

CLIENT: It's what other people say. Mostly. My anger is not a problem for me.

THERAPIST: But it's a problem for other people?

CLIENT: Yes?

THERAPIST: How so?

CLIENT: They're scared of what might happen when I get mad.

THERAPIST: OK, I'll bite. What happens when you get mad?

CLIENT: Bad shit happens.

THERAPIST: Like what?

CLIENT: People get hurt. I have broken other people's bones. Noses make a nice popping sound when they break, and you get a real good crack when you hit someone in the mouth and their jaw slams into their skull. I have beat people until they passed out.

THERAPIST: Got it. So people are worried about you hitting th-

CLIENT: [*Interrupting*] Not just hitting them. Beating the f*** out of them so bad they go to the hospital.

THERAPIST: That's serious. You can do some real damage.

CLIENT: [*Proudly*] You bet I can.

THERAPIST: Is there other bad shit that happens when you get mad? Do you yell? Break stuff?

CLIENT: Yes. Both. Well, not yelling exactly. I'll get a little loud, and my voice kind of changes to let people know I'm mad. I might say something nasty. I can be very nasty. I have made people cry. Not just women or feminine gay men—straight guys, too. I can tear you a new asshole with my fists and with my words [*proudly*].

THERAPIST: Sounds like you are someone people should definitely not mess with.

CLIENT: Absolutely.

THERAPIST: OK. Other people think you have an anger problem and are scared of your anger, but you're the one talking to a therapist, not them. What do you want to get from our conversations?

CLIENT: They're not entirely wrong. It would probably be good for me to have better control over my anger.

THERAPIST: Why? Does losing your temper cause problems for you?

CLIENT: Come on. Seriously?

THERAPIST: Yes, seriously. I'm a middle-aged White guy who grew up in the Philadelphia suburbs. You're a young Black man who grew up in a city. Winston-Salem isn't Philly, but still. I've read a lot about what it's like to grow up Black, and I've got some Black friends and some Black clients, but it is not my day-to-day and never was. Like many angry guys I've worked with, I think your anger works for you, not against you. And you've pretty much said that. So, what do you want to get from therapy?

CLIENT: Damn [*laughs*].

THERAPIST: Huh?

CLIENT: Of the five, no . . . wait . . . six therapists I've worked with when I was in group homes and after that, plus all the other staff members at those places, no one has ever said that to me.

THERAPIST: Said what?

CLIENT: "Middle-aged White guy" [*laughs*]. I'm sorry [*laughs again*].

THERAPIST: [*Pauses*] It's all right. I said it, and it's true. It's also part of how we work together. I'm gonna ask you to be straight with me about who you are, what you do, and why you do it. That means I need to be clear with you about who I am, what I can do to help you, and the limits of my abilities.

CLIENT: Shoot, man. You're different.

THERAPIST: I am. And I'm not letting you off the hook. If you're going to talk to me, what do you want to talk about?

CLIENT: People piss me off. A lot. And I think my life would probably be easier if I didn't go crazy on them.

THERAPIST: People meaning your mom?

CLIENT: Yeah. I love my mama and don't want to hurt her. She's my mother, y'know? And she's got breathing problems and all sorts of other problems. I don't want to kill her, but sometimes when I get mad at her, I just want to kill her.

THERAPIST: I get it. The anger makes you want to hurt her and think about hurting her, even though she's your mom and you love her.

CLIENT: Yes.

THERAPIST: Anyone else you're worried about hurting? Or anything else you're worried might happen when you get angry?

CLIENT: Her husband also lives with us, but I don't mind killing him.

THERAPIST: Come again?

CLIENT: He's not my dad, and I wouldn't feel bad. But my mama would be upset, so I don't want to kill him, but if I did, I wouldn't be upset. My mama would be mad at me, and that would be a problem.

THERAPIST: I just met you, and I can't decide if you're kidding or not.

CLIENT: Kidding. Mostly [*laughs*]. But for real, that's how I think. He doesn't mean much to me, and if I had to kill him, I would, and I wouldn't be sad about it or upset or anything. But I don't have any reason to kill him. We mostly leave each other alone.

THERAPIST: Thanks for letting me know how you think.

A few important things happened during this conversation. By not getting caught up in the damage he could do or had done, I made N'Shawn the focus, not his violence. Plenty of other people in his life focused on that, and centering the damage meant highlighting other people's reactions to and perceptions of N'Shawn. I made an effort to focus on his actual self and his concerns, not everyone else's reactions and concerns, which was why I repeatedly asked what he wanted to get from therapy. This choice meant that I accepted his decision to enact the masculine criterion of violence.

I also wanted to establish that we were partners who could work together. To do that, I needed to accept his use of violence and recognize the ways violence helped him achieve masculine status (which I discuss later in this chapter). I also needed to downplay the importance of my own achievements because I would be asking him to downplay his by acknowledging the ways violence caused him problems. He had already shown respect by coming to see me in my office and being flexible to meet my availability, and when I met him in the waiting room I had invited him to call me either "Andrew" (consistent with my White culture) or "Dr. Andrew" (consistent with his Black culture), whichever he preferred. And I would again diminish the distance between us with my "middle-aged White guy" description, a phrase he and I continued to use when there seemed to be cultural misunderstanding.

And then I listened. A lot. Not just that first day, but over the next few weeks, I listened as N'Shawn told me his story. I repeatedly reflected his story back "to make sure I'm understanding you"; at times, this included asking for "middle-aged White guy clarifications" about terms I was unfamiliar with. As he spoke, I also expressed surprise and support, and I sympathized with his anger and told him that I was impressed with some of his accomplishments. I didn't judge or express concern about any of the past violence he reported. That first day, on the way out, he held my arm, and we walked side by side.

Starting in the second session, we met remotely (voice only) because the family didn't have a reliable means of transportation. Over the next few weeks, I kept listening, and I continually showed N'Shawn that I understood him, his frustrations, and especially his pain. And the more I listened, the more he talked. I rarely challenged him directly, instead asking—or suggesting—how he could express his anger today in ways that kept him safe, didn't risk further damage to himself, and didn't put him at risk of interacting with the police or going to jail. (N'Shawn often told me that he'd be fine in jail but, given how much control he liked to have over his surroundings, I didn't really believe him.)

Themes in N'Shawn's Therapy

My work with N'Shawn focused on two themes: his anger and being emotionally vulnerable. I saw the anger as the source of his violence and understood that the violence was primarily reactive: N'Shawn was violent only when he felt attacked and needed to defend himself. I also believed that his anger was cover for a wide range of tender emotions, including sadness, hurt, and feelings of abandonment.

Like many men with anger issues, N'Shawn had literally fought for the things he had: self-respect and a certain amount of safety because of his fear-inspiring reputation. According to N'Shawn, he had always inflicted more damage than he had taken, and thus he had never lost a fight. N'Shawn needed the respect and safety because when he was 7 he had been forcibly raped (anally penetrated) by an older male family member. And then again, by an extended family member, at age 10, and by a boy from the neighborhood, at age 12. N'Shawn had attempted to fight back in each instance, but his assailants were all at least 5 years older and thus bigger and stronger. The first of his assailants had been jailed (because he was a legal adult and had raped others, who reported the event).

About 2 weeks after that third rape, 12-year-old N'Shawn ambushed his most recent assailant and beat him with a bat. It was the first time N'Shawn had been able to defend himself and the first time he felt powerful. In a conversation with me he explained that this constituted defending himself because it prevented future assaults from that boy and sent a message to others in the neighborhood that N'Shawn was not someone to mess with. He acknowledged that his attack was also driven by a desire for revenge by inflicting comparable—or more—pain on his assailant than had been inflicted on him.

In the week after he had delivered that beating, N'Shawn discovered something else: Other kids in his neighborhood, and even kids in school who didn't live in his neighborhood, began treating him differently. They showed him respect, which was based on violence and a fear of violence. Inspiring fear and respect, and the deference that came with it, was a new experience for N'Shawn. The combination of his own feelings of being powerful and the newly found peer respect gave N'Shawn two more things he had never experienced before: feelings of status and safety. Almost overnight, he had gone from someone small, weak, and forgettable to someone to be feared and whose good side you wanted to be on.

N'Shawn stayed on this path. He wouldn't back down from anyone, but he also found ways to fight only when he needed to because someone was a legitimate threat to his safety. He didn't fight the gang members in his neighborhood because he didn't see them as a threat to his safety, and they didn't see him as a rival because he wasn't selling drugs or interfering with their activities. N'Shawn didn't use his status or other people's fear of him as a way to take advantage of others because he had been taken advantage of and didn't want to do it to anyone else. He just wanted to be left alone. N'Shawn told me he fought only for the purpose of protecting himself and only when he needed to do so.

Self-protection was N'Shawn's underlying approach to everything. He had had sex with a number of people, but almost exclusively as hookups with gay or bisexual men, or allowing straight guys to explore what it was like to be with another man. N'Shawn admitted to having one boyfriend, when he was 19. That young man broke up with N'Shawn because N'Shawn wouldn't open up to him or say "I love you" even after they had been together for several months. Many years after that relationship, N'Shawn acknowledged to me that was the most open he'd ever been with a partner but that he wasn't sure that he'd loved that young man. N'Shawn told me he wasn't willing to get close to anyone because that made him vulnerable.

N'Shawn as an Angry Man

Many people don't understand men's anger, especially for someone like N'Shawn, whose anger seemed to be easily aroused and was often expressed violently. But with N'Shawn, and for many violent men, anger is their primary mode of defense against a hostile world. It's a defense that keeps them from being physically and emotionally harmed again. Anger tells other people to back off, and it works the vast majority of the time.

In Chapter 6, I discussed protecting others as a way to find a place in society and as an element of masculinity. N'Shawn's anger and violence were primarily due to the pain of being raped, repeatedly, and he used them strictly for self-protection; he never fought to protect someone else. That makes N'Shawn very different from men who adopt the protector role. In the world of emotion and American gender norms, anger holds a unique place. It is an emotion boys and men are allowed to have and allowed to express freely (David & Brannon, 1976). We expect men to control their feelings and how they display their feelings. Anger and lust are the only exceptions to this dictate. The permission to feel anger, but nothing else, may explain why many men channel any kind of negative emotion into anger. Commentator Don Long (1987) described anger as the "male emotional funnel system" (p. 315) for exactly this reason. And a year into therapy, N'Shawn acknowledged that all his "bad" feelings came out as anger. It's no wonder many people view men's anger as inherently unpredictable and dangerous: Many men display anger instead of the sadness, anxiety, or another tender feeling that others might expect.

One useful thing about anger, and especially anger in its function as the male emotional funnel system, is that there is almost always something to be mad about. It might be something that happened at work, or school, in public; a sports team that is doing poorly; some industry or governmental system that is blocking him from getting something he wants; or something else yet again, but whatever it is, it can become the focus of his anger. And, by converting his sadness or anxiety or frustration or disappointment into anger, he can use the anger to work off some of the emotional energy.

MASCULINITY AND THE ANGRY MAN TYPE

From the perspective of the multi-faceted masculinity framework, the masculine criterion to which N'Shawn most strongly adhered was his willingness to use violence. Unlike criteria such as breadwinning and protecting others, violence is almost always a means to an end. For N'Shawn, and most of the violent men with whom I have worked, violence is a means of protecting oneself from harm and hurt.

Violence provides a straightforward path to masculine achievement because guys who can beat other people up are seen as Man Enough. Those who do so repeatedly can move from being Man Enough to being The Man (see Chapter 2), at least among the people who know them.

For some men, their ability to use violence to protect themselves becomes their identity; these men have a masculine type known as "tough guy" or "fighter." This was certainly true for N'Shawn; the toughness that brought him safety also brought him fear-based respect, social status from his age mates, and self-confidence. This kind of violence is readily available in American media. Examples range from *The Fast and Furious*'s (R. Cohen, 2001) Dominic Toretto and his repeated use of violence to protect his chosen family to superheroes who use violence to save the United States or the Earth. The most obvious example may be The Incredible Hulk, who (used to) warn people "Don't make me angry. You wouldn't like me when I'm angry."

Benefits of Being an Angry Man

For N'Shawn, and many angry men with whom I have worked, threatening violence was a means of creating safety. It also brought a certain sense of power and status. The conversion of sad and anxious feelings into anger provides a way to make those vulnerable and unpleasant emotions go away; this was certainly true for N'Shawn. This conversion allows him to shift the focus away from those uncomfortable feelings and onto a feeling (and possibly a target) that is familiar and comfortable. When a man is given the opportunity to express his anger to friends, they often offer some type of support, and thus his depressed or anxious (or whatever) feelings might get soothed without him having to show any "weakness" associated with sadness, crying, anxiety, or not being able to take care of his own business.

The physical experience of anger can be its own benefit. Anger brings energy and focus, which may provide their own distraction from hurt feelings. Sadness is associated with a loss of energy, and both sadness and anxiety are characterized by a lack of focus. But if a man's anger can trigger the fight in his fight–flight–freeze reaction to danger, then he will experience a physiological shift that also changes his emotional state.

Once a man has learned to control his anger in ways that prevent him from getting into trouble, he may be able to channel that anger into something useful. Anger related to some kind of inequality or unfairness often reflects a deep-seated value, such as equality. In situations where this is the case, the connection between anger and values may fuel his passion and allow him to work on the problem, whether that is done through participation in a community organization, use of his professional skills, or some other means.

Challenges of Being an Angry Man

Perhaps the biggest psychological concern in working with angry men is the repeated conversion of anxiety, sadness, and other tender feelings into anger. Although it may provide relief in the moment, this emotional funnel system can become a self-reinforcing feedback loop that helps him avoid directly processing sadness, anxiety, shame, and other tender feelings. Metaphorically, it is comparable to obsessive-compulsive behavior, in which the compulsive behavior is anger.

The tendency to convert any hurt into anger also has deleterious effects on interpersonal relationships. N'Shawn's tendency to get angry after interpersonal slights, even when accidental, made it difficult for him to keep friends. He had very little experience apologizing or accepting apologies in ways that would repair a relationship or rebuild trust after difficulty had occurred.

When I was a new therapist, back in the 1990s, there was professional discussion of clients having *low frustration tolerance*. That is part of the dynamic here. Being prevented from obtaining a goal—whether that goal is friendship, completing a work task, making an appointment, or something else—can cause frustration. This was evident in N'Shawn's interpersonal relationships; I also saw it when he had to navigate the helping systems (medical, transportation, services for the blind, etc.). If he couldn't get the support he was seeking in a relatively straightforward manner, he would get frustrated and stop dealing with that system or organization.

Venting to a friend can be difficult for angry men. For guys like N'Shawn, who struggle to be vulnerable, it can be hard to focus on the cause of the hurt behind the anger. And because N'Shawn had difficulty keeping friends, he didn't always have someone to talk to. Other angry men with whom I have worked had friends who tended to feed their anger instead of exploring the reasons behind the anger. I find it useful to help my angry clients think about whom they should talk to when they're angry: someone who will be supportive while they are venting and who will help them calm down instead of keeping them amped up or encouraging them to engage in violence.

Men who tend toward violence in response to feelings of sadness or hurt can be prone to violence in interpersonal relationships. This is particularly common among men with an insecure attachment style, either resistant or avoidant (Shaver et al., 2011). If his partner threatens to move out, which would almost certainly cause him to feel rejected, then his risk of committing subsequent violence—including murder—increases significantly (Stith & McMonigle, 2009); this finding is based on male–female couples, but I believe it is also true of male–male couples. I will also note that the vast majority of school shootings are committed by teen boys or young men and follow some type of social rejection (Leary et al., 2003), paralleling the pattern seen in couples.

Intersectional Issues

Adopting an intersectional lens raises additional concerns. We know that men of color experience school-based punishment (e.g., suspension and expulsion) at higher rates than their White peers. Anger, and especially any violence that follows it, is a common reason boys face these penalties. N'Shawn certainly had faced such punishment, on many occasions. Boys may find these experiences unfair because the adults don't ask and don't understand why a boy has acted in the way he has, leaving him to feel as though he hasn't been heard. When this happens repeatedly, boys lose faith in the idea that schools and school personnel can be trusted to treat them fairly. Boys may then adopt an antagonistic approach toward school and the people who work there, which, according to Michael Reichert and Joseph Nelson (2018), requires a relational approach to repair.

As adults, men who are Black, Latino, or of Native heritage have higher rates of being homicide victims than members of other racial and ethnic groups. Rates are high enough that homicide qualifies as one of the 10 most common causes of death among those ethnic groups (Centers for Disease Control and Prevention, 2011; Liu et al., 2023). These homicides are mostly committed by a male assailant whom the victim knows, and the death is most likely to occur in a house (or apartment or back yard), involves a firearm, and is preceded by some type of argument (Liu et al., 2023). To me, that sounds a lot like two guys got into an argument during which someone got mad and pulled a gun, and then someone died.

N'Shawn's anger, and the violence that followed, provided him with a tangible benefit: People began to fear him. This is often labeled "respect," and it gave him a certain amount of status and, thus, safety. There is nothing novel about this, or unique to N'Shawn; violence is a male-specific method of obtaining status. Boys and men who can't obtain status in other ways may see violence as a legitimate choice for obtaining masculinity's achievements. I believe this choice is more common among boys whose lives are impoverished in ways they can't hide, especially boys from families of low socioeconomic status (SES). A lack of other means of obtaining status may also mean that boys are unable to refuse a fight, because refusing to fight can mean a substantial loss of masculine status. Boys of color tend to be overrepresented among low-SES populations (Shrider & Creamer, 2023). Similarly, I suspect boys from middle- and high-SES families who are prone to anger and violence choose to become bullies and thus are nominally willing to fight, even if they never actually do.

When displayed in front of White men or women, the anger of Black men may be perceived as especially problematic. This is the result of the

American history of racism and the legacy of distrust and misunderstanding it continues to create among White people. Stereotypical and prejudicial beliefs increase the likelihood that White people will see Black men as especially likely to become violent and possibly also as especially destructive when violent (Alexander & Alexander, 2021). Given their fears of destructive violence, White people may preemptively act to defend themselves, potentially through their own use of violence.

WORKING WITH N'SHAWN AND OTHER ANGRY MEN

N'Shawn and I worked together for approximately 3 years. About 6 weeks into our work together, we started meeting twice per week; all of our work was remote, with the exception of our initial session. Our therapeutic work focused extensively on his anger; we explored the current and past hurts behind his anger as well as ways to express that anger and ways to reduce the likelihood that his anger will be triggered. N'Shawn and I also explored his struggles to trust others, a common struggle among victims of (all types of) childhood abuse.

Treatment Plan

N'Shawn said he wanted to gain greater control of his anger, so that is where we started, and helping him with his anger would be the primary focus of our work. In the beginning, we focused on the twin elements of (a) helping him control his anger so he didn't have an angry outburst that turned violent and (b) verbalizing that anger to me in the forms of venting and processing. After he had gained skill in these tasks—in particular, the ability to process his anger—we shifted to a broader discussion of emotions as well as alternate methods of releasing angry energy that were under his control and did not hurt others.

We also engaged in some identity work. As a fully able teen and young adult, N'Shawn could readily be an angry, violent young man whom other folks would fear. However, as a blind man with the associated mobility issues, that identity was no longer effective.

Finding the Hurt Behind the Anger

I work with angry energy in my office in a manner similar to how I was taught to work with sad energy in my office: I try to help my clients get it out.

I have no problem sitting with a client who sobs for 10 or 20 or 30 minutes, and I may facilitate some of that sobbing before my clients are settled enough to process their feelings verbally. Similarly, I have learned to sit with clients who are angry and need to expel that angry energy before they can process it verbally. For many guys who are comfortable expressing their anger (even if they don't express it in a healthy way), talking and processing can occur only after a physical release of angry energy.

My willingness to listen to N'Shawn when he was angry, and to do so at length, was a novel experience for him. For the first time, he had an audience he could vent to. Because anger brings energy with it, N'Shawn could verbalize his anger for 20 or 30 minutes at a time. Part of my role was to listen and facilitate that energy release so that by the time we were done, the angry energy was spent. At times, it was like riding a roller coaster. N'Shawn had a good vocabulary and a good imagination; I knew he was winding down when he started making jokes. Other clients run out of energy and become quiet, with longer pauses between comments. If I'm not sure, I'll reflect that they seem to be slowing down or that their anger is burning out; I never ask "Are you done?" because that can make the anger itself sound like a problem, or it can sound dismissive.

During our third session, N'Shawn shared a recent experience that had made him angry. This was the first time he had shared something like this, and it occurred a few minutes into that day's session. Our conversation sounded something like this:

CLIENT: Can I tell you what happened yesterday?

THERAPIST: Sure. What happened yesterday?

CLIENT: I needed a cigarette, and I couldn't get one from anybody.

THERAPIST: What do you mean?

CLIENT: I was in my room watching TV, and I wanted to smoke. I knew I was out of cigarettes, so I went in the other room, and I asked my mom if she could get me a cigarette. (N'Shawn's mother is on oxygen and does not smoke, so his request was really for his mother to ask another member of the household for a cigarette on N'Shawn's behalf.) She said I would need to get one myself. So I asked her if her husband was around, and she told me "No, he's at work." Then I asked if my sister was around, and she said "No, she's at work." And then I was like, "Then why did you tell me to ask other people if you knew they weren't home?!" [*Starting to sound angry*] And she said that it's not her job to make sure I have cigarettes and I'm like, "But you knew they weren't home! Why tell me to ask people you know aren't here to be asked?!"

THERAPIST: Whoa. Yeah. Why would she say something like that?

CLIENT: Right? And then I'm like, "Well, I guess I'll just go back in my room then," and she's like, "Why don't you stay out here and hang out with me?", and I'm like, "You just told me to ask people who aren't here for a smoke. Why would I want to hang out with you?" and she's like, "Fine, just go back to your room then."

THERAPIST: [*Speaking over him a little*] I'm thinking that wasn't good . . .

CLIENT: No, it certainly was not good. [*Becoming more angry*] So then I started to get mad, like, real mad. I'm thinking "Why would you tell me to do something that you know I can't do? And then why would you think I wouldn't be mad at you and that I'd want to hang out with you? Besides, I didn't come out of my room to hang out with people, I only came out to get a smoke, anyway!"

THERAPIST: OK, you're thinking that she's an idiot. What did you say or do?

CLIENT: I went in my room and slammed the door after me because I know that makes her mad.

THERAPIST: Did it work? Did it make her mad?

CLIENT: I don't know. How should I know, and what makes you think I'd care? [*Louder*] I was in my room and she didn't come in, and that's all I know.

THERAPIST: OK, so what happened next?

CLIENT: Then I kept thinking about how I wanted a cigarette and how dumb it was that she told me to ask people who weren't there.

THERAPIST: Let me make sure I really understand this. Did she say anything like "They'll be home soon," or would she know their schedules and when they'll get home?

CLIENT: I don't know what she knows. She probably knows her husband's schedule, but I don't know if she knows my sister's schedule. What does it matter? I wanted a cigarette and couldn't get one!

THERAPIST: And that pissed you off.

CLIENT: Very much, yes.

THERAPIST: Because you couldn't get the help you wanted.

CLIENT: That's right.

THERAPIST: So what happened next? How long did you stay angry?

CLIENT: I don't know. A while. I tried to chill out, but I kept thinking about how she seems to be able to help everyone else get what they need, but she can't help me. And that just made me madder.

THERAPIST: Like, she doesn't take care of you the way you want to be taken care of?

CLIENT: Exactly. She's my mama, and when I went blind she was like "Come home and I'll take care of you," and so I did. But she's not doing a very good job. And I still don't have a cigarette! [*Angry again*]

THERAPIST: Wait, you still don't have a cigarette?

CLIENT: [*Chuckles*] No.

THERAPIST: Why are you laughing?

CLIENT: I got a cigarette last night from her husband when he came home from work and I smoked it. And now I'm out again and I won't get paid again until Thursday because that's the first day of the month.

THERAPIST: And today's only Monday, so you can't buy any cigarettes for 3 more days.

CLIENT: Yep.

THERAPIST: So I want to know, how much do you smoke?

CLIENT: Not much, just one or two a day.

THERAPIST: It seems like you got really mad at your mom when she told you to ask other people who weren't there.

CLIENT: I did. I sure did. I have a long fuse and a big explosion. When I get mad, everyone knows I'm mad. It's none of this little snarky comment stuff or being passive-aggressive bullshit. When I'm mad, people know I'm mad.

THERAPIST: And how long does your anger last?

CLIENT: It depends, but it usually passes pretty quick.

THERAPIST: How long is pretty quick? Ten minutes, 5 hours?

CLIENT: It depends on what's going on, but the longest is probably 2 or 3 hours, and that's when I'm really f— mad.

THERAPIST: Good to know.

While N'Shawn was venting, I made an effort to get to know the whole story and do so in a way that helped him vent all of the emotional energy. At times, I felt like I was probing for additional anger, such as when I asked "Why would she say something like that?" or said "You're thinking she's an idiot." My purpose was to have him release as much of his angry energy as possible, in addition to wanting to understand his anger as fully as possible.

After he had vented and had calmed some, we processed the incident. At first, I wanted to learn more about his anger. In that dialogue, which occurred during our third session, N'Shawn reported being upset when he couldn't borrow a cigarette from someone, and his anger was extensive. I explored how quickly he had become upset and how upset he had become (which seemed disproportionate to learning he couldn't get a cigarette). As time and therapy went by, I started asking N'Shawn to rate the intensity of his anger and, a few weeks later, the severity of the events that prompted his anger. We started with a simple scale—"a little," "a medium amount," "a lot"—and eventually shifted to a 1–10 scale when he found he needed to make finer distinctions. This strategy helped him recognize that his response was often disproportionately high.

Men who have a history of anger and violence may have difficulty recognizing, verbalizing, and coping with their tender feelings. This was certainly true for N'Shawn; instead of talking about how someone had disappointed him, or how frustrated he was by someone's behavior, he would go directly to anger and, on occasion, thoughts of revenge. I deliberately commented that he wasn't being taken care of (in the ways that he wanted to be), and he picked up that language. In this exchange, his adoption of my language ("getting help" and "being taken care of") is momentary, but that moment told me I was on the right track. I continued to identify not being taken care of as a source of his anger, and he began to adopt this framework and started using it on his own. Later, I added his disappointment at not being taken care of, and N'Shawn again acknowledged this was the case and then adopted my framework.

As I reflected different feelings back to N'Shawn, he slowly adopted my language and was able to recognize these feelings on his own. He also started to gain experience coping with these feelings directly, but almost all his experience in coping with tender emotions were from childhood or within therapy, which meant he had no adult experiences of receiving comfort from a friend or family member.

Helping Men Release Their Anger

N'Shawn ultimately became better at expressing anger in ways that were less harmful to other people (and his relationships with them) and, more important, he got better at recognizing the things that made him angry and developed some strategies for dealing with these situations. He gained the ability to contain his anger and restrain himself from making angry outbursts. With me, he could vent his anger and frustrations verbally (and often at length). Together, we would figure out ways to minimize his exposure to these triggers. N'Shawn acknowledged that he had never had someone with whom he could be this emotionally open or who would tolerate listening to him for so long. To facilitate work on his anger, and with the awareness that he didn't have any other outlets for his anger, after the first 6 weeks of therapy we started meeting twice per week.

I often encourage my clients who get angry on a regular basis to find someplace where they can yell in order to release some of their angry energy. For men who say yelling is sufficient, we talk about where they can do that: in their house, the backyard, a park or the woods, or even their car. We also talk about how and when they can get privacy while yelling, including having discussions about who they are worried might overhear them.

Some of my clients have difficulty imagining just yelling on their own. For them, a playlist of angry music to scream along to can be helpful. Again, we talk about how, when, and where they can use this playlist. For clients who can get privacy only in their car and might need to drive (instead of sitting in a parked car), I typically encourage them to drive on a highway between cities (not through a city) because it provides an opportunity to drive (and scream) without stopping for lights and stop signs. I don't want a client to have to stop yelling because there is another driver watching him when stopped at a red light. We also talk about a "calm down" or "peace out" or "restorative" playlist to switch to after the angry energy is spent. I often encourage my clients to create playlists with music they own so they don't have to be bothered by a streaming service giving them music that doesn't fit their angry or calming mood.

For my clients who need to get their angry energy out physically, I have a heavy bag in my office; a lot of guys tell me hitting a pillow doesn't work because the pillow doesn't offer the kind of resistance or solidity they want when hitting something. I've also had guys tell me that punching a pillow or a chair doesn't feel right because those things aren't solid enough and they're worried they might damage them. I've never had anyone tell me they're worried about breaking a heavy bag.

With respect to releasing anger, it is generally acknowledged that having only a physical release is ineffective. When this is the only strategy a client has, I agree that a physical release isn't therapeutically helpful because it's just a physical outlet that may—or may not—change their feelings in the moment. However, for clients actively working in therapy who have repeatedly demonstrated an ability to control and process the hurt feelings behind the anger, I find physical releases can help create long-lasting reductions in anger.

The rules for a client using a heavy bag to vent anger—whether in my office or at his home—are simple. Use of the bag is limited to anger; it's not there for a workout. Boxing gloves are required (and I provide them). I tell clients to punch straight ahead and keep the fist, wrist, and elbow in a straight line. This is called a *jab* in boxing. I tell them not to punch by coming around from the outside (called a *roundhouse*) because this risks damage to the wrist if not done properly. When they're done punching, we wait for 2 to 3 minutes. Many guys will go for a second and even a third round of hitting. I gauge this the same way I gauge whether or not a client is done sobbing. Then we talk about why they were mad and what they might do differently next time, similar to what I might do with a client who has been crying.

For my clients who don't want to hit something, or don't want to hit something in front of me, I suggest they create a "break box" at home, and sometimes I provide one in my office, or outside, say, in a parking lot. There can be something very satisfying about causing destruction. The break box consists of a large, wide-bottomed heavy-duty rubber tub with sides that are at least 1 foot tall; these are sold in 30 or 50 gallon sizes. Place one or two bricks (or a cinder block) in the bottom of the tub; this provides something solid to aim for that will cause dishes to break. Those bricks also add a little extra weight that helps prevent the tub from moving around. Safety goggles are recommended. Find an old set of plates/china and throw the plates and cups into the tub one at a time, aiming for the bricks at the bottom. Many of my male clients tell me they also yell while breaking things at home. At the end, you—or your client—will also need to sweep up any pieces that have bounced out of the bin. Then, process the feelings behind the anger. For clients who do this at home, I instruct them to wait 10 or 15 minutes after they stop before interacting with anyone else, so their feelings have time to settle.

Building Trust

When N'Shawn was a teen and an adult, anger was often the result of being let down by someone who said they were going to do something to help him/take care of him, being disrespected ("dissed"), or having someone explicitly violate his trust. These led to discussions about how he expected other people to treat him, facilitated the shift to addressing emotional vulnerability, and initiated explicit discussion of trust.

Many of my male clients don't really understand trust. I blame this in part on stereotypical portrayals of males in the media. In comedies, action films, and sports, there isn't much discussion about trust. But if you consume female-oriented media, you are much more likely to find discussions about when and how much to trust someone, especially after they have previously caused harm. Any show that's got drama or focuses heavily on interpersonal relationships is likely to include these kinds of conversations.

I start talking about trust in terms of favors and practical support, with a focus on identifying the people a guy can rely on to lend him $10 or $20 without question, pick him up if his car breaks down, or get him to an appointment on time. Then I talk about emotional trust, the kind he would want before talking about his feelings or revealing any deep secrets. Once it is clear to me that a client understands these distinctions, we will talk about which forms of trust are necessary with different types of friends: buddies, friends, good friends, and best friends (see also Chapter 4). If he has been, or is, in a dating relationship or had experience hooking up, we will also discuss the types of trust involved in these relationships (Garfield, 2015; Mutchler & McDavitt, 2011; Smiler & Heasley, 2016; Way, 2011, 2013). After N'Shawn and I had discussed trust in this way, I began talking about the different types of trust when I reflected his feelings and the sources of his hurt feelings back to him. A few weeks later, he had adopted this language and provided it spontaneously.

Because most of my male clients haven't really thought about these different forms of trust, they also haven't thought about how two people might develop a trusting relationship, so when I ask a male client about building trust I'm often told "It takes time." Time can be sufficient when you see people day in and day out and have the opportunity to observe them in a range of situations, as happens with classmates and coworkers, but it's not sufficient for adults who don't experience those settings. I provided some psychoeducation to N'Shawn and explained that building trust is something that happens through experience, not time. First, I asked him if there were people he had known for a long time—people from school, the neighborhood, his house of worship, coworkers, and so on—that he didn't trust even though they had never wronged him. He promptly acknowledged that there were many such people whom he knew by name and on sight but with whom he had never had a meaningful conversation with and thus didn't trust.

Then I asked if he had ever given these people the chance to earn his trust. After a moment's reflection, he acknowledged he hadn't. And then we began to discuss the process of having someone earn his trust, emphasizing the ways in which this (a) was a process, (b) required direct experience, and (c) did not have a guaranteed outcome (because trust could be earned or not). As part of learning to trust new people, I suggested that N'Shawn find some small things he might do to gauge people's trustworthiness. That might be asking someone to loan him $10 even though he didn't actually need to borrow the money, just to see if they would do it. In the form of a second request a few weeks later, he might also explore their reaction if he needed a few extra days to repay that $10.

We also identified a small thing in his life that required emotional trust. N'Shawn had never particularly hidden his sexual orientation, but he also wasn't a stereotypical or flamboyant gay man, so people didn't automatically assume he was gay. He agreed that telling people he was gay didn't seem like a big deal to him and that telling others about his sexual orientation could serve as a way to gauge their trustworthiness with emotional content. N'Shawn assured me that it would not be a problem if he was wrong and someone shared the news of his sexual orientation. (I'd learned that Black communities, at least here in the southern United States, where I practice, are not as accepting of gay Black men as my own White community is.) In this conversation we also discussed ways he might include references to being gay that varied in their directness, such as referencing an experience in a gay club, mentioning a boyfriend, or saying "As a gay man, I. . . ." Other people's reactions to these statements helped him learn whom he could trust with personal information and in what ways he could trust them.

Reducing Triggers

The idea that people's emotions are triggered by specific people, places, or actions is one with which most therapists, and many Americans, are familiar.

We began referring to the things that made N'Shawn angry as "triggers" in order to help him more specifically identify them. Then I highlighted the feelings that lay behind the anger, much as I did in the second dialogue example. These discussions initially occurred when we were processing events after he had become angry and calmed down.

One of N'Shawn's key strategies for controlling his anger was becoming more selective about whom, when, and under what circumstances he asked for both practical support and emotional support. Said differently, he was trying to reduce his triggers. Instead of indiscriminately relying on any family member who happened to be around for any type of support he needed, he learned who was willing to provide the practical help a blind man needed (including simple things, e.g., not leaving shoes in the hallway, where he could trip over them) and whom he could talk to about things that were bothering him. During these discussions we also addressed his expectations of others and thus were able to make his angry episodes less frequent and less intense.

One goal was to reduce the frequency with which N'Shawn was triggered. Once a situation or person has been identified as a trigger, the client and therapist attempt to develop strategies to minimize the amount of time the client spends in that situation or with that person. Another solution is to reduce the client's sensitivity to that trigger. Preventative strategies are also a common approach because they may eliminate the client's need to interact with the triggering person or situation entirely (e.g., by not running out of cigarettes). N'Shawn and I used all of these approaches, but with somewhat limited success because of his impoverished financial status and his dependence on others.

Helping Angry Men Redefine Themselves

N'Shawn had an ongoing struggle to redefine himself. A survivor of repeated sexual abuse, he found a new identity as a teen (through violence), as well as status and fear/respect, by being easily angered and a tough guy. As James Marcia explained in 1966, identity formation requires the exploration of options and an active commitment to (one of) those options. N'Shawn was just starting to explore other identity options when he had his stroke; specifically, he had been working on a nursing degree so he could help other kids like him. That degree program would have provided classroom and internship experiences that allowed him to explore what it was like to be a nurse. During the 2 years of his program, he would have had the opportunity to shift between his old angry identity and his new nurse identity. It is possible that by the end of the program his new identity as a nurse would have become his dominant identity and his angry identity would have been a minority element.

N'Shawn's stroke—which left him with some mobility issues and caused his blindness—took his tough guy identity away. It also ended his schooling and took away the possibility of obtaining an identity as a nurse. Although people were afraid of his temper, no one was particularly afraid of a blind man who had a bad leg. When he had his stroke, N'Shawn was entering adulthood and starting to explore ways of being that didn't involve toughness, and those options were new to him. The result was that I was working with a tough guy who could no longer be tough but had no experience being anything else. He had lost his identity and didn't have any alternatives he could easily explore, and thus he struggled to figure out what identity he might build or adopt now.

N'Shawn's unwillingness to risk any type of embarrassment or appearance of weakness, which were contrary to his tough image, contributed to his resistance and hampered our work on this issue. N'Shawn's reliance on other people for transportation, as well as the limitations of accessing the internet only through a mobile phone (while blind!), further limited his ability to explore other identities and modes of being.

N'Shawn responded to his stroke in the way that was most comfortable and familiar to him: He closed up and protected himself. But that strategy doesn't lend itself to exploring other identities or roles. N'Shawn's need to rely on others who weren't entirely reliable didn't help, either; each time they let him down he would slip into his old role and become angry. N'Shawn ultimately concluded that the family members with whom he lived ranged in their levels of trustworthiness with respect to practical support and his physical health, but he didn't feel they were particularly trustworthy regarding emotional support. He had lost the friends he had made prior to his stroke, and he stayed at home, except for medical appointments, and thus he had few opportunities to meet new people and make new friends.

CONCLUSION

Men get angry; anger is one of the few emotions they are allowed to express freely. Some men get angry easily and seem to always be angry. N'Shawn was such a man. His ever-present anger stemmed from multiple rapes he had experienced as a child and the lack of appropriate care after being raped. And N'Shawn's anger worked for him. After he expressed his anger by seeking revenge on his third rapist, N'Shawn gained a modicum of safety, and the respect of other kids in his neighborhood, and this helped him be The Man. He had never experienced any of those things before, and he continued to endorse the masculine criterion of violence and his image as an angry man. Unfortunately, he had never really developed other strategies that would help him feel like that, and now that he had had a stroke and become blind, he was again having experiences of not being cared for in the ways he felt he needed.

N'Shawn is hardly unique: Many men feel more comfortable showing anger instead of tender emotions, such as sadness or anxiety. That anger can not only hide those feelings but also shift the way he feels into something else. If the anger fuels violence, as it did for N'Shawn, he may also be able to gain a sense of safety and self-respect, as well as respect/fear from others and an enhanced status.

After establishing a connection by making sure that I heard what he wanted, and communicating that he and I were partners in the therapy, we worked on his anger. This occurred in two stages. In the first stage, we worked on his ability to control his anger and to process it. From there, we explored the people and situations that trigger him and identified strategies to reduce the impact of those triggers. I also reviewed some strategies that have been effective with other clients, but we determined that these weren't appropriate for N'Shawn given his physical limitations and the family's financial status. N'Shawn and I also engaged in some identity work, but his willingness and opportunity to explore other identities were limited by poverty, reduced physical abilities, and an unwillingness to take risks.

8 THE PLAYER

JOHN'S CASE

John was a 26-year-old heterosexual, White, cisgender, unmarried, man. He was handsome and had a well-muscled body, good social skills, and plenty of self-confidence. John enjoyed hanging out with his buddies, was competitive in martial arts at the local level, and had a small collection of firearms. He also painted and often used death imagery, such as skulls (with and without roses), in his works.

John came to therapy at his father's encouragement. He was unhappy and felt like his life wasn't going anywhere. He wanted more, but he wasn't sure what he wanted more of. John wasn't failing to launch: He had been promoted twice by the security firm he worked for and now helped manage security for special events. John had also been engaged to a college girlfriend but ended their 5-year relationship when he discovered she had been cheating on him with one of her coworkers for the past 2 years. That was a year before he entered therapy, and he acknowledged that he hadn't felt quite the same since he had discovered the cheating.

https://doi.org/10.1037/0000499-008
Clinical Work With Men: Understanding Masculinity in Psychotherapy, by A. P. Smiler

From my perspective, therapy started smoothly. We were building a good therapeutic alliance, and John seemed to be experiencing some relief from his symptoms. During our fourth session, John shared something that would (re)shape our work together:

CLIENT: Doc, I need to tell you something.

THERAPIST: OK.

CLIENT: I've been hooking up a lot lately.

THERAPIST: Yeah . . .

CLIENT: Like, a lot.

THERAPIST: OK. And that's a problem?

CLIENT: Well, yeah. Wait—you don't think it's a problem?

THERAPIST: As long as you're not hurting anyone or taking advantage of anyone, go for it. Have fun. Just use condoms so you don't get a disease or have a kid before you want one.

CLIENT: [*Surprised*] That's not what I was expecting you to say.

THERAPIST: In today's jargon, I'm "sex positive." As long as you're being safe, and you're being honest with your partners, I don't have any concerns about you hooking up. [*Short pause.*] But it seems like you have some concerns about hooking up? Or hooking up a lot?

CLIENT: Yeah.

THERAPIST: What's bothering you about hooking up?

CLIENT: It's just [*sighs*]. . . . It's not what I want to be doing right now. I'm 26, I have a career, and hooking up feels like, I don't know, like a college kind of thing. I shouldn't be doing that anymore.

THERAPIST: Because you're a "grown-up"?

CLIENT: [*Chuckles*] Yeah. No. Something like that. Look, hooking up is. . . . Well, it's immature. It's fine when you're just a kid in college, but I graduated 5 years ago, and I should be better than that. Hooking up is fun, but it's also pointless. I should be working on finding a girlfriend and getting married, not having sex with random girls.

THERAPIST: I'm going to play devil's advocate here. Do you enjoy the hookups you're having?

CLIENT: Yeah, they're fine. It's always fun with a new person.

THERAPIST: So the sex is fine; the problem is that hooking up feels immature, like you should be past this?

CLIENT: Yes. Exactly.

THERAPIST: How much, or maybe how often, are you hooking up?

CLIENT: Every 2 or 3 weeks.

THERAPIST: And how often do you jerk off? You don't have to answer, but it'll help me understand what's going on.

CLIENT: Every day or every other day. Why did you ask?

THERAPIST: Because if the only time you had an orgasm was when you hooked up, then I'd ask why you don't masturbate. But since you masturbate every day or every other day, then you're not hooking up because it's the only way to come.

CLIENT: No. Definitely not [*laughs*].

THERAPIST: OK. So why do you think you keeping hooking up?

CLIENT: I really don't know. I'll go out to a bar to hang out, maybe chill out after a difficult few days at work. I'll be there, and then all of a sudden, I'll see a girl or a group of girls who look like they're my age, and I'll start talking to them. And if there's someone I find attractive and she seems open to hooking up, I'll try to get with her.

THERAPIST: Are you going to these bars to hang out solo or with friends?

CLIENT: Sometimes it's just me alone, but sometimes I meet some of my guy friends.

THERAPIST: So you're not really looking to hook up when you leave the house, but you also know it's a possibility. I notice you're going to a bar and not a regular sit-down restaurant or a coffee shop or some other place where hooking up would be more difficult.

CLIENT: True.

THERAPIST: So your choice of destination says you're open to hooking up and makes it a possibility for the evening.

CLIENT: True.

THERAPIST: This might be a weird question, but what's fun about hooking up?

CLIENT: Uh, the sex?

THERAPIST: But you can masturbate at home, so why go find a random partner?

CLIENT: Oh. Huh. I know I can jerk off, and I will if I don't find someone. But it's kind of a challenge to find a girl and see if I can get her to have sex with me.

THERAPIST: So you like the challenge of finding a new partner?

CLIENT: Yes.

THERAPIST: Anything else?

CLIENT: You never quite know what's going to happen. I mean, I know I want to have sex with her, but you don't know if it'll be sex, penetration, or just oral or what. Or if it'll just be one time or more than once.

THERAPIST: So you like the surprise?

CLIENT: Yeah. I pretty much know what's going to happen if I'm playing with myself.

THERAPIST: Fair enough. OK. So you like the challenge and the surprise of not knowing what'll happen. Is there anything else that makes hooking up better than staying home and entertaining yourself?

CLIENT: I don't think so . . .

THERAPIST: Is there a chance that a hookup could turn into a relationship?

CLIENT: No.

THERAPIST: Why not?

CLIENT: Because. . . . Look. This is gonna sound bad.

THERAPIST: That's all right. I don't judge. And I want to understand what you're thinking so I can help you.

CLIENT: All right. It's kind of hypocritical. A girl I hook up with won't become a dating relationship because she's a slut. I know that I'm being just as slutty as she is, but that's the way it is. Honestly, the one time I tried to make a hookup into a relationship, I kept wondering if she thought I was a slut, so I ended it.

THERAPIST: Thank you for being honest. Uh, that one time. How long did it last?

CLIENT: About a week, but it was during college, so we got together like three times that week. I couldn't decide if she was actually into me or just wanted me for sex, so I ghosted her.

THERAPIST: Anything like that happen since then?

CLIENT: No. I pretty much won't talk to the girl after we hook up.

THERAPIST: Understood. OK. So hooking up is fun because it's a challenge; there's some suspense related to the unknown. I guess there's a novelty or new-ness factor because you don't know who she'll be or what she'll be like. But on the downside, you're 26, well out of college, and have started your career, and hooking up every 2 or 3 weeks feels immature. Maybe even wrong.

CLIENT: Yeah. You've got it.

THERAPIST: And you feel like you should be finding someone to marry?

CLIENT: Exactly. So what do I do?

I learned several things from this conversation. One was that John wanted to stop hooking up with random people because he thought it was immature and something that someone his age, or at this point in his career, shouldn't do. He didn't say hooking up was wrong, or bad, or immoral, just that it was something he shouldn't be doing any more. I also learned that John had some awareness of and insight into his own behavior, including ways in which he could hold double standards that were hypocritical.

Perhaps the most interesting thing I learned from this conversation was that John really enjoyed about hooking up was the pursuit and not knowing if he would be able to hook up with a particular woman or not. As we explored his motive—pursuit and a lack of certainty about whether or not he and a certain woman would hook up—John's desire for accomplishment became apparent. His desire for accomplishment also helped me understand his comment about hooking up as pointless; hooking up was a short-term activity that didn't lead to anything, which made it different from dating, with its implicit goal of marriage.

When I asked about his relationship with his ex-fiancée, John told me that at the time they got engaged, they'd been together for 4 years, were living together, loved each other, and had both started their careers. To John, proposing marriage seemed like the obvious next step, even though he was in no rush to get married and they hadn't put any effort into planning a wedding. As he reviewed their relationship with me, he was able to see ways in which the relationship had lost its excitement and that he had become bored. Like many couples in which one or both people are trying to work their way up the company ladder, they devoted more time, energy, and attention to their careers than to their relationship. The fact that she worked a standard Monday-through-Friday, 9-to-5 job, and his hours varied between days (for planning) and evenings/weekends (when the events occurred) added an extra degree of difficulty in finding time to be together when they could both be fully present.

I want to highlight one process element that helped me connect with John, helped deepen our connection, and allowed him to open up further. When John first spoke about hooking up a lot, I wasn't judgmental and accepted his behavior. I shared that I was sex positive, because I am, and because I wanted him to be comfortable defining the aspects of hooking up he saw as problematic. As you know, John told me that he thought hooking up was immature and that he should stop doing it. But he could have told me he was having erectile difficulties or other sexual performance issues, exploring some form of kink, had been exploring his sexual orientation, or some other issue, and I would have responded the same way: with acceptance and enough curiosity to allow him to define his problem.

Themes in John's Therapy

I conceptualized John's therapy as focusing on his desire for a long-term relationship in which he could be emotionally intimate and monogamous. Doing so required attention to two issues: (a) masculine conceptualizations of sexuality and promiscuity and (b) his insecure attachment style.

I like attachment theory's focus on early relationships as a model for later relationships, so I told John about secure, avoidant, and resistant attachment types (Bowlby, 1969; Levine & Heller, 2010; see also Chapter 4, this volume). *Resistant attachment*, a type of insecure attachment that is also known as *ambivalent* or *anxious–preoccupied attachment*, consists of an intense but unstable bond in which the child values the connection with their secure base (e.g., caretaker) but is uncertain if their secure base also values the connection and will take care of them, especially when the child needs them. The child resists separation because of a fear that their secure base may not be available the next time they are needed. John found himself reflected in the description of resistant attachment, and this understanding informed our exploration of John's adult relationships and his hookups.

We also explored his understanding of relationships based on the experiences he had growing up. Like many children, John's parents divorced when he was young (age 3). John lived with his mother after the divorce; his father was recruited into a better job and moved away. The minimal contact between John and his father—this was early in the cell phone era and before streaming video was common—minimized John's ability to rely on his father as a secure base. John's father remarried about 2 years later.

After the divorce, John's mother told him it would be just the two of them, which is not unusual. And as the only child from that marriage, John got a lot of his mother's time, energy, and attention—until she began a serious dating relationship when John was 7. She remarried when John was 9 and quickly had two more children. He continued to feel loved, but he didn't feel like he was as important to her as he previously had been, and thus his mother shifted from being a secure base to being unreliable (from John's perspective). The separations from both parents created John's resistant attachment style, and that resistant attachment was reflected in his current-day relationships with his mother and his father; he described both relationships as supportive but somewhat distant. These formative (and ongoing) experiences created his difficulty trusting that a romantic partner would consistently be there for him.

Using attachment theory (Bowlby, 1969; Levine & Heller, 2010), I helped John learn how to better explain his current focus on hookups. He talked about hookups as a way to control (or eliminate) the fear of separation (or loss of a relationship) because there was no expectation of any contact after the hookup. Then we deviated from the standard attachment script, and he spoke about the intensity of the experience of pursuing a woman over the course of an evening and the sense of accomplishment he felt when she would agree to have sex with him. From an attachment perspective, this could be seen as the usual intensity of a (re)union that is part of resistant attachment. I could have conceptualized his behavior as a re-creation of previous trauma with an attempt to master it. However, John's desire for accomplishment pointed to a rationale based in masculinity: the need for achievement.

For a heterosexual male following the standard sexual script, John viewed hooking up with a woman he had just met as an accomplishment. The heterosexual script directs him to take the initiative in flirting; to introduce the first (and most of the subsequent) elements of sexual contact; and to do these things while making the object of his attention feel comfortable, flattered, and attractive, all while not acknowledging the seduction as it occurs. During the course of an evening, he will probably be (quickly) rejected by several women when he initiates conversation or starts flirting, and he may face other rejections that take a little more time before one or both of them decides they are not the right people for tonight. Throughout, he is expected to take the lead and repeatedly make the next move while finding the right thing to say or do. This is a difficult task that requires good interpersonal skills and confidence in those skills. When it's going well, it's exciting, but a guy has to control the excitement or he might ruin the seduction.

John as a Player

John's masculinity centered on promiscuity as well as on a substantial desire for achievement. During college—before he had entered his 5-year relationship—his friends recognized his ability to hook up as a form of masculine achievement, and thus he was Man Enough. There were some stretches of college when he hooked up regularly and earned more props from his friends, who called him "The Man."

John's desire for achievement furthered my understanding of why he chose to hook up: This was another area where he could compete and a venue that was almost always open, so to speak. John could try to hook up almost any time he wanted. Employment, on the other hand, doesn't work that way. He had had to compete for a job and compete for promotions, but those competitions didn't come along very often, especially as he moved up the company's hierarchy. John's workplace competition was also limited by his desire to stay within a 1-hour drive of his mother and half-siblings, which meant there were limited options if he wanted to change companies. And although John competed in his martial art—and often did quite well in local and regional tournaments—he saw the costs of increasing his practice time to compete in formal competitions every few months as not worth the benefits. But promiscuity? That "accomplishment" was available almost any time. Promiscuity also offered an obvious benefit: partnered orgasm.

I surprised John when I told him I thought his efforts to hook up were about achievement and not about partnered orgasm. He acknowledged that he hadn't considered the possibility, but as he looked back on his history, John recognized the accuracy of my statement.

MASCULINITY AND THE PLAYER TYPE

There are long-standing stereotypes of promiscuous men within American culture. Today, the most common term is "player"; "playboy," "ladies' man," and "Casanova" were more commonly used in prior generations. I'll use the current term, "player," which may be seen as having a neutral or negative connotation; the older terms all have negative connotations. Whichever term you prefer, the image is centered around a man who has sex with many partners; ongoing romantic relationships with those partners are optional. During earlier periods in American history the player may have seduced his (female) partner over a period of weeks or months, and he was understood as likely having multiple concurrent partners (without their consent to being one of many). For most of American history, being a player was not a socially acceptable way to demonstrate masculinity. I detailed these shifts in my first book, *Challenging Casanova: Beyond the Stereotype of the Promiscuous Young Male* (Smiler, 2013).

Prior to and through the 1960s, promiscuous men were seen as untrustworthy and viewed suspiciously; they certainly didn't fit the good-guy standard of the day. But things changed. In the 1970s, and for the first time ever, (broadcast) television gave us sexually promiscuous male protagonists on Top 20 TV shows who were popular with the general public: Fonzie on *Happy Days* and Hawkeye Pierce on *M*A*S*H* are two examples. They were the first promiscuous men who were primary characters we were supposed to like; the ratings their shows achieved, and the cultural phenomena they created, tells me we liked them quite a bit (Smiler, 2013).

In the multi-faceted masculinity framework, the most relevant masculine criterion is promiscuity. According to my research (Smiler, 2013), there is no widely agreed-on definition of promiscuity, but three or more sexual partners per year for 3 consecutive years seems like a reasonable cutoff to me; other researchers (e.g., Humblet et al., 2003) have drawn the line at five or more partners. In the research I reviewed for *Challenging Casanova* (Smiler, 2013), the available data suggested that no more than 5% of men fit this criterion. Most of those studies were conducted before hookup apps became commonplace, so it is possible the percentage has increased, but I'd be surprised if more than 10% of men have three or more sexual partners per year for 3 (or more) consecutive years.

Being promiscuous is a way for boys and men to demonstrate masculine achievement. Guys who can legitimately claim to have had many partners are considered Real Men and, if his body count is high enough (as defined by his community), he may be seen as The Man. John achieved this status during the first 2 years of college. Some groups of young men will go to a club together with a goal of everyone hooking up, which makes their demonstrations of promiscuity (partly) public; the initial event and retelling those stories serves as a form of male bonding among these groups and can help the guys maintain their masculine status (Flood, 2008). Promiscuity may provide masculine achievement only among a man's peers; one national survey found that only 1% of American adults rated "having success with women" as the most important aspect of masculinity (Sand et al., 2008).

As I stated, there are readily recognizable stereotypes built around male promiscuity, including players. One study, conducted before cell phones were common, found that the stereotype focused on a well-dressed or stylish young man who was physically attractive, appeared to have ample spending money, and had good social skills (Green & Ashmore, 1998).

Benefits of Being a Player

At a minimum, being a player requires good social skills, whether digital or in person, and this takes some effort. The ability to start a conversation with someone you have never met before, create some amount of connection, have that person agree to have sex with you, and then maintain that as the two of you come together in person is not a trivial one. Hookup apps may have made that easier by ensuring that all of the potential people are willing to have sex with a random person and screening people on the basis of a particular set of characteristics, but there is no guarantee a potential partner will swipe right or respond to a guy's message. His ability to successfully navigate this type of interaction is likely to contribute to his self-esteem and self-confidence and may be a point of pride.

When I realize that a client who fits the player profile is confident in his social skills in hookup settings but not in other settings, such as work or family interactions, I typically explore why there is a difference. These comparisons can lead to identification of important *third variables* (or modifying factors), such as equality/inequality with conversational partners or the importance of a clear goal (hooking up) that readily allows him to determine if he is on the path to success. Some clients tell me they understand the rules of hooking up but not the rules in other social settings.

Players are also risk-takers, at least in this one realm. The process of hooking up requires a guy to take risks: He doesn't get to have sex with someone he's just met unless he's willing to risk being repeatedly turned down (at a bar or party or on an app) until he finds a willing partner. In the therapeutic setting, he may be more willing to eventually take a risk and try something new.

Being a player requires several skills that may be useful in the therapeutic setting. These include the ability to interpret and work with other people's emotions. During his first interactions with a potential new partner, a man needs to recognize and react to that person's verbal and nonverbal signals, including signs of interest and disinterest. Whether in person or in a digital format, continuing to try to communicate with someone who isn't interested in him is a waste of his time and effort. In therapy, clients can use their ability to interpret and work with other people's emotions to better understand their own feelings.

Challenges of Being a Player

The most obvious challenge associated with being a player may be the external risks. Promiscuous men are at greater risk of catching a sexually transmitted infection or having an unplanned pregnancy. They also are more likely to cheat on a monogamous partner (Dariotis et al., 2008; Humblet et al., 2003; Lansford et al., 2010). If he has been caught cheating, he may have received an ultimatum to attend therapy or have the relationship end, and so he may have little commitment to therapy.

Several players with whom I have worked have not been particularly attentive to their own feelings. They can readily assess whether they are in a good or bad mood, and even name those moods: happy, sad, mad, excited, anxious, and other common labels. However, they're not particularly good at understanding what prompted their mood, especially when that's a mild to moderate mood, such as "a little depressed." Without that insight, they can distract themselves from those (minor) bad moods, but they can't resolve or soothe their own hurt feelings. Hooking up provides a reliable distraction that requires several hours and all of their attention, and it often leads to good feelings through physical sensations (i.e., orgasm) and a sense of accomplishment.

Players often report difficulties sustaining long-term, emotionally intimate relationships; this was certainly the case for John. They may arrive for therapy because they are tired of bouncing from one relationship to the next, or they may start therapy after cheating on a partner. When men identify cheating as (part of) the problem and seek therapy of their own volition, it indicates they are likely to actively engage with therapy. In this case, they are more likely to engage with questions about why they cheat, the quality of their current relationship, and what they're missing.

Many players fear being hurt or abandoned by a long-term partner to whom they have chosen to open up and with whom they have become emotionally vulnerable. They may lack knowledge about how to start a relationship or how to maintain it. Sustaining emotional openness, intimacy, and vulnerability are all teachable skills, as is the ability to set boundaries and the ability to recover a connection after feelings get hurt. This is John's story, and it's particularly common among people with resistant attachment styles.

Some heterosexual men believe they do not have credible claims of masculine achievement in other realms, that their achievements are minimal and unstable, or that potential partners don't recognize their masculine achievements. They then shift their focus from masculine achievement in other realms (e.g., financial success, athletics) to masculine achievement through promiscuity with women. When women decline their attempts to be promiscuous, these men may channel all of their frustrations onto the women who have rejected them and to women in general.

Many heterosexual players have sexist beliefs. John acknowledged his when he spoke about double standards that positioned his hookup partners as sluts he wouldn't want to date (while also recognizing he was engaging in the same behavior). They may see hooking up with women as a conquest in which women have something to "give up." In this realm, some guys are particularly proud of their *game*, defined as their ability to talk someone into having sex with them. Although many players hold sexist beliefs, this is not a requirement for being a player. My impression is that men who came of age in the 2000s are less likely to be sexist than prior generations and more likely to recognize their own sexist beliefs. For example, John was generally respectful of his hookup partners. He didn't lie about who he was or let them believe that he was interested in a relationship when he was interested only in hooking up. John recognized that his own behavior was just as slutty as the women he was having sex with, and he rarely used denigrating terms with me when describing his female hookup partners. However, at the same time he also spoke about men as being more decisive and thus more capable in general and saw women as needing protection. This combination of beliefs is sometimes labeled *benevolent sexism*.

Intersectional Issues

There are several ways intersectionality influences perceptions of men's promiscuity and adoption of the player type, and age (or generation) is particularly important. There have been substantial shifts in America's perceptions of male promiscuity over the past few decades. Researchers have identified a greater acceptance of adolescent sexual activity and premarital or casual sex, especially among boys, since the 1980s (Garcia et al., 2012). As I noted earlier, promiscuous men didn't become Good Guys on TV until the 1970s. The 1980s gave rise to the teen sex comedy movie genre, in which a group a teen boys try to have sex; *American Pie* (Weitz, 1999) is probably the most familiar recent title here (Smiler, 2013).

The cultural changes in American sexuality didn't stop there. Kathleen Bogle's 2008 book *Hooking Up: Sex, Dating, and Relationships on Campus*, and the attention it was given by the news media, marked and furthered a shift to a period when young people increasingly saw sexual activity as something that did not require any type of romantic relationship, or even the suggestion of such a relationship. At that time, hookups, defined as sexual activity outside of a romantic relationship, and where any type of affectionate feelings were unexpected and unnecessary, had become an acceptable part of the culture (see also Epstein et al., 2009, and Garcia et al., 2012). The digital era has helped expand and reinforce the commonality of hookups among all ages. Thus, your client's age will tell you about the national cultural attitudes with which they grew up.

Among gay men, promiscuity is an accepted and even welcomed part of the culture. During the AIDS crisis of the 1980s–1990s, gay men's promiscuity became the focus of national attention, with conservative religious figures positioning the disease as a form of God's wrath and the Reagan administration choosing to mostly ignore the problem. In some cities, the owners of gay nightclubs and bathhouses refused to shut down their operations despite the efforts of public health officials (Shilts, 1987/2007). Public sentiment was very antigay at the time, but over the past few decades it has shifted. Because promiscuity is accepted in this community, gay male clients who find open relationships (aka *nonmonogamy*) appealing may experience greater acceptance and less resistance to this idea than their heterosexual peers. Furthermore, there is more awareness of open relationships and consensual nonmonogamy in the gay male community than other segments of society. (I discuss consensual nonmonogamy further later in this chapter.)

The vibe around male promiscuity is different in the Black community. During the slavery and Jim Crow eras, Black men were often accused of raping White women, and the White public perceived Black men's sexuality as being wild and uncontrollable (D. Roberts, 2021). This White perception of Black men's sexuality continues even today, but within the Black community the focus has more often been on efforts to reduce the relatively high rate of teen pregnancies and single-parent families. Some conservative White political observers have highlighted these pregnancies as part of their efforts to require the parents to marry in order to qualify for public assistance.

WORKING WITH JOHN AND OTHER PLAYERS

I have worked with John for approximately 3 years and continue to see him as I write this chapter. At first, we met every other week, but after approximately 1 year we switched to monthly meetings. He occasionally asks for an additional session, and at times when he's more stressed—or when his relationship is causing him stress—we return meeting every other week. During one of these times, we have addressed two issues in detail. One issue revolves around emotion and focuses on helping John better understand and be more open with his feelings; this necessarily includes discussions of his resistant attachment style. The other issue relates to the purpose behind his decision to be promiscuous and his desire for achievement.

Treatment Plan

John said he didn't want to keep having random hookups, so that was the initial focus of our therapeutic work. As illustrated in the opening dialogue, John was explicit in stating that he thought hooking up was immature. When I asked about his history, he was clear that only once had he ever knowingly hooked up with someone who was in a relationship; it's the only hookup he regretted. These answers convinced me that he was sincere about working toward this goal. If he had been driven to therapy by an ultimatum, or said something about being monogamous but not really believing in monogamy, then our initial work would have focused on helping him clarify what he really wanted and how to achieve that goal.

Over the next 3 years, John and I met biweekly or monthly, depending on how much support he felt he needed. He was content with this pace because it provided time for things to happen in his relationships that he could reflect on and we could discuss. I'll note that John seemed to enjoy therapy. He always arrived with an event or issue to discuss, never missed a session, and was diligent about rescheduling ahead of time if some type of scheduling conflict arose. We routinely talked about his romantic and sexual relationships but also had a detour of several months when he was debating pursuing an MBA. (He applied, was accepted, and attended.)

John had several relationships during those years, which gave us fresh material to process. We addressed John's desire for emotional connection, the factors that motivated him to hook up with new partners, and his long-term romantic and sexual goals. While doing so, I also came to recognize that John had a resistant attachment style, and that helped frame our work.

During these 3 years, John didn't stay single for more than about 2 months. He dated three different women, one for about 10 months, the second for about 6 weeks, and the third for over a year (and that is ongoing as I write this). He would typically try to hook up with someone else about 3 or 4 weeks after a relationship ended. When he would start telling me about the new woman in his life he routinely emphasized the possibility that she could be "the one" he'd marry and spend the rest of his life with. Working with John as he moved through each of these relationships gave me a lot of opportunities to understand how he approached his partners.

He was in love with the first of the two women and committed to the relationship. However, about 4 months into the relationship he started to get suspicious about how much and how often she messaged one of her colleagues. She ultimately broke up with John and started dating that coworker; whether she had sex with the coworker before breaking up with John is unclear.

The second relationship was with a woman he had met at a regional conference for security professionals. John liked her well enough, but she lived on the other side of the country. John wanted (or needed?) to spend time with her in person more often than once every 4 or 5 weeks, so the relationship fizzled. (This is an element of resistant attachment.)

The third relationship was with a woman named Yelena, a classmate he started to date near the end of the first semester in his MBA program. They had sex frequently during the first few months of their relationship, including some occasional lunchtime quickies. John said he liked the intensity and the spontaneity of these events.

Facilitating Emotional Connection

John and I had the following conversation approximately 20 months into therapy and 4 months into his relationship with Yelena, which seemed to be the time he typically started to encounter difficulties with his partner:

CLIENT: Yelena and I are starting to argue more.

THERAPIST: What happened? What did you argue about?

CLIENT: This past Friday we were doing a bar crawl with her friends. There's five—no, six—of us total, including us. Oh wait, maybe seven by this point because someone's boyfriend joined us. Uh, maybe just six at this point? Anyway, we've been to two bars and we're walking to the third and she's like "Let's go to my place and have a quickie and then we'll catch up with everyone." [*Pauses slightly and then continues when I don't say anything*] And I was like "No; you said you wanted me to spend time with your friends, so let's spend time with your friends." And she asked me again and then she started to kiss me and started to put her hands down my pants and I kind of pulled away from her and I'm like, "No; let's just go be with your friends."

THERAPIST: Did you really turn down sex with Yelena because you wanted to spend time with her friends? Because I remember 2 months ago when y'all got freaky in semipublic places.

CLIENT: No, not because of her friends. I just—I didn't really want to have sex right then. I'd had a bad day at work and a long work week—we had events I needed to staff three nights that week—and I was content to just be out and relax and not have to do much. Honestly, I would have been fine if we'd stayed home and cuddled up on the couch, but she'd made a point of making sure we were doing something with her friends because I'd only hung out with her friends one other time, and she said we needed to spend more time with her friends, so I'd gotten ready to be with her friends. And I was having a fairly good time. It was nice to be out somewhere and not have to think about the place's security or worry if everything was happening the way it was supposed to. And then we're walking from one bar to the next, we're holding hands, and we're toward the back of the group, and she's like, "My place is two blocks away. Let's go have a quickie." And I said no. I told her that she'd made it clear that she wanted me to spend time with her friends, and that's what I was doing.

THERAPIST: And I don't think you've told me about any times you've declined sex with Yelena, although you have talked about her sex drive being lower than yours . . .

CLIENT: No. There was one time when I was sick a few weeks ago that I said no, but that's it.

THERAPIST: I'm guessing this isn't the first time you've been tired, and I remember you telling me stories about the two of you getting freaky in semipublic places about 2 months ago, so what am I missing here? Why'd you say no this time?

CLIENT: Honestly?

THERAPIST: Yes please.

CLIENT: I just really wanted to be connected to her and know she was there for me and that I didn't have to do anything. Like I said, I'd have been fine if we were just hanging out on the couch.

THERAPIST: To be clear, you wanted the emotional connection?

CLIENT: Yes.

THERAPIST: And sex would have ruined that?

CLIENT: Sex is different. It's a physical connection and an emotional connection. I just wanted to let my feelings go and connect with her emotionally.

THERAPIST: Did you tell her that?

CLIENT: Uh . . .

THERAPIST: I think that's a "No, I didn't tell her that."

CLIENT: I did tell her, but not until we were in the middle of the argument.

THERAPIST: Why'd you wait? Why not tell her that at the beginning of the night? Or when she first suggested sex?

CLIENT: I don't know.

I learned a few things from this conversation. One was that John had reached a point in his relationship with Yelena where emotional connection was at least as important as sexual connection and that either of those could dominate in any particular moment. I also learned that John continued to struggle to openly share his emotions and instead would manage the situation so that his emotional needs were met without him having to verbalize those needs. He did that by highlighting Yelena's stated desire for John to spend time with her friends instead of sharing his own desire for emotional connection. This behavior is a manifestation of his resistant attachment: He wasn't sure if his new secure base, Yelena, would be there to hear and support his feelings.

I wasn't surprised that their emotional connection had become a central element of the relationship. My lack of surprise came from having seen this dynamic in John's other relationships. It also fit the definition of a relationship, not a hookup. If their relationship was going to be primarily about the sex, then there's minimal need to get to know about the other person's life, get to know each other's friends, and so on. Those aspects of connection are unnecessary for a hookup partner, whether that's a one-time hookup or an ongoing one. Sure, there might be some venting about a bad day that happens before or after the sex, but people generally think of hookups as having little or no emotional connection. But a dating relationship? That's expected to include real knowledge about your partner's work, their emotional life, friends, family, and so on (Bogle, 2008; Epstein et al., 2009; Garcia et al., 2012).

I also recognized that John was struggling with how to create and maintain an emotionally intimate and trusting relationship. We discussed the differences between a partner who gives you their attention because they're trying to get to know you and a partner who continues to give you their attention 6 months later because they've invested in you. John also worked to identify factors that would allow him to trust his partner and believe she would have his back and be open to hearing about and soothing his emotions, and do so reliably. This last piece initially led me to point out ways in which Yelena was demonstrating these traits, such as doing what she said she would do or demonstrating good boundaries.

In subsequent sessions, we explored John's reluctance to verbalize his wants and feelings. The dialogue illustrates John clearly acting on his feelings and his awareness of those feelings at the time, but he struggled to tell Yelena about his feelings until after they had started arguing. He and I had had this discussion before, but I heard something different as this behavior continued to appear in his relationship with Yelena. He said something like "I don't want to come across as a little bitch who's always in their feelings" and instead of focusing on the feeling piece, I highlighted the "little bitch" piece. When I asked what that meant, John talked about not wanting to come across as moody or caught up in his feelings. When I clarified that he wanted to be seen as reliable and consistent, he answered with an emphatic (and possibly exasperated) "YES!" John worked as a protector (see Chapter 6) and readily identified himself as such, but I had somehow failed to consider the ways in which being steady, reliable, constant, and in control of himself were necessary parts of his job that are often associated with masculinity. I switched to a discussion of (masculine) predictability and (feminine) unpredictability/moodiness, and that opened some new avenues of discussion about how he wanted to be seen.

Addressing Resistant Attachment

People with resistant attachment styles resist separation from their intimate partners, who serve as a secure base. For children, that secure base is typically the primary caregivers; for adults it is typically a long-term romantic partner or a best friend (and can be both; people can have multiple secure bases). As discussed earlier in this chapter, the attachment is labeled *resistant* because the individual finds it stressful to separate from their secure base because of fears that the secure base will not return. Individuals with resistant attachments do not resist creating connections; on the contrary, they are often eager to do so. Women are more likely to have a resistant attachment style than men (Levine & Heller, 2010).

Unfortunately for John, his history included several events (or traumas) when his secure base left him. The first was when his father moved to another state when his parents divorced. John recalled that after the divorce his mother said things like "It's the two of us against the world," and young John readily accepted this. However, when she got married again, and then had two children with her new husband, her attention (appropriately) shifted away from John, and he felt as though he had lost her. His college girlfriend cheated on him for a 2-year period, including when they were engaged, and thus he experienced an abandonment and betrayal from a previously reliable partner. (This is a partial replay of the events he had experienced with his mother.) All of this contributed to John having difficulty believing that someone would return to him after an argument.

I came to realize that John's resistant attachment style was prompting him to avoid any type of disagreement or argument with Yelena (and prior girlfriends) because he would become anxious if they argued: He feared an argument might prompt her to leave and thus indicate she was not his secure base. Instead, he routinely attempted to manage the situation and reduce his anxiety while avoiding openly disagreeing with Yelena.

John's fears that a partner might leave him, at any time, manifested in other ways. Somehow, he would always get permission from his girlfriends to share their phone locations though a tracking app, which allowed him to always know where she was (and he sometimes became suspicious if she was someplace new and unusual). He was very attentive, and I'll say overly attentive, to how long it would take his girlfriend to reply to a text, especially if her phone location indicated she was at home. At times, John would even drive by a girlfriend's apartment to see if she was, in fact, home. John recognized that these actions made him sound like a stalker, but he found it difficult to prevent himself from doing them when he was anxious and wanted (emotional) reassurance and wasn't getting it.

While he was dating Yelena, I asked him to read *Attached: The New Science of Adult Attachment and How It Can Help You Find—and Keep—Love* by Amir Levine and Rachel Heller (2010). Written for a general audience, the book describes the attachment system; the behaviors of people who have secure, resistant, and avoidant attachment styles; and how those styles manifest themselves. We worked through the book one (and occasionally two) chapter at a time, and John was readily able to apply the material Levine and Heller presented. From my perspective, the book is much better at helping people with resistant attachment styles than those with avoidant attachment styles (but I haven't yet found a book that really works for those folks).

Understanding Promiscuity, Intensity, and Achievement

Many of the promiscuous men I work with desire intensity, or novelty, or challenge. The process of hooking up with a new partner—identifying them, determining/creating their interest, and then proceeding to sex—is intense. There is a lot happening in a relatively short time, with many potential mistakes that would cause the hookup to fail. Sex with an ongoing partner can come to lack that intensity or novelty or challenge. Moreover, hook-up sex may be the only area of a man's life that provides intense or novel or challenging experiences: Work, time with his family of origin, and even hanging out with friends may be quite routine.

Approximately 3 or 4 months into a new relationship, John and his new partner would develop some habits that made spending time together and having sex more routine. Then, with these routines in place, the intensity dropped, and John would begin to question the relationship. If John's partner needed his help dealing with challenges in her life, or he needed her support to deal with challenges in his own life, such as when he changed jobs or his 12-year-old dog passed away, the intensity returned and he was more invested in the relationship.

Approximately 1 year after we shifted to less frequent sessions, John enrolled in the MBA program to improve his chances of moving into upper management. Shortly after his first semester started, and before he started dating Yelena, John reported that his interest in hooking up had decreased. He had made several changes prior to this point that might have explained his decreased desire to hook up. But John also acknowledged that for the first time in many years, he had an intense experience throughout the week while completing schoolwork and so he didn't really need to find additional intensity. John's use of hooking up as an intense experience suggested that his behavior was partly the result of being understimulated.

In the opening dialogue of this chapter, John and I talked about the benefits of hooking up other than partnered orgasm. In working through this issue with other clients, I sometimes ask how much time, energy, and attention a client devotes to this part of his life. Although there are different appearance standards for gay men and straight men, I want to know if he seems more invested in appearance—shaping his body and dressing it well—than average. I also want to know how frequently and how much time he is spending on dating and hookup apps, going to bars with the intent to hook up, and so on, to determine if hooking up is a primary nonwork activity. With some clients, I describe hooking up as a hobby that requires just as much time, energy, and attention as playing a sport or being in a band. These questions help us reposition hooking up as having nonsexual goals.

I might point out that hooking up is a choice and requires both skill and effort, especially if a client is hooking up in person at an event instead of using an app, such as Tinder or Grindr. For those clients, it may be an obvious choice, but it's still a choice. In reality, it's easier to stay home and masturbate than to have to choose the right person, flirt, and so on, and risk being turned down, as John and I discussed in the opening exchange. My promiscuous clients are also aware that most of their hookups lead to an orgasm that is of fine or good quality and that being with a longer term partner who knows what turns them on is more likely to lead to a (consistently) good orgasm that is sometimes great. All of this helps me shift the clients' attention away from the sex (and orgasm) and on to other motives.

Understanding Monogamy, Consensual Nonmonogamy, and Cheating

The cultural changes that sometimes are called a "hookup culture" have brought greater attention to open relationships, which are often labeled *consensual nonmonogamy* in the research literature. Open relationships rely heavily on both honesty and trust. Like any intimate relationship, open relationships are facilitated by greater self-knowledge, especially when it comes to the reasons an individual wants more than one partner or what they are seeking from those partners. As a therapist, my goal is to help my clients work through their issues and get to a point where they can have healthy (and respectful) intimate relationships. I don't have an inherent preference for the number of partners my clients are having those relationships with.

Having an open relationship requires the members of that relationship to work together to develop a set of boundaries that govern the nonmonogamy as well as the practices they will use to discuss the boundaries as time goes on. Some of those boundary questions address who is allowed as a partner (e.g., can it be someone with whom both members of the couple interact regularly? can it be strangers?), the frequency of contact with extradyadic partners (one-off encounters only, an ongoing partner only?), the location of these activities (in the couple's house? outside only?), the extent to which partners will be told when each other is meeting another sex partner, and the disease- and pregnancy-prevention strategies to be used. The need for ongoing discussion of these issues also is important to ensure that issues of discomfort, trust, and jealousy are being addressed regularly and in ways that will help the primary couple remain emotionally connected. These discussions are well beyond the scope of this book, but Tristan Taormino's (2008) *Opening Up: A Guide to Creating and Sustaining Open Relationships* and Jessica Fern's (2020) *Polysecure: Attachment, Trauma, and Consensual Nonmonogamy* are very good resources.

Dishonesty in bars, clubs, and other hookup settings is less common among the younger clients with whom I work, but it still exists. Regardless of my clients' age, I consistently encourage clients who are trying to hook up to be honest about what they are looking for during a hookup—a night of pleasure but not an ongoing relationship—and we talk about consent in sexual encounters. Younger men who have grown up in an era where consent has been emphasized, and with hookup apps (e.g., Tinder and Grindr), are more likely to expect and practice honesty and openness about sexual preferences; these have been much more a part of their socialization into sexuality than they have for older men.

Honesty is very important and, from my perspective, it is also a habit. In my experience, men who are willing to be dishonest during a hookup are more likely to be dishonest about other behaviors and are more likely to cheat on their partners. Cheating occurs when someone breaks an agreement they have made with their partner regarding sexual activity with others. It can occur in both monogamous relationships (where any type of sexual activity with someone else is off-limits) and nonmonogamous relationships (where certain behaviors and/or certain people may be off-limits). Men who cheat on their partners are more likely to be dishonest in other ways (Humblet et al., 2003).

CONCLUSION

As he started college, John's promiscuous behavior helped him develop a reputation as a player, become The Man, and achieve status among his male peers. But now, several years after graduation, he was trying to change his identity and abandon this masculine criterion. The identity pieces were straightforward (and I didn't discuss them directly, but his security work gave him an identity as a protector, and his decision to pursue an MBA would increase his credentials as a breadwinner). However, John's efforts to abandon the masculine criterion of promiscuity were less amenable to change, largely because random hookups served a range of other purposes he hadn't considered.

My discussions with John focused on other motives for hooking up, in particular the ways in which it provided a sense of achievement. For some men, hooking up may facilitate masculine achievement and provide status among their male peers; this seems to have been John's case during the beginning of his undergraduate career. Hooking up clearly built John's self-esteem; it was a task he was good at. And the skills inherent in that task—the ability to connect with others and respond to other people's emotions, as well as a willingness to take (some) risks—were ones I could rely on him to use in our therapeutic work.

John struggled in his romantic relationships because of his resistant attachment style, which was the result of significant separations from his parents. The anxious need for connection was one reason he would hook up. We also explored what he was looking for in a romantic relationship, as well as his ability to develop and maintain such a relationship, to help him address and better manage his resistant attachment and the anxiety it generated.

John was clear that his desire to stop hooking up was his own and was not coming from external pressure, and I believed him. As a result, we did not discuss open relationships, although I have addressed them briefly in this chapter. For some promiscuous men with whom I have worked, an open relationship seems more likely than a monogamous one to bring long-term happiness.

9 THE UNEMOTIONAL MAN

BART'S CASE

A 60-year-old heterosexual, White, cisgender man, Bart was well muscled but clearly overweight and could be described as a fireplug. He was employed as a maintenance worker for a family-owned company that managed two apartment complexes and a few rental houses. He had grown up helping his father fix things around the house, and he had furthered his skills when he enlisted in the Navy after high school and became an electrician's assistant. Bart told me he liked his job because it was a way to help people.

Bart was on his second marriage. He and his wife, Claire, had been married 12 years, and were raising one of their grandchildren, Liza, the 3-year-old daughter of Claire's son. Bart's son-in-law (Liza's father) was continually in and out of prison for a range of small offenses (petty theft, assault, low-level drug dealing). The child's mother had simply vanished one day after dropping 6-month-old Liza off with Bart and his wife; Liza's father was in jail at the time, and they didn't see him as reliable, so Bart and Claire legally adopted her.

https://doi.org/10.1037/0000499-009
Clinical Work With Men: Understanding Masculinity in Psychotherapy, by A. P. Smiler

Bart had three adult children from his first marriage but hadn't really been part of their childhood. He had begun to reconcile with his older son, but he was estranged from his daughter, who was the youngest of the three. Bart's middle child, a son, had been killed in an industrial accident 7 years ago when Bart was 53, and his older son was 23.

THERAPIST: So, what brings you to a therapist's office today?

CLIENT: My cardiologist thought it would be a good idea.

THERAPIST: Why did your cardiologist think it would be a good idea?

CLIENT: I have a heart condition, and nothing else I've tried has helped, so she thought it might be stress and told me to see a therapist.

THERAPIST: What else have you tried? Or, what are you doing right now to help your heart and reduce stress?

CLIENT: She gave me some medication. I also had a sleep study done a few years ago, they said I have sleep apnea, and I now have a CPAP [continuous positive airway pressure] machine that I use every night.

THERAPIST: OK.

CLIENT: She put me on a diet, but that didn't work.

THERAPIST: It didn't work?

CLIENT: I'm a meat-and-potatoes kind of guy. A salad is fine as an appetizer, or alongside my meal, but salad's not a meal. Vegetables aren't a meal.

THERAPIST: Got it. What else do you do for your heart?

CLIENT: That's it, really.

THERAPIST: You mentioned stress. Is there anything you do specifically to relieve or reduce stress?

CLIENT: No. I mean, we all have stress, right? It's not like we can avoid it.

THERAPIST: Fair enough, but sometimes we can reduce how much stress we have. What stresses you out?

CLIENT: My wife, mostly.

THERAPIST: Your wife? How so?

CLIENT: She's always on me to do this or do that around the house. My "honey do" list is at least a mile long and always growing.

THERAPIST: And—

CLIENT: And if Claire's watching me work, she's got to tell me how to do it. Like, I don't know? But she's always got to put in her two cents.

THERAPIST: That sounds very stressful.

CLIENT: Meh. It is what it is, and she's always tried to tell me what to do. Besides, it's not really hard stuff, just fixing things around the house.

THERAPIST: OK. What else is stressful in your life?

CLIENT: We're raising our granddaughter, and she can be a handful, let me tell you. Liza—that's her name—Liza's 3 years old. She's been with us since she was about 6 months old, and we legally adopted her around the time she turned 1. Her dad's good for nothing; he's in and out of jail for all sorts of petty stuff. Liza's mom wasn't worth a damn, either. One day when Liza was 6 months old and he was in jail, she asked us to watch the baby for a few hours. She dropped Liza off and vanished, never to be heard from again.

THERAPIST: Wow.

CLIENT: Yup.

THERAPIST: You said Liza's a handful. What do you mean?

CLIENT: That girl has quite a mouth on her, and when she doesn't want to do something there's nothing that can make her do it. She'll fuss and scream and throw a tantrum and go on and on and on.

THERAPIST: That sounds difficult.

CLIENT: It is.

THERAPIST: Is Liza better behaved for Claire?

CLIENT: [*Laughs*] No, she's worse with Claire. Claire can't control her at all.

THERAPIST: OK. So far, the stressful things in life are your honey-do list and taking care of Liza. Anything else? Are other parts of your relationship with Claire stressful? Is work stressful?

CLIENT: My relationship with Claire is all right. We argue a fair bit, but that's normal, right? I don't think I've got any more stress there than anyone else. And work is work. I'm a maintenance man for a couple that owns two small apartment complexes and a few rental houses here in town. I go in, fix stuff, and that's that. It's not particularly stressful.

THERAPIST: And you like the owners?

CLIENT: Yeah. They're good people.

THERAPIST: Good people. That's excellent. Are they also good bosses?

CLIENT: [*Laughs*] Yes, they're good bosses, too.

THERAPIST: So, let me make sure I understand what you're telling me. Your cardiologist, who you've been seeing for how many years?

CLIENT: About 15 years.

THERAPIST: And why'd you start seeing the cardio?

CLIENT: My PCP [primary care physician] sent me. Was worried about my weight, my stress, and thought I might have an arrhythmia.

THERAPIST: Do you? Have an arrhythmia?

CLIENT: Yes, but it's under control.

THERAPIST: OK. So 15 years ago, your PCP referred you to a cardiologist because of your weight and an arrhythmia. Since then, you've got medication and a CPAP for sleep apnea, and things are under control. But your cardio remains worried about your stress level, and you've already told me two or three times that you're no more stressed than other folks, even though you're raising your 3-year-old granddaughter who barely listens to you and your wife, your relationship with your wife has some arguing, and you've got a honey-do list a mile long. Is that right?

CLIENT: Yep.

THERAPIST: And you say your job isn't particularly stressful, but my mom managed apartments for most of my life and I've been both a renter and an owner, and I know that tenants are not patient when there's something wrong with their apartment. They want you to get there now, and they want you to fix it right now.

CLIENT: [*Laughs*] Yep. That's definitely how my job works.

THERAPIST: I think that's probably more stressful than a lot of other jobs. I mean, it's on you to fix the thing and fix it as quickly and cheaply as possible in order to keep the tenants and the owners happy, and I know that doesn't always happen.

CLIENT: No, it certainly does not.

THERAPIST: Which makes it sound more stressful than when you talked about it. Of course, you might just be used to it after all these years and so you don't really notice the stress.

CLIENT: Huh. I suppose that's possible.

THERAPIST: And 20 minutes ago, when I asked what you do for fun, you told me you don't really get to have fun, between taking care of Liza and handling the honey-do list.

CLIENT: That's true . . .

THERAPIST: Fun is an antidote to stress. It sounds like you might be more stressed than you think you are.

CLIENT: Maybe. But there's no point in complaining about it. Complaining doesn't make the stress any less. Life's hard, and I just need to deal with it.

Throughout our conversation, Bart's answers were direct and to the point. There was little to no additional description and nothing that might be considered unnecessary information. His answers were also emotionless and included no complaining. Bart shared his health information and his family medical history in the same fashion, with a steady voice that made me think he was assessing his health issues in the same way he might assess a malfunctioning HVAC system. His replies had a "Just the facts, ma'am" style, with no emotional content—no change in tone of voice and no explicit statement of feelings about anything, no feelings about his divorce, his estrangement from his children, the death of his younger son, or becoming a full-time parent (to his step-granddaughter) at age 57. The only exception was his clear love and affection for Liza.

The Main Theme in Bart's Therapy

From this beginning, our work would be dominated by one theme: getting Bart to take better care of himself, in particular, his mental health and emotional well-being. We began with stress and stress reduction. When I asked Bart to tell me about his stress and all the things that wear him out, he had no difficulty doing so. I asked Bart about his stress because that is the male-typed word for "worried" or "anxious." At work, there was a never-ending list of broken appliances and dumb things the tenants did. The maintenance department was also perpetually short-handed; Bart had worked for this family for 15 years, but the next most senior person had been there 3 years, and Bart saw him as working rather slowly and making repairs that were simply "good enough." The maintenance department always seemed to be hiring a new person, and they struggled to find employees. When Bart started working for this company, they had five people doing maintenance, including him. Bart now felt lucky when they had four employees.

Bart reported that his home life was highly stressful and said he was rarely able to relax at home. He described Liza as something of a terror, saying that she listened to him only sometimes and rarely listened to Claire. Bart also spoke about Claire's difficulty enforcing or maintaining any type of punishment for Liza for more than 15 minutes and described times when he would attempt to discipline Liza but Claire would undercut his efforts. Bart was the only earner in the family, and I never got a clear explanation as to why that was, except that Claire couldn't work because of her own physical health issues. In addition, given Bart's skill set, he was also responsible for any repairs and improvements at his own house. Bart enjoyed attending their church—both the religious and social aspects—but Claire did not, so he went infrequently and without her.

Bart as an Unemotional Man

For Bart, and for many of the unemotional men with whom I have worked, being unemotional is their primary strategy for dealing with uncomfortable emotions: They ignore them. They find this effective, at least in the short term. That was certainly the case for Bart: Ignoring his feelings let him get through the day without making any trouble or without making the existing trouble worse (e.g., by standing up for himself). There were numerous downsides, to this, however, including the lack of closeness with his son, his inability to say no, and the adverse impact of long-term stress on his body.

Bart was genuinely concerned about his physical health. And I'll note that he even used the word "concerned" instead of "stressed," which told me his anxiety was higher in this realm than in other realms. Bart understood his heart problems to be a combination of age and the wear and tear of his life, but he had never considered the impact of suppressing his feelings as part of that wear and tear.

As therapy progressed, I realized that Bart thought of his body as a tool or a machine to be maintained, much as he used tools and other machines for his work. Bart acknowledged that he wasn't always good at doing maintenance on his body—especially with respect to his weight—but he took his medication as prescribed and took care of injuries and other health issues promptly. Bart's conceptualization of his body as a tool is consistent with our conception of men as doers, according to which doing and getting the job done are prioritized, and how a guy gets the job done is largely irrelevant as long as the job gets done. Furthermore, the condition of the tool is not particularly important as long as the tool can do the job. If a tool wears out, or a machine is beyond repair, a guy can always borrow or buy another one. But that's not true for bodies. (This metaphor gets used in professional sports when people talk about players going to the dressing room "for repairs.")

MASCULINITY AND THE UNEMOTIONAL MAN TYPE

Men who show no or little emotion adhere to two interrelated masculine criteria: (a) emotional stoicism and (b) antifemininity. Adherence to these masculine norms can provide them with a self-respect, self-esteem, and part of an identity. That partial identity consists of "I'm not a woman." It doesn't say anything about who he is, only what he is not.

But what he is not is very important for many American men. Not acting like a woman/girl—the antifemininity just mentioned—qualifies as the primary guideline for male behavior, according to at least one researcher (O'Neil, 2015). Indeed, some of the most common jibes boys use to police each other's masculinity are direct manifestations of this directive, including statements like "Don't be such a girl!" (Reigeluth & Addis, 2016; Rosenberg et al., 2017). Directives like "Don't be a fag" and disclaimers such as "No homo" (i.e., implying no homosexual intentions) rely on the mid–20th-century description of gay men as gender inverted and, thus, womanly. And according to current American stereotypes, one of the defining characteristics of women (and gay men) is their emotionality.

As such, masculine directives to avoid emotional expression are at least partly related to directives to not act womanly. Unlike other masculine criteria I describe in this book, self-definition in this way is entirely relative to some other entity (i.e., women) instead of being reliant on oneself and some type of accomplishment. Over the course of treatment, I try to help unemotional men find another masculine criterion (e.g., providing, problem solving) on which they can rely to acquire masculine achievement. On rare occasions, I have had men decide to opt out of conforming to masculinity instead of shifting to another criterion. There was no need to do this with Bart; he was a guy who fixed things and fit the description of problem solvers I provided in Chapter 5.

The emotional stoicism norm directs men to minimize any emotional display by having a stiff upper lip. The idea that men are rational and women are emotional is widely held in American culture and is an all-or-none exaggeration of cultural stereotypes and real-world data that show differences between men as a group and women as a group. From the historical research I have read, I believe the associations of masculinity with rationality and femininity with emotionality shifted from being a peripheral to central component of gender stereotypes during the industrial revolution in the late 1800s and early 1900s. In a pair of books, the historian Peter N. Stearns (1979, 1994) detailed how this shift came about. He argued that men, and only men, were positioned as being calm, cool, and rational enough to understand the logic and functioning of machines, as well as the logic and functioning of large factories in which men and machines were conceptualized as forming a larger machine comprising organic and industrial components. Women weren't suited to this work because of their "well-known" propensity for emotional displays and hysteria. This distinction helped create and justify management of factory work as men's work.

The antifemininity norm is relevant because emotional expression, crying in particular, is categorized as feminine and thus something appropriate only for women. Bart's father had shamed Bart during his childhood for crying by invoking femininity when he called him a "sissy" and "girly." Adherence to these norms doesn't directly help a guy demonstrate his manliness; he won't be a Real Man or Man Enough by being stoic or not feminine. But he runs substantial risk of losing masculinity points and needing to reachieve his masculinity if he does show emotion, especially if he does so by crying, being overly excited (and especially giddy), or displaying high levels of anxiety. Exceptions are made for life cycle events (births, marriages, deaths, etc.) and for certain sporting events or major accomplishments. As a result, being unemotional can contribute to and facilitate his ability to adhere to other masculine criteria, and thus it can facilitate masculine achievement.

The positioning of men as rational and women as emotional is sufficiently central to American conceptions of men and women that it has been codified in psychological measures of adherence to gender stereotypes since the early 1900s (see reviews by Morawski, 1985, and Smiler, 2004). Interestingly, successive generations of male American undergraduates have shown stronger endorsement of stereotypical aspects of both masculinity and femininity from the mid-1970s through the early 2000s; this is also true for female undergraduates (Donnelly & Twenge, 2016; Twenge, 1997). I will also note a logical inconsistency: Although boys and men are told not to show emotion, there are two exceptions: (a) anger (see Chapter 7) and (b) lust (see Chapter 8). At the macro scale, I think it will be difficult to eliminate the problematic aspects of angry and lustful behavior while men's emotional range remains as limited as it is.

I do not think there is a specific masculine type that epitomizes men's lack of emotionality. We could talk about strictly logical male characters, such as Mr. Spock and Data from the Star Trek universe, but these versions of masculinity don't provide a guy with masculine achievement among other men (Smiler, 2006). However, violating the injunctions to be emotionally stoic and not demonstrate feminine characteristics can prompt questions about the extent of a man's masculine achievement and cause him to lose status, so I typically think of the lack of emotional expression as a means to an end: It's not an identity, or a type unto itself, but rather a characteristic that many men demonstrate.

In my clinical work, I think about emotionality as lying along a continuum that ranges from unemotional to highly emotional, comparable to other continua, such as introverted–extraverted, being an early adopter or late adopter of new technology, or being clean or messy. In Bart's case, he fixed things for his work and around his home, and he definitely fit my description of problem solvers (see Chapter 5).

The stereotype of men as unemotional has also entered the scientific world. Some researchers have discussed the "extreme male brain theory of autism" (Crespi et al., 2019, p. 1), which is characterized by a lack of emotional empathy and a tendency toward rule-based systemic thinking and has been shown to have clear male–female differences in diagnosis and evidence of underlying genetic differences. But the extreme male brain codifies a stereotype; substance abuse also has clear male–female differences and underlying genetic differences, but it has not been described as "extreme male coping" in the scientific literature.

Benefits of Being an Unemotional Man

One of the benefits of being unemotional is rarely or never losing one's temper. For some rational men, that calmness is important and may be a real point of pride. He might be someone who "never loses his cool" or "always has his head on straight" or "keeps calm no matter what." For Bart, and many of the men with whom I have worked, this aspect of masculinity gets highlighted during childhood because their tears were used against them. This was certainly the case for Bart, who was bullied and humiliated by his father for crying. I have heard similar stories from other guys who were bullied by neighborhood kids.

Men who show no emotion may be seen as always calm, and even reliable, especially if their ability to stay calm when things go wrong is associated with good problem solving or male-typed caretaking. This may be especially true for men who deal with a crisis, whether that applies to first responders (who rush toward danger) or lawyers and associated professionals, who work as fixers and clean up other people's messes.

Displaying little or no emotion is also a way to avoid calling attention to oneself. In current terminology, some people are all about drama and regularly broadcast their feelings to others. This attracts attention and thus is unmanly. Bart saw himself as a regular guy who just did his thing and minded his own business. He mostly just wanted to be left alone. Routinely displaying his emotions, and especially doing so loudly, would not fit that image.

Men who show little or no emotion may be particularly appealing to romantic partners who are highly emotional in an opposites-attract manner. Emotionally inexpressive men may be appealing to romantic partners who prefer men who don't express emotions because of their own negative experiences with other men whose emotions were expressed unpredictably or dangerously.

The Challenges of Being an Unemotional Man

A primary concern when working with unemotional men is their lack of awareness of their emotional side and the impact this has on their relationships and physical health. As Bart's case illustrates, not addressing the stress in an individual's life may contribute to hypertension. High levels of stress are associated with an elevated heart rate and can adversely affect blood flow, sleep, and other basic regulatory process. This is likely why hypertension is a primary risk factor for both heart disease and stroke, both of which are among the five leading causes of death in this country (Gillespie & Hurvitz, 2013). Bart's weight also adversely affected his health, and there was likely a link between his weight and his stress.

Like many unemotional men, Bart had difficulty connecting to others. The intimate connections that are central to close friendships and romantic relationships are emotional in nature; we talk about loving those people and categorize love as an emotion. Without the ability to recognize happiness, or even feel happy, and thus with little prioritization of those pleasurable moments, a man is unlikely to put forth the effort to form or maintain close connections. When Bart chose to back away from his son in order to avoid the emotional discomfort of that conflict, his relationships with him deteriorated.

Despite the negative effects of being unemotional, research has shown that men who strongly endorse the emotional control norm are less likely to seek therapy (O'Neil, 2015; Wong, Ho, et al., 2017). Stereotypes about therapy suggest it is focused strictly on emotions, with clients bearing their souls to therapists while crying. In response to this, and in an attempt to be more male friendly, I sometimes frame my clinical work as problem solving.

Although unemotional men may appeal to some romantic partners, men who seek therapy and begin to start expressing their feelings, especially negative emotions, are likely to encounter pushback from their partners. I often try to prepare my clients for these moments, explaining that the marriage is a system and that changes in one part of the system typically require changes in the other part of the system.

Intersectional Issues

Directives to be unemotional, and the choice to follow such directives, vary across subcultures. Richard Majors and Janet Billson (1992) wrote about the importance among Black boys and men of being emotionally inexpressive. Describing this as part of a "cool pose" they saw as common, Majors and Billson argued that coolness helps Black men develop and demonstrate social competence, pride, dignity, self-esteem, and respect while also demonstrating hostility toward the dominant culture that has mistreated them. They argued that this version of coolness could be used to restrain a man's anger, which could be dangerous to himself and others (see Chapter 7) and that this had descended from games enslaved men played with each other in order to help them learn how to hide anger from their enslavers.

Financial status and social class also play a role. As I detailed in Chapter 2, achievement is required to prove one's manhood. Doing so may be more difficult for men and boys who are financially impoverished because they may have few other ways to demonstrate masculine achievement. For them, not expressing emotion may be especially important for maintaining what little achievement they are able to claim. Such a dynamic would be more likely to appear among boys of color because they are more likely to be raised in such environments.

Emotional expression is part of the American stereotype of gay men, with such expression often positioned as extreme and over the top (Heasley, 2005; Herek, 1995). At the large-group level, gay men are typically more aware of, and more expressive of, their emotions than straight men, but not as much as the stereotypes indicate. The gay male community distinguishes among more stereotypically masculine "butch" and more stereotypically feminine "femme" men, recognizing the differences in levels of emotional expression (Sánchez et al., 2009), but there is no such distinction among straight men. Instead, straight boys and men need to bracket their emotional expression with phrases like "No homo," whether this is applied to actual friends or their love and admiration for professional athletes (Klugman, 2015; Pascoe, 2007).

WORKING WITH BART AND OTHER UNEMOTIONAL MEN

Bart and I have worked together for approximately 4 years, but our time together has been intermittent. We've met as often as every other week, but at times we've gone 3 or 4 months between appointments because he has difficulty getting time off, has to take care of his granddaughter while his wife is receiving medical treatment, or is receiving his own medical treatment. As a result, our meetings have been sporadic, and the work has been slow. Despite this inconsistency, Bart is dedicated to the work. I initially framed our work as helping him reduce and relieve stress, and we then shifted to setting boundaries as a method of preventing stress (by not taking on undue burdens). As in my work with Benny (Chapter 6), I then framed stress as an emotion and used this framing to help Bart discuss his emotions and explore his choice to show as little emotion as possible.

Treatment Plan

Bart began seeing me because he needed to address his stress, so that was the focus of our clinical work. I adopted an expansive approach to identifying sources of stress, and Bart didn't object, so our work addressed several elements of his life that were stressful. We began with simple venting of his stress and then moved to boundary-setting as a method of preventing stress. As I got to know Bart, I realized that he tended to suppress almost all of his feelings, so we explored the importance of identifying and expressing other feelings, with particular attention to ways in which experiencing happiness and other good feelings could offset stress. Although it's not included in the chapter, the expansion of Bart's range of feelings and his increased comfort expressing those feelings also lead to discussion of the losses he felt regarding his own father and his sons.

Reducing Stress

When I recognize that a man who believes strongly in not expressing his feelings has entered my office and that he is skeptical about therapy, I make an effort to find a small win (see Chapter 4) in the first or second session. It needs to be something he will be able to apply outside the office. For Bart, it was stress reduction strategies, such as taking the long way home after a day of work, much like I suggested to Benny, in Chapter 6. The efficacy of this strategy helped convince him that therapy could be helpful and that discussing his stress could be useful. In doing so, we sometimes actively engaged in problem solving, such as what he might say to his boss or his wife. This approach helped Bart see therapy in a masculine framework (problem solving) instead of a feminine one (emotional expression).

When we started, Bart would have spent the entire therapeutic hour venting his stress, if permitted. After about 25 minutes of this in one session, though, I interrupted and suggested that we focus on one thing he could do in order to reduce stress, and he agreed. This set the pattern for the basic structure of our sessions. Bart would vent for 20–30 minutes while catching me up on his activities and stresses from the past 2 or 4 weeks (because he could meet only every other week), and then we would focus on some aspect of his life. When I asked Bart who else he had to vent to, he said he didn't have anyone. When he complained about work, Claire would tell him to find a new job, and if he complained about Liza she would either one-up him with her own issues regarding the child or remind him that she also struggled with her. In both cases, he didn't feel heard or supported.

Because home and work were both highly stressful, we began by identifying some things he could do to de-stress between leaving work and arriving home. Bart lived about 15 minutes from his workplace and said that he was still thinking about work when he got home. In his job as a maintenance worker, Bart's day didn't end strictly at 5:00 p.m. because he couldn't leave maintenance tasks partly done. We decided to give him extra time between work and home to clear his head of work stress before he had to handle home stress. If he had a lot of energy to work off, he would take the long way home and spend about 30–40 minutes driving so the energy would have time to dissipate. If he was relatively low energy and just needed a few minutes to sit still before arriving home, he would leave work and sit in a park near his home while doing a simple breathing–meditation exercise for 10–15 minutes. Bart found both strategies useful and acknowledged that he had always tried to get home quickly because he thought Claire needed his help and would be upset. She didn't notice the extra time, but after 2 or 3 weeks she realized that Bart seemed less stressed when he got home.

We discussed some other strategies I have found useful with other clients, but Bart declined them. For example, I offered my voicemail as a place to vent. I ask that clients start by telling me they were just venting so I would know they aren't expecting a call back. Others have found stress reduction through writing a "punch list" of tasks they needed to accomplish, but Bart was provided with this kind of list at work, and the idea of a list didn't really apply to his nonwork stress. Other clients have written a "shit list" of all the bad things that happened that day; in essence, this is the opposite of a gratitude journal. Bart said he liked the idea but that he was highly unlikely to follow through with it.

Setting Boundaries

I continued to listen closely while Bart vented, and I soon realized that part of his stress was due to the fact that any time someone at work—management, a coworker, a tenant—asked him to do something, he always said yes. This was also true at home, with Claire, and, to a lesser extent, Liza. When I pointed this out, Bart explained that he liked helping people and really didn't mind, although there were times when he felt like his coworkers and his wife were taking advantage of him. In Bart's view, helping others was part of being a good Christian.

And then, a few weeks later, he was complaining about his boss asking him to start a job at 4:45 p.m. that would almost certainly take an hour, not the 15 minutes his boss thought, which meant he would be leaving work well after his 5:00 p.m. stop time. Bart got mad, reminded his boss of his need to get home to his wife and granddaughter, and his boss said that was fine and told him to go home and to handle this job first thing in the morning. I flagged this and asked Bart why, this time, he had said no. Bart said he was annoyed because the boss hadn't asked any of the other guys to handle this repair and felt like his boss might be taking advantage of him a little by asking for something this late in the day. Bart also said he was able to say no because he was taking Liza to a church event at 6:00 p.m. that evening and thus had a good reason to say no. He also realized that he was less patient than usual because he had banged his elbow against something during the prior job and was still in pain.

This event opened up a conversation about boundary-setting. I explained the basic ideas of boundary-setting: that Bart had the option of saying yes or no, that the relationship or setting set some constraints on his ability to say yes or no, that any choice he made would prompt other people to react in their own ways, and that he had to be ready to deal with such reactions. We talked about these principles over the next few sessions, especially the relational and setting constraints. Bart was clear about the extreme boundaries—he couldn't refuse to feed his granddaughter, and he couldn't refuse most work requests from his boss—but he became more comfortable with the idea that he might selectively object to some of Claire's requests at home or might more often refuse to start bigger jobs after 4:00 p.m. so he could more reliably leave at 5:00 p.m. And then, as if he were testing a repair he had just made, he started to test his ability to do this. At first, he would need to channel some of his anger in order to fortify himself before saying no, but after 2 or 3 months he gained the ability to say no, or "not now," according to his mood and how he was feeling at the time. Bart realized fairly quickly that saying no meant less stress for him.

Accessing Emotions

The incident with Bart's boss also opened up a conversation about emotions. During this stretch of therapy, I explained some of the basics of our emotional system. I described it as a source of information comparable to our five physical senses. The emotional system gives us information, and we choose how to act on that information. I further explained that anger is typically the result of being hurt, being afraid, or perceiving that something isn't fair, and that we can act on this information in whatever way we want: by getting angry, ignoring it, or doing something else that is healthier and helps us deal with the cause of the anger.

The next session was 4 weeks later. We typically met every other week, but Bart had canceled a session because of a medical appointment of Claire's. Bart began by providing updates on the things that had frustrated him over the last few weeks, as he usually did. Then he shifted the conversation:

CLIENT: I thought about what you'd said last time about saying no. So I tried it. It was last Thursday and—no wait, two Thursdays ago. Yeah, that's right. Two Thursdays ago.

THERAPIST: So, 2 weeks ago tomorrow? (We met on Wednesdays.)

CLIENT: Yes. Two weeks ago tomorrow. My boss asked if I would be willing to cover on-call (duties) for the weekend because one of the other guys, Max, couldn't do it because he had a trip to the beach. I was about to say yes and then I remembered what we'd talked about last time. I wanted to say no, but I couldn't; then I thought about how unfair it was that Max was getting out of his on-call shift—we're each expected to be on call every 4 weeks, but it's only for severe emergencies, like a broken pipe that's flooding an apartment. Anyway, I always do my on-call shifts as they're scheduled and make sure that anything I schedule for that weekend can be canceled at the last minute if I need to. And I'm thinking that Max has known for months that he was scheduled this weekend, and it's Thursday, and the boss is asking me, and then I started to get mad. And once I started to get mad, then I could tell the boss no. I didn't have to get as mad as that other time, either.

THERAPIST: That's awesome! I'm so glad you were able to do that.

CLIENT: [*Mildly pleased and possibly a little embarrassed*] Thank you.

THERAPIST: You said you couldn't say no at first and had to get angry before you could do it?

CLIENT: Yes sir.

THERAPIST: That's all right. It's easier to say no when we're mad than at other times. And you said you didn't have to get as mad as that other time you said no?

CLIENT: Yes sir.

THERAPIST: So that means it was easier than last time?

CLIENT: Yes, a little. I mean, after our conversation last time about the ways that I let people take advantage of me and they never really repay those favors, I walked out of here thinking I need to stop letting that happen. This fit the bill, and I wanted to say no right away, but couldn't. And then I remembered the anger part and that made it easier.

THERAPIST: Why'd you want to say no right away?

CLIENT: Max is fine doing maintenance, but he knew months ago that this was his weekend to work. If he'd come to me a few weeks ago and asked to trade weekends, I'd have said yes. But to ask on Thursday afternoon for the next day? Uh-uh. That's not right.

THERAPIST: And it was the boss asking you, not Max?

CLIENT: That's right.

THERAPIST: You said he was going to the beach?

CLIENT: Yeah. He'd told me at the beginning of the week.

THERAPIST: Did the boss say that?

CLIENT: Huh. No, he didn't. I wonder what Max told him.

THERAPIST: I'm going to come back to you. It sounds like the anger made it easier to say no.

CLIENT: Yes sir.

THERAPIST: That's one of the useful things about anger. One of the reasons why people get mad is when they think something is unfair. They might also get mad when they're threatened or hurt. The reason I'm saying this is because emotions serve a purpose; they tell us when things are good or bad for us. In maintenance terms, they're indicator lights. Anger tells you when something isn't working right; it's that little red light. Happiness tells you things are going well; it's that little green light.

CLIENT: Huh. I never thought about emotions that way.

THERAPIST: Emotions as a source of information about how things are going, you mean?

CLIENT: Yes sir.

THERAPIST: And does thinking about emotions as a feedback system change how you think about emotions?

CLIENT: Absolutely. It's like when I listen to a machine to hear the noise it's making when something goes wrong. My anger is the same way. Y'know [*makes noise of gears grinding*] is kind of the same as me getting upset with Liza because she's not doing what I want.

THERAPIST: Right. And the amount of upset tells you how important this is to you. It doesn't necessarily tell you why it's important or what to do, just how important it is.

CLIENT: Which is why sometimes what Liza does don't bother me but a little and why sometimes I want to explode?

THERAPIST: Exactly. And the difference between only being bothered a little and wanting to explode might be entirely about what Liza is doing, like she's about to stick a fork in an electrical outlet or you've already asked her ten times and she's still not doing what you've asked. On the other hand, it might be about how tired you are, or how hard of a day you had, or because you're already in a bad mood, or something else yet again.

CLIENT: Huh. This all makes sense. I wish someone had told me this before. I never knew any of this about anger.

Bart shared that he didn't like feeling angry and that it had bad connotations for him, so the fact that his anger helped him do something to reduce his stress was bothering him. He explained that when he was younger his father had often been angry and would yell at Bart, his brother, and his mother. The only times Bart could remember seeing his father happy were one Christmas (but just one) and one time when the family had won a raffle for a new set of living room furniture (couch, armchair, and coffee table) in the early 1970s.

When Bart or his brother misbehaved and their father was around, they would get beaten. (His mother rarely reported the boys' misbehavior to their father.) And even as boys of 8, 9, or 10 years of age, if they cried from a beating their father would get angrier, and the beating would get worse. He'd also call them weak, or sissy, or girly. Bart and his brother both learned to take their beatings stoically and, in the process, Bart shut down his emotions completely so his father wouldn't get upset at him for any type of emotional expression and thus couldn't call him girly.

Bart lived with ongoing fear of his father's anger until he was 16. One day, Bart arrived home from school earlier than usual because football practice had been unexpectedly canceled. When Bart got home, he discovered his father yelling at his mother and threatening her. Bart intervened on his mother's behalf, his father told him to get out of the way or he'd beat him to a pulp, and Bart stood his ground. The two men came to blows, and Bart managed to hurt his father badly enough that his father withdrew and Bart won the fight. After that, he was less scared of his father, and the two of them kept a respectful distance from each other—at least, as much as possible when living in the same house.

As discussions of Bart's father's anger progressed, Bart realized that he had spent most of his life avoiding his emotions so he wouldn't become angry and act like his father. In doing so, he had suppressed all of his feelings, not just anger. After he shared this story, I asked Bart how he felt about it. It took him a moment to reflect, and then he told me it made him sad: not that he was feeling sadness in the moment, more of a "sad it happened" and "sad he'd gone through that." As we continued to process that moment, I shared with him that sadness was the emotional system's response to the loss of something important. With this, I wanted to emphasize two things: (a) that I heard and respected Bart's sadness, and (b) that sadness served a specific purpose. We had already talked about the purpose of anger, and now we were talking about the purpose of sadness (which indicates a loss). With each new emotion we encountered, we continued to talk about the purpose associated with that emotion.

Bart's recognition of the ways his father's anger had shaped his childhood led to his recognition of other losses. Most important among these was his estrangement from his own children, which was largely due to Bart's first wife painting him in a bad light, violating their shared custody agreement, and otherwise making him look bad in front of the kids, and Bart's repeated decision not to fight back. His kids came to see him as an uninvolved parent who didn't care about them, a perception he didn't try to change until after he and his first wife had been separated for several years and the kids had started graduating high school and moving out of their mother's house.

Challenging the Emotional Stoicism Norm

I also challenged Bart's conceptualization of men as having little or no emotion and the masculine directive to not show emotion. Unlike the norms I have discussed in the six other case studies in this book, I almost always challenge this element of masculinity. I do so because of the range of negative effects described throughout this chapter.

One way I challenged Bart's belief idea that men are naturally unemotional is by providing a very brief description of the amygdala and its primary purpose as a processor of emotions. I also pointed to the amygdala's positioning as part of the midbrain or as a subcortical area, which makes the amygdala and emotional processing (a) biologically based; (b) present in all humans, regardless of gender; and (c) evolutionarily older than the areas used for rational thought, that is, the cortical areas that make up the forebrain. With clients who own cats, dogs, or horses, I share that the amygdala is common to all mammals, ask if their pets show some basic emotions, and sometimes ask if we humans have less emotional range than those creatures.

There are some culturally based exceptions to the prohibition against men showing emotion. I sometimes deliberately ask my clients to invoke their stereotypes as a method of helping them recognize that some men are expected to be emotional. Most of my clients readily agree that their stereotypical image that Italian men, as well as men of Latin descent, engage in high levels of emotional expression. Some of my unemotional clients find these stereotypes reassuring because it helps them recognize that some classes of men are emotional and thus gives them permission to be more emotional.

Connecting emotions to physiological sensations can help men recognize their feelings. Because those physiological sensations are automatic and physiological, men might decide that the associated feelings are also automatic and rooted somewhere in the body's response system. I'll ask, "What's going on inside your stomach?" or "Can you feel the tension in your forehead?" Then I'll interpret their body signals and translate them into emotion-focused language; for example, a jumpy stomach usually accompanies anxiety, and a smile reflects pleasure (Rabinowitz & Cochran, 2002). Although I don't use one, I've seen diagrams that have a circle of emotion words and a circle of physical sensations that often accompany those feelings. I have, however, seen emotion wheels (described shortly) that explicitly connect feelings to physical sensations.

Once Bart understood and accepted the connection between emotions and physical sensations, I explained my conception of the body's daily energy use. I told him the body has a certain amount of energy derived from food, sleep, and so on. For example, let's say that approximately 10% of this energy is dedicated to the body's physical systems (e.g., movement, digestion), 10% is dedicated to maintaining the emotional system, and 10% is for thinking. The remaining 70% can go wherever it's needed. I also explained that pain reduced the available energy. Bart indicated his understanding, and he acknowledged that he rarely devoted extra energy to his emotional system.

Identifying a Wider Range of Emotions

As Bart became more comfortable with the idea that emotions are important, and started to experience anger and sadness, I continued to provide psychoeducation about them. Although it sounds basic, men often need to learn to recognize and incorporate *feeling words* (e.g., "happy," "annoyed") into their working vocabulary, including a discussion of the most elementary emotions (e.g., mad, sad, glad, afraid). One technique I use with men who need structure in recognizing and labeling emotions is to suggest that they keep a diary in which they identify emotional reactions and record the situations in which the feelings occurred.

I have used emotion checklists on occasion (Levant & Pryor, 2025), but more often I use an emotion wheel (Garfield, 2015). I like Robert Plutchik's (1980) emotion wheel (see Figure 9.1) because it's got a relatively small

FIGURE 9.1. Robert Plutchik's Emotion Wheel

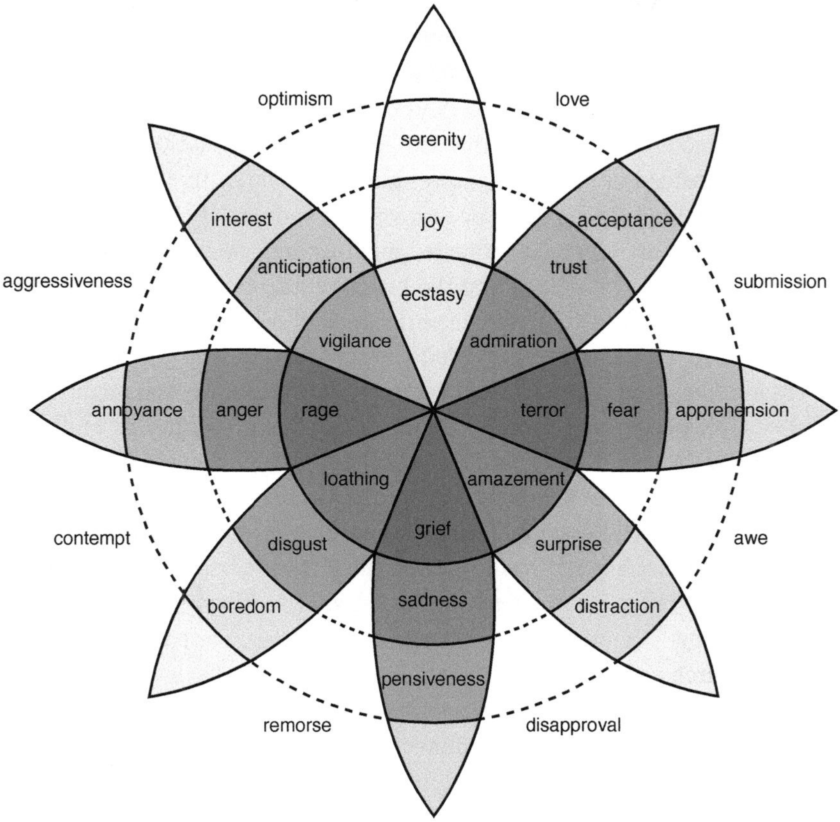

Note. By Machine Elf 1735, public domain, via Wikimedia Commons (https://commons.wikimedia.org/wiki/File:Plutchik-wheel.svg).

number of emotion words (exactly 32), and the visual is relatively simple and not overwhelming. For guys like Bart, who have suppressed or avoided their feelings for decades, this emotion wheel is the mildest entrance I can show them while also giving them a structure.

Explaining the structure of the emotion wheel is important because many men want to understand how things work; that was certainly true for Bart, who fixed things for a living. Plutchik's (1980) version illustrates and names eight emotion families, from low to medium to high intensity, and gives their opposites; for example, happiness and sadness are positioned opposite from each other. The image also identifies blends of two neighboring emotions. (I have some issues with Plutchik's opposites and his blends, but his emotion wheel is visually simple and clean and thus a good starting place.)

I use the emotion wheel often enough that I have laminated copies in my office for easy reference. One side has Plutchik's (1980) relatively simple version, and the other side has a more detailed emotion wheel with approximately 100 terms. Guys like Bart look at Plutchik's wheel, then look at the other one, and quickly return to Plutchik's version. As mentioned earlier, there are also emotion wheels that explicitly connect emotions to physical sensations instead of illustrating lower and higher intensity feeling words.

Having helped Bart experience anger and sadness, I chose to explore happiness with him next. He struggled mightily with this, identifying major life events, such as marriage and the births of his children, but little else. I find this to be a fairly common experience with men who (mostly) ignore their feelings. In response, I provided a range of synonyms for "happiness," including "pleasure," "peace," and "serenity." As a therapist, you might think of pleasure, peace, and serenity as specific forms of happiness and thus members of the same family, or they might be members of another emotional family, such as *calm*. To help Bart find positives in his daily life, I talked about these synonyms as different members of the happiness family; consistent with his tactile approach to the world, he described them as different "flavors" of happiness. Bart then identified playing with Liza, watching repaired machines function properly (especially when the gears/work parts were visible), and his time at church as things that made him happy. On the basis of his descriptions, I distinguished his experiences as *happy*, *pleased*, and *peaceful* (respectively), but I didn't insist that he immediately adopt my terminology. He was still new to this (happy) family and trying to sort things out.

CONCLUSION

On average, American men are less emotional than women, and American stereotypes sometimes paint men as completely emotionless. In fact, men's emotional inexpression is often contrasted with women's high levels of emotional expression, and this distinction is often portrayed as one of the fundamental differences between the two groups. Directives to be unemotional are so fundamental to our conception of what it means to be manly that a guy who centers his masculinity on this principle cannot use it to achieve masculine status. An unemotional man is just a man. American masculinity doesn't see this as an achievement, but failure to adhere to this criterion can mean a loss of masculine status and designations that one is not Man Enough.

Bart, who also fits the description of a problem solver (Chapter 5), clearly followed directives to be unemotional. He had started suppressing his feelings in childhood and, now age 60, had been diagnosed with hypertension that was at least partly caused by his unwillingness to express feelings. He attributed his hypertension primarily to stress. I translated "stress" as "worried," and we met for several years to help him bring his stress under control. He eventually did bring it under control, and some of the signs of his cardiovascular issues improved.

My work with Bart included some joint problem solving of stressful issues in his life that he had largely just accepted as part of daily life and "dealt with." Bart felt that others often took advantage of him, so I taught him how to set boundaries. In this chapter, I have described some of the work we did to help him access a broader range of emotions, as well as some strategies for helping men directly challenge the belief that men do not have, or should not show, feelings.

10 CONCLUSION

In Chapter 1, I argued that men deserve culturally competent care so they will have better experiences in therapy that will lead to better outcomes. I also argued that masculinity is complex, as are men. To help you develop the cultural competence necessary for work with men, I introduced the multifaceted masculinity framework (MFMF) and then, in Chapters 3–9, presented case studies of seven different men, each of whom highlighted a different approach to masculinity.

The MFMF describes four facets of masculinity:

1. Masculinity's criteria: These are the dos and don'ts by which men live, such as "Men should be effective problem solvers" and "Men should not be feminine." There are many such directives, too many for any single man to live by, and they have changed over the years.

2. Masculinity's achievement: *Achievement* refers to the rewards men reap when they adhere to masculine criteria, such as the status of being Man Enough or even The Man. The tenuous nature of masculine achievement prompted researchers Joseph Vandello and Jennifer Bosson (2013) to describe masculinity as "hard won and easily lost" (p. 101).

https://doi.org/10.1037/0000499-010
Clinical Work With Men: Understanding Masculinity in Psychotherapy, by A. P. Smiler

3. Masculinity's types: These types encompass the range of roles that men might play, such as jocks, rebels, and nerds. But these types are not created equal—some come with more social status and approval than others. These types can also be thought of as *stereotypes*, *identities*, or even *parts*.
4. Masculinity's negotiations: These are the decisions men make regarding their specific enactment of masculinity, on the basis of their own values and desires, as well as the opportunities available in their environment. Negotiations, masculine and otherwise, are the bread and butter of therapy.

Each of the seven case studies highlighted a specific masculine criterion and a type closely associated with that criterion. I discussed breadwinners and protectors and problem solvers, as well as men who were angry or self-sufficient. In doing so, I explored how a single criterion—and the type associated with it—can have a substantial impact on many parts of a particular man's life.

Chapter 5's Murray, for example, was a problem solver. Solving problems was how he approached many elements of his life, including interpersonal relationships. He used his problem-solving skills so that he would be useful to other people, but he struggled to determine whether people actually liked him. Murray's problem solving also created substantial problems with his wife, who often complained that he didn't really hear or understand her.

Recognizing and accepting choices regarding masculine criteria is an element of creating connection with male clients. Throughout my work with the clients portrayed in the case studies, I accepted these men as they were and tried to help them improve their lives in ways that made sense to them and were consistent with their masculine type, consistent with Seidler et al.'s (2018) recommendations about building rapport. I detailed this in Chapter 7 in my discussion of N'Shawn's violent behaviors, which echoed my reaction when Chapter 6's Benny first spoke about hitting his son. In Chapter 8, my acceptance of John's hookup behavior is also rooted in this acceptance of masculinity and dovetails with the sex-positive approach that has become more prominent over the past decade or two.

Some of the case studies highlighted the role of masculine achievement. For N'Shawn, masculine achievement provided safety and a (fear-based) respect he had never experienced before. Gary's story, presented in Chapter 3, highlighted masculine achievement in a different way. He struggled with how to implement his desire to be a (financial) provider because he had envisioned himself achieving masculinity through a breadwinner role, but that role didn't match his personality, skills, and values. When he refocused on being Man Enough, he was able to identify and find a job that better matched who he was, and his depressive symptoms abated. This shift in Gary's masculine achievement is an example of direct change in a client's formulation of masculinity; John's efforts to decrease his promiscuity is another.

Because this is a book for therapists, I have highlighted the problems associated with each of the sets of criteria/type. I also have discussed the strengths associated with each set of criteria/type because masculinity (and men) have both positives and negatives (Englar-Carlson & Kiselica, 2013; Kiselica, 2010; Kiselica et al., 2016), and identifying these strengths is a way to build rapport (Seidler et al., 2018). For breadwinners, protectors, and problem solvers, those strengths include a set of skills and a sense of competence that is based on those skills, respect from others, and a place in society. Other types provide specific skills, such as the unemotional man's ability to stay calm in a crisis and the self-sufficient man's ability to take care of himself. Your ability to identify and discuss the positive elements of masculinity with male clients is likely to help them feel seen and understood and thus to facilitate the development of a solid therapeutic alliance. Depending on a client's therapeutic needs, those positives may help address his issues.

I also have described *action empathy*, which is defined as demonstrating care by doing something to (attempt to) help someone else. Men often engage in action empathy to relieve a relationship partner's distress. This was illustrated briefly in Murray's case; his efforts to try to solve people's problems were how he showed he cared. Action empathy can also be seen elsewhere in the book. It's part of the driving force behind Gary's efforts to be an effective breadwinner and Benny's efforts to protect his family. Your ability to recognize action empathy for what it is, an expression of emotion, can help your clients recognize that they have some ability to recognize other people's emotions and that emotions aren't an inherently bad thing. In heterosexual relationships, giving a man credit for this "emotional" behavior can help address claims he's not aware of other people's feelings.

Problem solving is another strength that many men possess, and it was illustrated in several chapters. It was the explicit focus in Murray's story. In Chapter 4, I described how Sam's self-sufficiency was facilitated by his ability to solve problems on his own, and unemotional Bart's (Chapter 9) job doing maintenance could be thought of as a continuous exercise in problem solving (i.e., of how to fix things). Gary asked that his therapy focus on problem solving, not coping, and thus we focused on finding a job that fit him better. Seidler et al. (2018) discussed problem solving as a means of tailoring language; it is also action oriented and future focused, consistent with the idea that men are doers.

The process of therapy is unfamiliar to many men, which may explain why Seidler et al.'s (2018) review found that so many authors highlighted the importance of explaining to clients how therapy works. I have summarized treatment planning in each of the seven case study chapters. Most of those chapters include examples of identifying therapeutic goals, with N'Shawn's case including the most detailed example. Sam's recognition of my ability to improve his decision making by prompting him to consider relational factors was something he and I discussed, and although I reference that in Chapter 4 I didn't specifically illustrate that conversation.

The range of masculinity-related issues I have discussed illustrates some of the complexity inherent in working with men. However, men's issues are not limited to the ways masculinity shapes and affects their lives, and in each chapter I identified other therapeutic issues that were part of the treatment and (in some cases) interacted with masculinity. Perhaps the most detailed of these discussions related to the overlap between Sam's masculine self-sufficiency and his avoidant attachment style; I also addressed the interplay between John's resistant attachment style and his sexual promiscuity. In Benny's story, I provided a detailed discussion of the impact of the sexual victimization of boys in order to highlight ways in which masculinity creates a differential impact for male victims. Boundary-setting (Gary, Bart), general anxiety (Murray), and difficulties creating and maintaining friendships (Sam, N'Shawn) were the subject of discussion in other chapters.

My selection of case studies was intended to illustrate diversity. One of the seven case studies presented in this book features a man of color. I also presented two gay men, two men who had physical limitations, and three who did not complete undergraduate degrees. Because some critics have expressed concern that the literature on gay men is overly focused on body image, sexually transmitted infections, and health management (Parent & Bradstreet, 2017; Sánchez, 2016), I highlighted other issues that gay men encounter. As a White man who works primarily with White clients, I am always struck by how much smaller, and how less interdependent, the White definition of family is compared with other racial and ethnic groups, a topic I addressed in Chapter 4. As always, it is important to understand that any given member of a demographic group is an individual and that their behavior may not be typical of that group.

Before signing off, I'd like to thank you for reading this book. I hope it helps you better understand your male clients, identify their hidden strengths and weaknesses, and think about them in a more detailed manner. As I said at the beginning of this book, men are complicated.

References

Addis, M. E. (2011). *Invisible men: Men's inner lives and the consequences of silence*. Times Books.

Addis, M. E., & Mahalik, J. R. (2003). Men, masculinity, and the contexts of help seeking. *American Psychologist, 58*(1), 5–14. https://doi.org/10.1037/0003-066x.58.1.5

Alexander, L., & Alexander, M. (2021). Fear. In N. Hannah-Jones, C. Roper, I. Silverman, & J. Silverstein (Eds.), *The 1619 project: A new origin story* (pp. 97–124). One World.

American Psychological Association. (2000). Guidelines for psychotherapy with lesbian, gay, and bisexual clients. *American Psychologist, 55*(12), 1440–1451. https://www.apa.org/practice/guidelines/glbt.pdf

American Psychological Association. (2007). Guidelines for psychological practice with girls and women. *American Psychologist, 62*(9), 949–979. https://doi.org/10.1037/0003-066X.62.9.949

American Psychological Association. (2015). Guidelines for psychological practice with transgender and gender nonconforming people. *American Psychologist, 70*(9), 832–864. https://doi.org/10.1037/a0039906

American Psychological Association. (2017). *Ethical principles of psychologists and code of conduct* (2002, amended effective June 1, 2010, and January 1, 2017). https://www.apa.org/ethics/code

American Psychological Association, Boys and Men Guidelines Group. (2018, August). *APA guidelines for psychological practice with boys and men*. https://www.apa.org/about/policy/boys-men-practice-guidelines.pdf

American Psychological Association, Girls and Women Guidelines Group. (2018, February). *APA guidelines for psychological practice with girls and women*. https://www.apa.org/about/policy/psychological-practice-girls-women.pdf

Andreassen, C. S. (2014). Workaholism: An overview and current status of the research. *Journal of Behavioral Addictions, 3*(1), 1–11. https://doi.org/10.1556/JBA.2.2013.017

Aosved, A. C., Long, P. J., & Voller, E. K. (2011). Sexual revictimization and adjustment in college men. *Psychology of Men & Masculinity, 12*(3), 285–296. https://doi.org/10.1037/a0020828

APA Task Force on Psychological Practice With Sexual Minority Persons. (2021, February). *APA guidelines for psychological practice with sexual minority persons*. American Psychological Association. https://www.apa.org/about/policy/psychological-sexual-minority-persons.pdf

APA Task Force on Race and Ethnicity Guidelines in Psychology. (2019, August). *Race and ethnicity guidelines in psychology: Promoting responsiveness and equity*. American Psychological Association. https://www.apa.org/about/policy/guidelines-race-ethnicity.pdf

Arnett, J. J. (2000). Emerging adulthood: A theory of development from the late teens through the twenties. *American Psychologist, 55*(5), 469–480. https://doi.org/10.1037//0003-066x.55.5.469

Baltes, P. B., & Baltes, M. M. (1990). Psychological perspectives on successful aging: The model of selective optimization with compensation. In P. B. Baltes & M. M. Baltes (Eds.), *Successful aging: Perspectives from the behavioral sciences* (pp. 1–34). Cambridge University Press. https://doi.org/10.1017/CBO9780511665684.003

Baltes, P. B., & Freund, A. M. (2003). The intermarriage of wisdom and selective optimization with compensation: Two meta-heuristics guiding the conduct of life. In C. L. M. Keyes & J. Haidt (Eds.), *Flourishing: Positive psychology and the life well-lived* (pp. 249–273). American Psychological Association. https://doi.org/10.1037/10594-011

Barber, B. L., Eccles, J. S., & Stone, M. R. (2001). Whatever happened to the jock, the brain, and the princess? Young adult pathways linked to adolescent activity involvement and social identity. *Journal of Adolescent Research, 16*(4), 429–455. https://doi.org/10.1177/0743558401165002

Basile, K. C., Smith, S. G., Kresnow, M., Khatiwada, S., & Leemis, R. W. (2022). *The National Intimate Partner and Sexual Violence Survey: 2016/2017 report on sexual violence*. Centers for Disease Control and Prevention. https://www.cdc.gov/nisvs/documentation/nisvsreportonsexualviolence.pdf

Bem, S. L. (1974). The measurement of psychological androgyny. *Journal of Consulting and Clinical Psychology, 42*(2), 155–162. https://doi.org/10.1037/h0036215

Bem, S. L. (1993). *The lenses of gender*. Yale University Press.

Bhatia, M. (2014). Going deep: Using sports to engage men therapeutically. In A. B. Rochlen & F. E. Rabinowitz (Eds.), *Breaking barriers in counseling men: Insights and innovations* (pp. 52–64). Routledge.

Blazina, C., & Bartone, A. (2016). Moving beyond essentialism in the contemporary psychodynamic psychology of men: Implications for theory and research. In Y. J. Wong & S. R. Wester (Eds.), *APA handbook of men and masculinities* (pp. 105–122). American Psychological Association. https://doi.org/10.1037/14594-005

Bogle, K. A. (2008). *Hooking up: Sex, dating, and relationships on campus*. New York University Press.

Bowlby, J. (1969). *Attachment and Loss, Vol. 1: Attachment*. Basic Books.

Brooks, G. R. (2017). Counseling, psychotherapy, and psychological interventions for boys and men. In R. F. Levant & Y. J. Wong (Eds.), *The psychology of men and masculinities* (pp. 317–345). American Psychological Association. https://doi.org/10.1037/0000023-012

Busette, C. (2018, March 14). *A new deal for poor African-American and Native-American boys*. Brookings Institution. https://www.brookings.edu/blog/fixgov/2018/03/14/a-new-deal-for-poor-african-american-and-native-american-boys/

Butler, J. (1990). *Gender trouble: Feminism and the subversion of identity*. Routledge.

Canetto, S. S. (2015). Suicide: Why are older men so vulnerable? *Men and Masculinities, 20*(1), 49–70. https://doi.org/10.1177/1097184X15613832

Canetto, S. S., & Lester, D. (2002). Love and achievement motives in women's and men's suicide notes. *The Journal of Psychology, 136*(5), 573–576. https://doi.org/10.1080/00223980209605552

Centers for Disease Control and Prevention. (2011). *Leading causes of death by age group, race/ethnicity males, United States, 2010*. Retrieved December 1, 2017, from https://www.cdc.gov/healthequity/lcod/men/2010/LCODrace_ethnicityMen2010.pdf

Chen, Y.-Y., Cai, Z., Chang, Q., Canetto, S. S., & Yip, P. S. F. (2021). Caregiving as suicide-prevention: An ecological 20-country study of the association between men's family carework, unemployment, and suicide. *Social Psychiatry and Psychiatric Epidemiology, 56*(12), 2185–2198. https://doi.org/10.1007/s00127-021-02095-9

Christidis, P., Lin, L., Conroy, J., Stamm, K., & the American Psychological Association Center for Workforce Studies. (2019, April). *2008–2017: Master's and doctoral degrees awarded in psychology*. American Psychological Association. https://www.apa.org/workforce/publications/2017-postsecondary-data/report.pdf

Cohen, J., & Brooks, R. A. (2014). *Confronting school bullying: Kids, culture, and the making of a social problem*. Lynne Rienner.

Cohen, R. (Director). (2001). *The fast and the furious*. Universal Pictures.

Collins, L. (2020, August 31). Miss America's history-makers and rule-breakers. *The New Yorker*. https://www.newyorker.com/magazine/2020/09/07/miss-americas-history-makers-and-rule-breakers

Connell, R. W. (1995). *Masculinities*. University of California Press.

Connell, R. W., & Messerschmidt, J. W. (2005). Hegemonic masculinity: Rethinking the concept. *Gender & Society, 19*(6), 825–859. https://doi.org/10.1177/0891243205278639

Cook, J. M., Anderson, C., Simiola, V., & Ellis, A. E. (2018). Top ten questions male sexual abuse survivors want to know from health care research. *Journal of Aggression, Maltreatment & Trauma, 27*(8), 867–882. https://doi.org/10.1080/10926771.2018.1446481

Cooper, A., & Smith, E. L. (2011, November). *Homicide trends in the United States, 1980–2008*. U.S. Department of Justice. https://bjs.ojp.gov/content/pub/pdf/htus8008.pdf

Crespi, B., Read, S., Ly, A., & Hurd, P. (2019). AMBRA1, autophagy, and the extreme male brain theory of autism. *Autism Research and Treatment*, Article 1968580. https://doi.org/10.1155/2019/1968580

Dariotis, J. K., Pleck, J. L., Astone, N. M., & Sonenstein, F. L. (2011). Pathways of early fatherhood, marriage, and employment: A latent class growth analysis. *Demography, 48*(2), 593–623. https://doi.org/10.1007/s13524-011-0022-7

Dariotis, J. K., Sonenstein, F. L., Gates, G. J., Capps, R., Astone, N. M., Pleck, J. L., Sifakis, F., & Zeger, S. (2008). Changes in sexual risk behavior as young men transition to adulthood. *Perspectives on Sexual and Reproductive Health, 40*(4), 218–225. https://doi.org/10.1363/4021808

David, D., & Brannon, R. (1976). The male sex role: Our culture's blueprint for manhood and what it's done for us lately. In D. David & R. Brannon (Eds.), *The forty-nine percent majority: The male sex role* (pp. 1–48). Addison-Wesley.

Donnelly, K., & Twenge, J. M. (2016). Masculine and feminine traits on the Bem Sex-Role Inventory, 1993–2012: A cross-temporal meta-analysis. *Sex Roles, 76*, 556–565. https://doi.org/10.1007/s11199-016-0625-y

Eisler, R. M. (1995). The relationship between masculine gender role stress and men's health risk: The validation of a construct. In R. F. Levant & W. S. Pollack (Eds.), *A new psychology of men* (pp. 207–225). Basic Books.

Eisler, R. M., & Skidmore, J. R. (1987). Masculine gender role stress: Scale development and component factors in the appraisal of stressful situations. *Behavior Modification, 11*(2), 123–136. https://doi.org/10.1177/01454455870112001

Ellis, A. E., Simiola, V., Mackintosh, M.-A., Schlaudt, V. A., & Cook, J. M. (2020). Perceived helpfulness and engagement in mental health treatment: A study of male survivors of sexual abuse. *Psychology of Men & Masculinities, 21*(4), 632–642. https://doi.org/10.1037/men0000313

Englar-Carlson, M., & Kiselica, M. S. (2013). Affirming the strengths in men: A positive masculinity approach to assisting male clients. *Journal of Counseling & Development, 91*(4), 399–409. https://doi.org/10.1002/j.1556-6676.2013.00111.x

Epstein, M., Calzo, J. P., Smiler, A. P., & Ward, L. M. (2009). "Anything from making out to having sex": Men's negotiations of hooking up and friends with benefits scripts. *Journal of Sex Research, 46*(5), 414–424. https://doi.org/10.1080/00224490902775801

Erikson, E. H. (1963). *Childhood and society* (2nd ed.). Norton.

Faludi, S. (1999). *Stiffed: The betrayal of the American man*. William Morrow.

Feirstein, B. (1982). *Real men don't eat quiche*. Pocket Books.

Fern, J. (2020). *Polysecure: Attachment, trauma, and consensual nonmonogamy*. Thornapple Press.

Fincher, D. (Director). (1999). *Fight club*. Fox 2000 Pictures, Regency Enterprises, Linson Films.

Flood, M. (2008). Men, sex, and homosociality: How bonds between men shape their sexual relations with women. *Men and Masculinities, 10*(3), 339–359. https://doi.org/10.1177/1097184X06287761

Garcia, J. R., Reiber, C., Massey, S. G., & Merriwether, A. M. (2012). Sexual hookup culture: A review. *Review of General Psychology, 16*(2), 161–176. https://doi.org/10.1037/a0027911

Garfield, R. (2010). Male emotional intimacy: How therapeutic men's groups can enhance couples therapy. *Family Process, 49*(1), 109–122. https://doi.org/10.1111/j.1545-5300.2010.01311.x

Garfield, R. (2015). *Breaking the male code: Unlocking the power of friendship*. Gotham Books.

Gartner, R. B. (1999). *Betrayed as boys: Psychodynamic treatment of sexually abused men*. Guilford Press.

Gartner, R. B. (2017a). *Trauma and countertrauma, resilience and counterresilience: Insights from psychoanalysts and trauma experts*. Routledge.

Gartner, R. B. (Ed.). (2017b). *Understanding the sexual betrayal of boys and men: The trauma of sexual abuse*. Routledge.

Gillespie, C. D., & Hurvitz, K. A. (2013). Prevalence of hypertension and controlled hypertension—United States, 2007–2010. *Mortality and Morbidity Weekly Review, 62*(Suppl.), 144–148.

Gilmore, D. D. (1990). *Manhood in the making: Cultural concepts of masculinity*. Yale University Press.

Good, G. E., Schopp, L. H., Thomson, D., Hathaway, S., Sanford-Martens, T., Mazurek, M. O., & Mintz, L. B. (2006). Masculine roles and rehabilitation outcomes among men recovering from serious injuries. *Psychology of Men & Masculinities, 7*(3), 165–176. https://doi.org/10.1037/1524-9220.7.3.165

Gottman, J. (1994). *Why marriages succeed or fail: What you can learn from the breakthrough research to make your marriage last*. Simon & Schuster.

Gough, B., & Novikova, I. (2020). *Mental health, men, and culture: How do socio-cultural constructions of masculinities relate to men's mental health and help-seeking behaviour in the WHO European Region?* (Health Evidence Network Synthesis Report No. 70). WHO Regional Office for Europe. https://www.ncbi.nlm.nih.gov/books/NBK559706/pdf/Bookshelf_NBK559706.pdf

Green, R. J., & Ashmore, R. D. (1998). Taking and developing pictures in the head: Assessing the physical stereotypes of eight gender types. *Journal of Applied Social Psychology, 28*(17), 1609–1636. https://doi.org/10.1111/j.1559-1816.1998.tb01692.x

Halberstam, J. (1998). *Female masculinity*. Duke University Press.

Hannah-Jones, N., Roper, C., Silverman, I., & Silverstein, J. (Eds.). (2021). *The 1619 project: A new origin story*. One World.

Heasley, R. (2005). Queer masculinities of straight men: A typology. *Men and Masculinities, 7*(3), 310–320. https://doi.org/10.1177/1097184X04272118

Helmreich, R. L., Spence, J. T., & Wilhelm, J. A. (1981). A psychometric analysis of the Personal Attributes Questionnaire. *Sex Roles, 7*(11), 1097–1108. https://doi.org/10.1007/BF00287587

Herek, G. M. (1995). Psychological heterosexism in the United States. In A. R. D'Augelli & C. Patterson (Eds.), *Lesbian, gay, and bisexual identities over the lifespan* (pp. 321–346). Oxford University Press.

Herek, S. (Director). (1989). *Bill & Ted's excellent adventure*. Interscope Communications, Nelson Entertainment.

Humblet, O., Paul, C., & Dickson, N. (2003). Core group evolution over time: High-risk sexual behavior in a birth cohort between sexual debut and age 26. *Sexually Transmitted Diseases, 30*(11), 818–824. https://doi.org/10.1097/01.OLQ.0000097102.42149.11

Iwamoto, D. K., & Kaya, A. (2016). Asian American men. In Y. J. Wong & S. R. Wester (Eds.), *APA handbook of men and masculinities* (pp. 285–297). American Psychological Association. https://doi.org/10.1037/14594-013

Kilmartin, C. (2014). Using humor and storytelling in men's work. In A. B. Rochlen & F. E. Rabinowitz (Eds.), *Breaking barriers in counseling men: Insights and innovations* (pp. 20–29). Routledge.

Kiselica, M. S. (2010). Promoting positive masculinity while addressing gender role conflict: A balanced theoretical approach to clinical work with boys and men. In C. Blazina & D. Shen-Miller (Eds.), *An international psychology of men: Theoretical advances, case studies, and clinical innovations* (pp. 131–160). Routledge.

Kiselica, M. S., Benton-Wright, S., & Englar-Carlson, M. (2016). Accentuating positive masculinity: A new foundation for the psychology of boys, men, and masculinity. In Y. J. Wong & S. R. Wester (Eds.), *APA handbook of men and masculinities* (pp. 123–143). American Psychological Association. https://doi.org/10.1037/14594-006

Klugman, M. (2015). "I love him in an absolutely gay way": Heterodox fragments of the erotic desires, pleasures, and masculinity of male sports fans. *Men and Masculinities, 18*(2), 193–213. https://doi.org/10.1177/1097184X15584911

Lansford, J. E., Yu, T., Erath, S. A., Pettit, G. S., Bates, J. E., & Dodge, K. A. (2010). Developmental precursors of number of sexual partners from ages 16 to 22. *Journal of Research on Adolescence, 20*(3), 651–677. https://doi.org/10.1111/j.1532-7795.2010.00654.x

Leary, M. R., Kowalski, R. M., Smith, L. H., & Phillips, S. (2003). Teasing, rejection, and violence: Case studies of the school shootings. *Aggressive Behavior, 29*(3), 202–214. https://doi.org/10.1002/ab.10061

Lee, T. (2021). Inheritance. In N. Hannah-Jones, C. Roper, I. Silverman, & J. Silverstein (Eds.), *The 1619 project* (pp. 293–305). One World.

Leiner, D. (Director). (2004). *Harold & Kumar go to White Castle*. Senator International, Kingsgate Films, Endgame Entertainment.

Levant, R. F., & Pryor, S. (Eds.). (2025). *Assessing and treating emotionally inexpressive men*. Routledge.

Levant, R. F., Rankin, T. J., Williams, C. M., Hasan, N. T., & Smalley, K. B. (2010). Evaluation of the factor structure and construct validity of scores on the Male Role Norms Inventory—Revised (MRNI-R). *Psychology of Men & Masculinity, 11*(1), 25–37. https://doi.org/10.1037/a0017637

Levine, A., & Heller, R. S. F. (2010). *Attached: The new science of adult attachment and how it can help you find—and keep—love*. TarcherPerigee.

Levinson, D. J. (1996). *The seasons of a woman's life*. Knopf.

Levinson, D. J., Darrow, C. N., Klein, E. B., Levinson, M. H., & McKee, B. (1978). *The seasons of a man's life*. Knopf.

Lew, M. (2004). *Victims no longer: The classic guide for men recovering from sexual child abuse*. Harper Perennial.

Lin, L., Stamm, K., Christidis, P., & the American Psychological Association Center for Workforce Studies. (2018, May). *Demographics of the U.S. psychology workforce: Findings from the 2007–16 American Community Survey*. American Psychological Association. https://www.apa.org/workforce/publications/16-demographics/report.pdf

Liu, G. S., Nguyen, B. L., Lyons, B. H., Sheats, K. J., Wilson, R. F., Betz, C. J., & Fowler, K. A. (2023). Surveillance for violent deaths—National Violent Death Reporting System, 48 states, the District of Columbia, and Puerto Rico, 2020. *Morbidity and Mortality Weekly Report, 72*(5), 1–38. https://doi.org/10.15585/mmwr.ss7205a1

Liu, W. M. (2005). The study of men and masculinity as an important multicultural competency consideration. *Journal of Clinical Psychology, 61*(6), 685–697. https://doi.org/10.1002/jclp.20103

Long, D. (1987). Working with men who batter. In M. Scher, M. Stevens, G. E. Good, & G. A. Eichenfield (Eds.), *Handbook of counseling and psychotherapy with men* (pp. 305–320). Sage.

Lorre, C., & Prady, B. (Executive Producers). (2007–2019). *The big bang theory* [TV Series]. Chuck Lorre Productions; Warner Bros Television Studios.

Machado, A., Hines, D., & Matos, M. (2016). Help-seeking and needs of male victims of intimate partner violence in Portugal. *Psychology of Men & Masculinity, 17*(3), 255–264. https://doi.org/10.1037/men0000013

Mahalik, J. R., Locke, B. D., Ludlow, L. H., Diemer, M. A., Scott, R. P. J., Gottfried, M., & Freitas, G. (2003). Development of the Conformity to Masculine Norms Inventory. *Psychology of Men & Masculinity, 4*(1), 3–25. https://doi.org/10.1037/1524-9220.4.1.3

Majors, R., & Billson, J. M. (1992). *Cool pose: The dilemmas of Black manhood in America*. Touchstone.

Marcia, J. E. (1966). Development and validation of ego-identity status. *Journal of Personality and Social Psychology, 3*(5), 551–558. https://doi.org/10.1037/h0023281

Marshall, G. (Director). (1990). *Pretty woman.* Touchstone Pictures, Silver Screen Partners IV.

Mary Kay Letourneau. (2025, August 7). In *Wikipedia.* https://en.wikipedia.org/wiki/Mary_Kay_Letourneau

McDaniel, M., Simms, M., Monson, W., & Fortuny, K. (2013, August). *Imprisonment and disenfranchisement of disconnected low-income men.* Urban Institute. https://aspe.hhs.gov/system/files/pdf/56191/rpt_imprisonment.pdf

Minkin, R. (2023, November 13). *Most American workers say their boss is capable, confident and fair.* Pew Research Center. https://www.pewresearch.org/short-reads/2023/11/13/most-american-workers-say-their-boss-is-capable-confident-and-fair/

Morawski, J. G. (1985). The measurement of masculinity and femininity: Engendering categorical realities. *Journal of Personality, 53*(2), 196–223. https://doi.org/10.1111/j.1467-6494.1985.tb00364.x

Mutchler, M. G., & McDavitt, B. (2011). "Gay boy talk" meets "girl talk": HIV risk assessment assumptions in young gay men's sexual health communication with best friends. *Health Education Research, 26*(3), 489–505. https://doi.org/10.1093/her/cyq069

National Center for Education Statistics. (2017). *Indicator 24: Degrees awarded.* https://nces.ed.gov/programs/raceindicators/indicator_ree.asp

Nellis, A. (2021). *The color of justice: Racial and ethnic disparity in state prisons.* The Sentencing Project. http://www.sentencingproject.org/wp-content/uploads/2016/06/The-Color-of-Justice-Racial-and-Ethnic-Disparity-in-State-Prisons.pdf

Ng, C. J., Tan, H. M., & Low, W. Y. (2008). What do Asian men consider as important masculinity attributes? Findings from the Asian Men's Attitudes to Life Events and Sexuality (MALES) Study. *Journal of Men's Health, 5*(4), 350–355. https://doi.org/10.1016/j.jomh.2008.10.005

Ojeda, L., & Organista, K. C. (2016). Latino American men. In Y. J. Wong & S. R. Wester (Eds.), *APA handbook of men and masculinities* (pp. 299–318). American Psychological Association. https://doi.org/10.1037/14594-014

O'Neil, J. M. (2015). *Men's gender role conflict: Psychological costs, consequences, and an agenda for change.* American Psychological Association. https://doi.org/10.1037/14501-000

Orenstein, P. (2020). *Boys and sex: Young men on hookups, love, porn, consent, and navigating the new masculinity.* Harper.

Parent, M. C., & Bradstreet, T. C. (2017). Gay, bisexual, and transgender masculinities. In R. F. Levant & Y. J. Wong (Eds.), *The psychology of men and masculinities* (pp. 289–314). American Psychological Association. https://doi.org/10.1037/0000023-011

Pascoe, C. J. (2007). *Dude, you're a fag: Masculinity and sexuality in high school.* University of California Press.

Pew Research Center. (2015, December 17). *Parenting in America: Outlook, worries, aspirations are strongly linked to financial situation.* https://www.pewresearch.org/social-trends/2015/12/17/parenting-in-america/

Phillips, T. (Director). (2009). *The hangover* [Film]. Legendary Pictures, Green Hat Films, BenderSpink.

Pleck, J. H. (1981). *The myth of masculinity*. MIT Press.

Pleck, J. H. (1995). The gender role strain paradigm: An update. In R. F. Levant & W. S. Pollack (Eds.), *A new psychology of men* (pp. 11–32). Basic Books.

Plutchik, R. (1980). *Emotion: Theory, research, and experience: Vol. 1. Theories of emotion*. Academic Press.

Putnam, R. (2000). *Bowling alone: The collapse and revival of American community*. Touchstone.

Rabinowitz, F. E., & Cochran, S. V. (2002). *Deepening psychotherapy with men*. American Psychological Association. https://doi.org/10.1037/10418-000

Real, T. (1997). *I don't want to talk about it: Overcoming the secret legacy of male depression*. Scribner.

Reeves, R. V. (2024). *Of boys and men: Why the modern male is struggling, why it matters, and what to do about it*. Brookings Institution Press.

Reichert, M. C., & Nelson, J. D. (2018). I want to learn from you. In N. Way, A. Ali, C. Gilligan, & P. Noguera (Eds.), *The crisis of connection: Roots, consequences, and solutions* (pp. 344–360). New York University Press.

Reigeluth, C. S., & Addis, M. E. (2016). Adolescent boys' experiences with policing of masculinity: Forms, functions, and consequences. *Psychology of Men & Masculinity, 17*(1), 74–83. https://doi.org/10.1037/a0039342

Reiner, A. (2020). *Better boys, better men: The new masculinity that creates greater courage and emotional resiliency*. HarperOne.

Roberts, D. (2021). Race. In N. Hannah-Jones, C. Roper, I. Silverman, & J. Silverstein (Eds.), *The 1619 project: A new origin story* (pp. 45–62). One World.

Roberts, S. (2024, September 28). Bill Lucy, pioneering labor and civil rights leader, dies at 90. *The New York Times*. https://www.nytimes.com/2024/09/28/us/bill-lucy-dead.html

Rochlen, A. B., McKelley, R. A., & Whittaker, T. A. (2010). Stay-at-home fathers' reasons for entering the role and stigma experiences: A preliminary report. *Psychology of Men & Masculinity, 11*(4), 279–285. https://doi.org/10.1037/a0017774

Rochlen, A. B., & Rabinowitz, F. E. (2014). *Breaking barriers in counseling men: Insights and innovations*. Routledge.

Rochlen, A. B., Suizzo, M.-A., McKelley, R. A., & Scaringi, V. (2008). "I'm just providing for my family": A qualitative study of stay-at-home fathers. *Psychology of Men and Masculinity, 9*(4), 193–206. https://doi.org/10.1037/a0012510

Rosenberg, A., Gates, A., Richmond, K., & Sinno, S. (2017). It's not a joke: Masculinity ideology and homophobic language. *Psychology of Men & Masculinity, 18*(4), 293–300. https://doi.org/10.1037/men0000063

Salsberg, E., Quigley, L., Mehfoud, N., Acquaviva, K., Wyche, K., & Silwa, S. (2017, October). *Profile of the social work workforce*. Health Workforce Research Center. https://hsrc.himmelfarb.gwu.edu/sphhs_policy_workforce_facpubs/16/

Sánchez, F. J. (2016). Masculinity issues among gay, bisexual, and transgender men. In Y. J. Wong & S. R. Wester (Eds.), *APA handbook of men and masculinities* (pp. 339–356). American Psychological Association. https://doi.org/10.1037/14594-016

Sánchez, F. J., Greenberg, S. T., Liu, W. M., & Vilain, E. (2009). Reported effects of masculine ideals on gay men. *Psychology of Men & Masculinity, 10*(1), 73–87. https://doi.org/10.1037/a0013513

Sand, M. S., Fisher, W., Rosen, R., Heiman, J., & Eardley, I. (2008). Erectile dysfunction and constructs of masculinity and quality of life in the multinational Men's Attitudes to Life Events and Sexuality (MALES) study. *The Journal of Sexual Medicine, 5*(3), 583–594. https://doi.org/10.1111/j.1743-6109.2007.00720.x

Schmitt, D. P., & International Sexuality Description Project. (2003). Universal sex differences in the desire for sexual variety: Tests from 52 nations, 6 continents, and 13 islands. *Journal of Personality and Social Psychology, 85*(1), 85–104. https://doi.org/10.1037/0022-3514.85.1.85

Schwartz, R. C. (2021). *No bad parts: Healing trauma and restoring wholeness with the internal family systems model.* Sounds True.

Scorsese, M. (Director). (2013). *The wolf of Wall Street.* Red Granite Pictures, Appian Way Productions, Sikelia Productions, EMJAG Productions.

Seidler, Z. E., Rice, S. M., Ogrodniczuk, J. S., Oliffe, J. L., & Dhillon, H. M. (2018). Engaging men in psychological treatment: A scoping review. *American Journal of Men's Health, 12*(6), 1882–1900. https://doi.org/10.1177/1557988318792157

Shaver, P. R., Segev, M., & Mikulincer, M. (2011). A behavioral systems perspective on power and aggression. In P. R. Shaver & M. Mikulincer (Eds.), *Human aggression and violence: Causes, manifestations, and consequences* (pp. 71–87). American Psychological Association. https://doi.org/10.1037/12346-004

Shields, S. A. (2008). Gender: An intersectionality perspective. *Sex Roles, 59*(5–6), 301–311. https://doi.org/10.1007/s11199-008-9501-8

Shilts, R. (2007). *And the band played on: Politics, people, and the AIDS epidemic* (20th anniversary ed.). St. Martin's Press. (Original work published 1987)

Shrider, E. A., & Creamer, J. (2023, September 12). *Poverty in the United States: 2022.* https://www.census.gov/library/publications/2023/demo/p60-280.html

Singer, B. (Director). (2000). *X-men.* Marvel Entertainment Group, The Donners' Company, Bad Hat Harry Productions.

Singh, A., & dickey, l. m. (Eds.). (2017). *Affirmative counseling and psychological practice with transgender and gender nonconforming clients.* American Psychological Association. https://doi.org/10.1037/14957-000

Smiler, A. P. (2004). Thirty years after the discovery of gender: Psychological concepts and measures of masculinity. *Sex Roles, 50*(1–2), 15–26. https://doi.org/10.1023/B:SERS.0000011069.02279.4c

Smiler, A. P. (2006). Living the image: A quantitative approach to delineating masculinities. *Sex Roles*, *55*(9), 621–632. https://doi.org/10.1007/s11199-006-9118-8

Smiler, A. P. (2011). Sexual strategies theory: Built for the short term or the long term? *Sex Roles*, *64*(9–10), 603–612. https://doi.org/10.1007/s11199-010-9817-z

Smiler, A. P. (2013). *Challenging Casanova: Beyond the stereotype of the promiscuous young male*. Jossey-Bass.

Smiler, A. P. (2014). Resistance is futile? Examining boys who actively challenge masculinity. *Psychology of Men & Masculinity*, *15*(3), 256–259. https://doi.org/10.1037/a0037286

Smiler, A. P. (2019). *Is masculinity toxic? A primer for the 21st century*. Thames & Hudson.

Smiler, A. P. (2024). Understanding masculinity: A multifaceted organizing framework. *Psychology of Men & Masculinities*, *25*(4), 357–374. https://doi.org/10.1037/men0000495

Smiler, A. P., & Heasley, R. (2016). Boys' and men's intimate relationships: Friendships and romantic relationships. In Y. J. Wong & S. R. Wester (Eds.), *APA handbook of men and masculinities* (pp. 569–589). American Psychological Association. https://doi.org/10.1037/14594-026

Spence, J. T., & Helmreich, R. L. (1978). *Masculinity and femininity: Their psychological dimensions, correlates and antecedents*. University of Texas Press.

Spencer, M. R., Garnett, M. F., & Miniño, A. M. (2024, March). *Drug overdose deaths in the United States, 2002–2022* (ATA Brief No. 491). National Center for Health Statistics. https://doi.org/10.15620/cdc:135849

Stearns, P. N. (1979). *Be a man! Males in modern society*. Holmes & Meier.

Stearns, P. N. (1994). *American cool: Constructing a twentieth-century emotional style*. New York University Press.

Stith, S. M., & McMonigle, C. L. (2009). Risk factors associated with intimate partner violence. In D. J. Whitaker & J. R. Lutzker (Eds.), *Preventing partner violence: Research and evidence-based strategies* (pp. 67–92). American Psychological Association. https://doi.org/10.1037/11873-004

Stone, O. (Director). (1987). *Wall Street*. American Entertainment Partners, Amercent Films.

Substance Abuse and Mental Health Services Administration. (2021, October 23). *Racial/ethnic differences in mental health service use among adults and adolescents (2015–2019)* (Pub. No. PEP21-07-01-002). https://www.samhsa.gov/data/sites/default/files/reports/rpt35327/2021NSDUHMHChartbook.pdf

Sussell, A., Peterson, C., Li, J., Minino, A., Scott, K. A., & Stone, D. M. (2023). Suicide rates by industry and occupation—National Vital Statistics System, United States, 2021. *Morbidity and Mortality Weekly Report*, *72*(50), 1346–1350. https://doi.org/10.15585/mmwr.mm7250a2

Swedo, E. A., Aslam, M. V., Dahlberg, L. L., Niolon, P. H., Guinn, A. S., Simon, T. R., & Mercy, J. A. (2023). Prevalence of adverse childhood experiences among

U.S. adults—Behavioral Risk Factor Surveillance System, 2011–2020. *Morbidity and Mortality Weekly Report, 72*(26), 707–715. https://doi.org/10.15585/mmwr.mm7226a2

Tajfel, H., & Turner, J. C. (1979). An integrative theory of intergroup conflict. In W. G. Austin & S. Worchel (Eds.), *The social psychology of intergroup relations* (pp. 33–47). Brooks/Cole.

Tannen, D. (1990). *You just don't understand: Women and men in conversation*. Morrow.

Taormino, T. (2008). *Opening up: A guide to creating and sustaining open relationships*. Cleis Press.

Taris, T. W., Van Beek, I., & Schaufeli, W. B. (2012). Demographic and occupational correlates of workaholism. *Psychological Reports, 110*(2), 547–554. https://doi.org/10.2466/03.09.17.PR0.110.2.547-554

Thoits, P. A., & Virshup, L. K. (1997). Me's and we's: Forms and functions of social identities. In R. D. Ashmore & L. Jussim (Eds.), *Self and identity: Fundamental issues* (pp. 106–133). Oxford University Press.

Thompson, E. H., Jr., & Bennett, K. M. (2015). Measurement of masculinity ideologies: A (critical) review. *Psychology of Men & Masculinity, 16*(2), 115–133. https://doi.org/10.1037/a0038609

Turner, J. C. (1999). Some current issues in research on social identity and self-categorization theories. In N. Ellemers, R. Spears, & B. Doosje (Eds.), *Social identity: Context, commitment, content* (pp. 6–34). Blackwell.

Twenge, J. M. (1997). Changes in masculine and feminine traits over time: A meta-analysis. *Sex Roles, 36*(5–6), 305–325. https://doi.org/10.1007/BF02766650

Twohy, D. (Director). (2013). *Riddick*. One Race Films, Radar Pictures, Riddick Canada Productions.

Uniform Crime Reporting Program. (2016, December 12). *FBI releases 2015 crime statistics from the National Incident-Based Reporting System, encourages transition*. https://ucr.fbi.gov/nibrs/2015/resource-pages/nibrs-2015_summary_final-1.pdf

U.S. Bureau of Labor Statistics. (2022). *National Census of Fatal Occupational Injuries in 2021* [News release]. https://www.bls.gov/news.release/archives/cfoi_12162022.pdf

Vandello, J. A., & Bosson, J. K. (2013). Hard won and easily lost: A review and synthesis of theory and research on precarious manhood. *Psychology of Men & Masculinity, 14*(2), 101–113. https://doi.org/10.1037/a0029826

Vandello, J. A., Bosson, J. K., Cohen, D., Burnaford, R. M., & Weaver, J. R. (2008). Precarious manhood. *Journal of Personality and Social Psychology, 95*(6), 1325–1339. https://doi.org/10.1037/a0012453

Voyer, D., & Voyer, S. D. (2014). Gender differences in scholastic achievement: A meta-analysis. *Psychological Bulletin, 140*(4), 1174–1204. https://doi.org/10.1037/a0036620

Way, N. (2011). *Deep secrets: Boys' friendships and the crisis of connection*. Harvard University Press.

Way, N. (2013). Boys' friendships during adolescence: Intimacy, desire, and loss. *Journal of Research on Adolescence, 23*(2), 201–213. https://doi.org/10.1111/jora.12047

Wedgwood, N., Connell, R., & Wood, J. (2023). Deploying hegemonic masculinity: A study of uses of the concept in the journal *Psychology of Men & Masculinities*. *Psychology of Men & Masculinities, 24*(2), 83–93. https://doi.org/10.1037/men0000417

Weitz, P. (Director). (1999). *American pie*. Zide/Perry Productions, Universal Pictures.

Wexler, D. B. (2014). Approaching the unapproachable: Therapist self-disclosure to de-shame clients. In A. B. Rochlen & F. E. Rabinowitz (Eds.), *Breaking barriers in counseling men: Insights and innovations* (pp. 30–40). Routledge.

Wong, Y. J., Ho, M.-H. R., Wang, S.-Y., & Miller, I. S. K. (2017). Meta-analyses of the relationship between conformity to masculine norms and mental health-related outcomes. *Journal of Counseling Psychology, 64*(1), 80–93. https://doi.org/10.1037/cou0000176

Wong, Y. J., Liu, T., & Klann, E. M. (2017). The intersection of race, ethnicity, and masculinities: Progress, problems, and prospects. In R. F. Levant & Y. J. Wong (Eds.), *The psychology of men and masculinities* (pp. 261–288). American Psychological Association. https://doi.org/10.1037/0000023-010

Woodhams, C., Lupton, B., & Cowling, M. (2015). The presence of ethnic minority and disabled men in feminised work: Intersectionality, vertical segregation and the glass escalator. *Sex Roles, 72*(7–8), 277–293. https://doi.org/10.1007/s11199-014-0427-z

Index

A

B

D

E

F

G

T

About the Author

Andrew P. Smiler, PhD, is an award-winning author, therapist, and psychologist living in Winston-Salem, North Carolina. His therapeutic practice focuses on helping teenage boys, adult men, and their families live happier, healthier, and more productive lives. Dr. Smiler is a past president of the American Psychological Association Division 51, the Society for the Psychology of Men and Masculinities, which recently recognized him as Practitioner of the Year (2025). He is also a past board chair of MaleSurvivor (https://www.malesurvivor.org). He is the author of several books, including *Is Masculinity Toxic? A Primer for the 21st Century* (2019), *Dating and Sex: A Guide for the 21st Century Teen Boy* (2016), and *Challenging Casanova: Beyond the Stereotype of the Promiscuous Young Male* (2013), and is coauthor of the best-selling textbook *The Masculine Self* (7th ed., with Christopher Kilmartin; 2024). You can visit his website at https://andrewsmiler.com.